WOMEN IN THE ATLANTIC REVOLUTIONS

WOMEN IN THE ATLANTIC REVOLUTIONS

The Basque Case

Dr. Iker Echeberria Ayllón

Center for Basque Studies,
University of Nevada–Reno
2026

UNIVERSIDAD DEL PAÍS VASCO | EUSKAL HERRIKO UNIBERTSITATEA

This book was published with generous financial support from the Basque Government.

Center for Basque Studies
University of Nevada, Reno
1664 North Virginia St,
Reno, Nevada 89557 usa
http://basque.unr.edu

Copyright © 2026 by the Center for Basque Studies and the University of Nevada, Reno

Series: Diaspora and Migration Studies Series #21

ISBN-13 (paperback) : 978-1-967179-03-9 | ISBN-13 (epub) : 978-1-967179-04-6

All rights reserved.

Library of Congress Cataloging-in-Publication Data

Names: Echeberría Ayllón, Iker author

Title: Women in the Atlantic revolutions : the Basque case / Iker Echeberria Ayllón.

Description: Reno, Nevada : Center for Basque Studies Press, [2026] | Series: Diaspora and migration studies series ; 21 | Includes bibliographical references and index. | Summary: "The book aims to analyze the role of Basque women within the conflictive context of the Atlantic Revolutions. Especially focused on the Spanish War of Independence and the American Independence processes, where the Basque community played a fundamental role, the book brings us closer to the discourses on femininity developed around their role within the war conflict, their performance beyond the hegemonic and normative speeches of the period or the participation of the Basque community within these processes"— Provided by publisher.

Identifiers: LCCN 2025051958 (print) | LCCN 2025051959 (ebook) | ISBN 9781967179039 paperback | ISBN 9781967179046 epub

Subjects: LCSH: Women, Basque—Political activity—Atlantic Ocean Region—History | Women, Basque—Social conditions—Atlantic Ocean Region | Revolutions—Atlantic Ocean Region—History

Classification: LCC HQ1162 .E24 2026 (print) | LCC HQ1162 (ebook)

LC record available at https://lccn.loc.gov/2025051958

LC ebook record available at https://lccn.loc.gov/2025051959

Printed in the United States of America

Cover image credit: Plate 7 from "The Disasters of War" (Los Desastres de la Guerra): 'What courage!' (Que valor!) Goya (Francisco de Goya y Lucientes) 1810 (published 1863).

CONTENTS

vii Preface

ONE
1 Basque Women Rebelling in the Early Modern Age

TWO
23 The Female Preeminence of the Basque Coast

THREE
32 A Lady on the Military Front

FOUR
47 On Some Female Canons

FIVE
59 Basques in Mexico

SIX
65 Basque "Support" for the Crown

SEVEN
73 (Basque) Women in the Atlantic Revolutions

EIGHT
103 Building Heroines for the Nation

NINE
117 The Problem of the Virile Woman in War Times

TEN
126 The Punishment Suffered by Women

ELEVEN
131 The Noncitizen

142 Conclusion
153 Bibliography
187 Index

PREFACE

"The Spaniard who does not know America, does not know what Spain is." This famous quotation belongs to the poet Federico García Lorca. And how right he was, although imagine being Basque! I remember a night walking through the center of Mexico City with my friend Anney. We were walking toward the Zócalo from the Alameda. While many appreciate the Zócalo's hustle and bustle, the Latinoamérica Tower, and its dozens of sellers and shops, I stopped in front of the San Francisco temple where the chapel of the Basque Brotherhood of Aránzazu once stood. When we arrived at the palace of Emperor Agustín de Iturbide, on the same street, I attempted to explain to Anney the importance, now invisible, of those Basque Americans born in the eighteenth century. A proud Mexican, she seemed fed up, although without losing that joy that so characterizes her, of hearing about the Basques. With each step, not yet at the Zócalo, full of Basque ghosts, she became restless. That's when she asked me, half-joking, half-serious: "Iker, you're a historian, what do you think my life would have been like if you hadn't conquered us?" I was only able to respond with the first stupid thing that came to my mind, full of well-intentioned clichés. Even with my answer, I felt like I was attacking her, embarrassed, not knowing what to add. In reality, I wanted to find comfort in my own answer. Centuries may have passed, but I felt the temporal distance in my own way.

As night falls, something intimate and fascinating happens next to the Zócalo. On one of the sides of the cathedral, where there used to be ancestral monuments, a ritual is performed or, rather, experienced. Anney takes me there. I do not intend to reveal here the emotions that this event awoke in me or those that I witnessed. The following work does not answer the question posed by my friend, but it *is* an attempt to get closer to one.

CHAPTER ONE

Basque Women Rebelling in the Early Modern Age

This book aims to analyze the history and influence of Basque women in the context of the Atlantic Revolutions. The main argument laid out in these pages may seem strange to the reader. After all, there are few historiographical works that address the issues raised. In the eighteenth century, public space, like so many other issues, was a man's thing. But nothing could be further from the truth.

I would like to begin by pointing out that Basque women have been part of the most turbulent political and social events during the early modern history. As this work focuses on the geopolitical context known as the Atlantic Revolutions, it seems imperative to recognize some of the elements and dynamics that have been linked to this period.

Between the sixteenth and early nineteenth centuries, the seven territories of present-day *Euskal Herria* or Basque Country—that is, the provinces of Labourd, Soule, and Lower Navarre in France and the provinces of Gipuzkoa and Álava, the Kingdom of Navarre, and the Lordship of Biscay in Spain—witnessed many popular movements, rebellions, revolts, and riots, some based on consumers' fury and others on their excitement. From these events, there are two aspects that I would like to highlight: the role played by women, on the one hand, and their links with the Atlantic world, on the other.

In 1550, we observe a female presence in the antiseigniorial revolt that took place in Moretín, Kingdom of Navarre.[1] Two decades later, in 1570, women participated in a *cencerrada* in Olite, an exercise of community justice that, at the time, was considered a "skillful and ruthless method of political criticism." In the small, mostly illiterate rural communities of the period, "political control mechanisms" of an oral nature such as *cencerradas* or *matracas* were fundamental,[2] although the immediate case seems very simple: as a protest against a wedding, women disguised themselves with "shawls and false beards, carrying cowbells, axes and all kinds of instruments."[3]

Despite male prominence, women again took part in the antiseigniorial revolt of Larraga and the antitax riot of San Martín de Unx in 1593.[4] These subsistence riots, against the imposition of taxes or in defense of improving the rebels' socioeconomic conditions, are linked to the classic concept of moral economy, revolts in which women traditionally participate, as E. P. Thompson says. Because women functioned as guardians of the home, some of their main tasks were feeding and protecting the family as well as reproductive work that demands, in crisis situations, their direct intervention; hence "the initiators of the riots were, frequently, women."[5]

These disturbances in central Navarre seemed to diminish in the following century. At least as far as conflicts involving women are concerned, the Kingdom of Navarre yields interesting numbers: ten cases throughout the sixteenth century, four in the seventeenth, and seven more in the eighteenth. According to Javier Ruiz Astiz, this decline was probably due to the control exercised "by civil and religious authorities," eager to transmit a certain "ideal of social reform."[6]

Reviewing all the Basque territories, these conflicts shifted in the late seventeenth century to coastal areas. The explanation for this phenomenon is multifactorial, although the importance gained by the Atlantic world seems decisive.[7]

Except for central and southern Navarre, the Basque Country lacks an extensive agricultural area; it is a territory turned toward the sea, at least since the Middle Ages: "On both sides of the Pyrenees there were territories turned towards the sea and its resulting economic activities, very lucrative jobs in the context of a customs regime that turned border areas into free trade zones. For this reason, when we talk about popular revolts embodied by peasant sectors, we also observe a great prominence of the coastal urban world."[8]

Since the seventeenth century, many of the conflicts took place in urban areas, centers where popular indignation exploded. Thanks to a limited rural space, without large expanses for the farming of Mediterranean cereals, the demographic and economic influence exercised by the urban centers located on the coast and the political, economic, and demographic prominence acquired by the areas of Atlantic influence—a phenomenon that would happen on a European scale in the early modern age—the Basque Country would turn its activity to the sea, as a kind of "thalassocracy."

With the beginning of the conquest of America, its rise can be seen. Its mastery of Atlantic navigation placed maritime pilots, shipowners, and shippers in privileged positions, a situation that we observe in the foundation of the College of Biscayan Pilots in Cadiz[9] or in its notable influence within the institutions in charge of managing Spain's commercial monopoly in America, such as the House of Trade of Seville or its Consulate of Merchants.[10] People like Juan Sebastián Elcano, the first to circumnavigate the world, or Andrès de Urdaneta, responsible for discovering the navigation route that united Asia with America, serve as models for the rest of the Basque sailors.[11]

Another element that helps us understand the success of Basque movement to America is related to the poverty of its territory. The Basque Country, geographically mountainous, humid, and narrow, lacks large areas for the cultivation of cereals, an aspect that has influenced its history. On the one hand, we have the aforementioned influence of the maritime coast and its resulting economic activities,[12] its urban development, and the absence of an extensive rural world. On the other hand, the consolidation of its *foral* systems later in the period—its own legal rules, since these regimes used, among others, the argument of poverty.[13] This meant extending the privileged status of nobility to all its natives, the so-called universal nobility.[14] Cereal production and demand also showed a deficit throughout the early modern age, which explains another of its great peculiarities: the Basque Country was established as a commercial free-trade zone for the importation of grain and other products, with its customs located inland, on the line marked by the Ebro River.[15]

The territory's narrowness finally caused a phenomenon of singular importance. The farms came to be owned by small producers, creating small plantations that forced, in some way, the concentration of wealth. Without the possibility of distributing the family property equally among heirs, a widespread practice in the rest of the Spanish monarchy, families in the north of the peninsula were forced to opt for the monolithic inheritance of family assets.[16] This single-heir system generated a significant human surplus, where the second sons of the lineage often chose, among other options, to immigrate to the New World.[17]

Thanks to these peculiarities, the Basque migration to America was successful. For decades, especially from the second half of the seventeenth century, emigrants from Basque lands were employed in the Carrera de Indias—a monopolistic maritime navigation and trade system between the Spanish Monarchy and its American territories, particularly administrative positions. The status of nobility was a great advantage; Basques stood out in the world of trade and controlled, to a large extent, mineral extraction.[18] In this ordered emigration, the formation of solid migratory chains, preexisting social links—the uncle-nephew relationship, the determination of a local boss, or the support of countrymen—that these individuals used for centuries without the need to create new connections,[19] became indispensable.

As a result of all this, late in the early modern age an important Basque network was established in America and its main cities. Courtiers; merchants;[20] Basque political institutions; Basque-Navarrese devotional brotherhoods;[21] transatlantic commercial monopolistic companies, such as the Royal Guipuzcoan Company of Caracas (Real Compañía Guipuzcoana de Caracas, RCGC);[22] or enlightened organizations with a notable Atlantic dimension, such as the Royal Basque Society of Friends of the Country (Bascongada, RSBAP), help illustrate this phenomenon: during these centuries, the Basques built a network of political and economic influence throughout the vast Hispanic monarchy, the so-called Basque lobby.[23]

The Basque Country's Atlantic-centric economy also explains other related elements. First, American products had a major influence on the region's economy. For example, 23 percent of legal silver shipments arriving in Seville from America ended up in the Basque Country.[24] The profitability of these products also contributed to one of the Basque coast's main activities: smuggling. It is estimated that due to the absence of customs on the coast, during the seventeenth and eighteenth centuries, the illegal circulation of American products, including cocoa, silver, and tobacco, became one of the most important industries in Gipuzkoa.[25] This Atlantic impact had a political dimension, as well, specifically as influenced by the descendants of Basque emigrants, including, of course, women, within the different independence processes that swept through the American continent.

Returning to the revolts that shook the Basque territory, the main one was in the seventeenth century: the Vizcaya Salt Rebellion of 1631–34.[26] Women played a fundamental role in its outbreak. One of this rebellion's great peculiarities is its complex nature, for it was never limited to the classic subsistence riot: "'peasant fury,' littoral crisis, commercial and urban crisis, tax protests, the situation of the Crown, etc. Everything came together to provoke and configure the final result of this set of contradictions."[27] These sociopolitical dimensions make this revolt unique.

Despite its traditionalism—"its main goal was to purify the traditional social relations that had been attacked"[28]—"it was the women of the popular levels who raised their voices in a public, political and radical discourse."[29] There were three women-led moments in the conflict: they made demands on behalf of the insurgents, they arbitrated with the authorities, and they helped in the escape of an instigator.[30] Part of the speech put forward by the Biscayan women from the rural world, those who went to the city of Bilbao in the most turbulent days, pointed out the economic differences, defending legal and social equality: "now our sons and husbands will be mayors and councilors, and not the traitors who sell us the republic. . . . Why should the women of these Lords be called, and we not, and why should they go around very elegant and bejeweled? . . . In Biscay we are all equal. . . . We will all have to live, eat and dress equally, we are as good as them."[31]

"The leading role is assumed by a collective voice that suggests the chorus of classical tragedy. . . . They represent the voice of the people, the interests of the community, but they do not lead the real action."[32] And this characteristic is one of the keys—the relationship of the insurgent women with speech. According to writers of the period, such as Juan Luis Vives or Fray Luis de León, women had to remain silent, limiting their sphere of social action following an ideal associated with silence, modesty, and prudence.[33] This model may have prevailed throughout the modern centuries, although it is also true that, in moments of social tension, women raised their voices. How is it possible that social reality was so far removed from the scope of the most distinguished dissertations?

The ideal of the honest, modest, and submissive woman spread throughout much of society, although it never ceased to be an aspiration, an illusion. Limited to the home, women could use speech to achieve one of their most important social functions: effective control. In the small communities of modern centuries, whispering was a basic mechanism of surveillance, punishment, and social control, a tool to confine the most divergent.[34] It was called "women's throne," according to Jean-Jacques Rousseau.[35] The androcentric and patriarchal system would grant women part of this function by making use of speech, a task that reveals an interesting systemic contradiction. The "infrapolitics" of subordinate groups, according to Steve Hidle, consisted of a rumor comparable to a "formative stage in the development of public opinion,"[36] an aspect that fits with Thompson's statements about women's roles as initiators of the rebellions. They were, ultimately, responsible for transmitting the most indignant messages.

Against this threat, contemporary writers interfered, describing women as impostors. However, women could also use a second mechanism, the plea. Much more in line with the canons and desires of a society flooded by changing androcentric schemes, the plea must be understood as a tool "to formulate requests and to harmonize relations between men and women."[37] Women would use this device to obtain a benefit from authorities, so the feminine culture of the period had the plea as an attribute of its identity.[38] Plea and whisper can therefore be linked to the "strategic use of gender."[39]

Between 1631 and 1634, Biscayan women played an essential role in transmitting part of the information that was spread throughout the territory as rumor.[40] The end of the crown's maritime blockade brought the Salt Rebellion of Biscay to a close. Later, the salt tax that started the revolt was eliminated. However, the territory accepted the restoration of the Veeduría del Contrabando—the person in charge of fraud control, a relevant position as fraud was increasing with the increase in American trade.[41]

As the century progressed, there were three riots with female presence: Bermeo in 1672, Fitero in 1675, and Ugarre between 1683 and 1692. In the case of the small Biscayan town Bermeo, women were the protagonists of a small issue: one ordinary morning, they went to the dock to buy grain, and the day ended with protests against speculation.[42] In the Basque-French case of Ugarre, they stalked the representative of Louis XIV, Claude Charron, after the confiscation of a salt convoy. All this occurred among events that led the rioters to try to kill the guards of the Ferme.[43] Sometimes, without having to start the most violent acts, women participated in the action, although always using speech, which could end up inciting violence.

In the eighteenth century, there was a strong rise of popular protests, revolts where women participated in many ways. The Matxinada of 1718 stands out, an antitax riot over the transfer of customs to the coast that stirred up part of the population and ended with the success of the *matxinos* (rebels).[44] After the business strike organized by Guipuzcoan merchants and the return of customs to the interior, the RCGC was established in 1728, another milestone in the history of Atlantic relations.[45] Meanwhile, the crown managed to increase its control over illegal trade by establishing a new antismuggling judge.[46]

At these events, women once again showed the power of their voices, since, according to critics of the period, "they participated in everything, fanning the flames with their evil tongues."[47] Furthermore, they also participated in the riots that took place in Bilbao, which ended with the murder of Deputy General Enrique de Arana: "shortly after dawn, an innumerable multitude of their troops could already be seen in the nearby mountains, in much greater numbers and with more weapons than the days before they carried out their plan, and their women were undoubtedly loaded with baskets to carry what they stole."[48]

The same thing happened at the beginning of the nineteenth century during the Zamacolada, when, according to one witness, "the women, who are the worst in all the riots, began to insult the men . . . and then they, crowding around us, snatched them [the prisoners] from our arms."[49] In the French Basque Country, crowds of women took part in the riots, as in Saint Jean de Luz in

1726,⁵⁰ Sara in 1773, or Hasparren in 1784. In this last rural town, two thousand women were mobilized.⁵¹

As we see in these examples, women's speech is crucial, a chorus that transfers the messages and ignites, according to the most critical voices, the most indignant ones. Speech becomes women's great instrument for political and social action, rumors that influence the rest of the community.⁵² And speaking of its use, the Basque language predominates: in the serious events that happened in Saint Jean de Luz in 1748, the women rebelled after misinterpreting a pamphlet written in French.⁵³ In Hasparren in 1784, "the intendant's negotiations with the women were delayed until the arrival of Abbot Haramboure, who acted as translator and mediator."⁵⁴

The link between the Basque language, the use of words by women, and popular insurrections could be important, in fact. The problem is that there are no sources that preserve the most indignant messages in the form of a stanza or pamphlet. With some exceptions,⁵⁵ these manifestations were spread from valley to valley orally, not written down. Few studies indicate the presence of this type of text in seventeenth-century Navarre or in the aforementioned case of Saint Jean de Luz.⁵⁶ What is the reason for such a gap?

One of the reasons, although not the only one, could be related to *bertso*. These poetic compositions, sung and improvised, are still part of the Basque oral culture today. In the Old Fuero (law) of Biscay of 1452, there was a warning about "women who have a reputation for being shameless troublemakers in neighborhoods and who write verses and songs as defamatory pamphlet."⁵⁷ In other words, these women were female *bertsolaris* who practiced satire as a critical and offensive expression. It is a form of community entertainment, one of the oldest Basque cultural expressions and performed, although not exclusively, by women. Bertso has always been linked to gossip and the exhibition of popular discontent. It is no coincidence that most of the pamphlets preserved to date align with the geographical limits of the Basque language—that is, they are written in Spanish and published in the territories with the greatest Spanish influence.[58]

In this regard, I highlight two of the previously mentioned elements: the impact of American products and the influence of this Atlantic universe in the Basque territory. Many of the disturbances were caused by the monarchs' desire to impose taxes on colonial products, such as salt, but also by their attempt to suppress the legal and fiscal autonomy of these territories, in a clear centralizing dynamic. The problem of customs, their absence and supervision, is directly related to the traffic of these American goods, whose consumption soared between the seventeenth and eighteenth centuries.[59]

This was the case of Labourd in 1784, where women played a key role during protests against the tobacco and salt tax authorities.[60] Two years earlier, in Mendionde, customs officials were attacked during protests against the imposition of taxes and the tobacco monopoly. During the first day, two hundred women peacefully surrounded the customs offices. The next day, more than one thousand women, armed with spikes and lances and supported by three hundred men, stormed the building.[61]

The female influence within these movements was so important that, during this period, the riots were also known as "émotions des ces femmes" (emotions of these women). In the insurrections that happened between 1773 and 1784 in the French Basque Country, 26.8 percent were attended by women, of whom 36.6 percent were charged.[62] "Between 1660 and 1789, the gender split in the anti-tax revolts in Languedoc shows a clear decline in the female presence as the chronology progresses, however, in Labourd we do not see such a drop."[63] In the province of Álava, meanwhile, small peasant communities hurled insults at the Tobacco Revenue guards, even using violence against them.[64] In the Kingdom of Navarre, women attended nearly 8 percent of the riots.

And what about across the Atlantic? The fact is that the role played by women is similar, if not identical. Through the centuries, especially during the Atlantic Revolutions, American women played an essential role. We see this in the American antitax revolts against the British Crown and throughout Hispanic America.

In the *comunero* revolt that took place in Socorro, New Granada, in 1781, several women contributed. It was the classic antitax protest, where a woman called Manuela Beltrán sparked the insurrection by publicly rejecting an edict from the crown and shouting, "Long live the king, death to bad government."[65] That same year, in Maracaibo, more women joined the protests.[66] Another example is the plot that took place in Venezuela in 1797 to establish an independent republic, abolish slavery, and create a free market; the wives of the main leaders joined in.[67] However, one of the most important rebellions to occur was the one led by Túpac Amaru II that swept through the regions of Bolivia and Peru in those years. His wife, Micaela Bastidas, like other indigenous women, played an essential role.[68]

In some of the events that led to the independence proclaimed by the Congress of Venezuela on July 5, 1811, we observe the intervention of women. A year earlier, for example, a popular rally took place in Bogotá's main square to demand the formation of a republican junta. Among the attendees were women from Bogotá's high society. Some events were violent: the viceroy's wife was arrested and taken to Divorcio, a detention center for women. During her transfer, she was attacked by a group of women.[69]

Farther north, in eighteenth-century Mexico, 25 percent of rural protests were led by women, who were described as "aggressive, insulting and rebellious." The void left by men, who migrated seasonally to work far from their villages, influenced this reality.[70] This participation continued with their later intervention in the Bajío rebellion led by Miguel Hidalgo. In both the Old and the New Worlds, women played central roles in uprisings, fulfilling actions characteristic of the female gender. One of the most interesting interpretations, furthermore, is its relationship with later political events. In both the American and Hispanic American cases, there will be a direct connection between these popular and "traditional" riots and future independence movements.

Back in the Basque Country, another interesting trend emerged that could be related to women's involvement in insurrections: female crime in Vizcaya was around 10 percent,[71] a statistic that rises to 20 percent in its coastal towns.[72] What is the reason for such an increase? The answer can be found, although not categorically, in one of the most singular phenomena of the period: the feminization of the Basque coast.[73]

NOTES

1. Javier Ruiz Astiz, "La participación de las mujeres en los desórdenes públicos: Análisis de su presencia en la Navarra moderna," *Sancho el Sabio* 33 (2010): 24.
2. José Carlos Enríquez Fernández, "Cultura popular, Charivari y fiesta: Los procesos de regulación represiva de las tradiciones lúdicas de las clases plebeyas vizcaínas (siglos XVII–XIX)," *Zainak: Cuadernos de Antropología-Etnografía* 26 (2004): 525–45; Javier Ruiz Astiz, "Herramientas de transmisión comunitaria: Libelos y pasquines en la Navarra moderna," *Historia y Comunicación Social* 14 (2009): 87–110; Javier Ruiz Astiz, "Cencerradas y matracas en Navarra durante el Antiguo Régimen: Funciones y objetivos," *Hispania* (2013): 237–45.
3. Ruiz Astiz, "La participación," 30.
4. Ruiz Astiz, "La participación," 21, 27.
5. Pilar Pérez-Fuentes Hernández, *"Ganadores de pan" y "amas de casa": Otra mirada sobre la industrialización vasca* (Bilbao: UPV/EHU, 2004); Edward P. Thompson, *Tradición, revuelta y conciencia de clase: Estudios sobre la crisis de la sociedad preindustrial* (Barcelona: Crítica, 1984), 109.
6. Ruiz Astiz, "La participación," 17–18.
7. John H. Elliott, *Imperios del mundo atlántico: España y Gran Bretaña en América, 1492–1830* (Madrid: Taurus, 2006); John H. Elliott,

España, Europa y el mundo de ultramar (1500–1800) (Madrid: Taurus, 2010).
8. José Ángel Lema Pueyo, "De 'Ipuzkoa' a la hermandad de villas de Gipuzkoa (ss. VI–VX)," in *Síntesis de la Historia de Gipuzkoa*, ed. Álvaro Aragón Ruano and Iker Echeberria Ayllón (Donostia: Diputación Foral de Gipuzkoa, 2017), 208–10; Alberto Angulo Morales and Iker Echeberria Ayllón, "Furias de consumidores y voces femeninas: Las resistencias anti-fiscales en tierras de vasconia (1634–1804)," in *Resistencias campesinas en los espacios rurales de Europa y América durante la Edad Moderna*, ed. Rubén Castro Redondo and Pablo F. Luna (La Plata, Argentina: Universidad Nacional de La Plata, Facultad de Humanidades y Ciencias de la Educación; Ensenada, Mexico: IdIHCS; Santander, Spain: Universidad de Cantabria, HisMundI 7, 2024), 341–74.
9. Fernando Txueka Isasti, "El Colegio de Pilotos Vizcaínos de Cádiz. La otra historia marítima de los vascos: Del Mare Nostrum al Pacífico," *Itsas Memoria. Revista de Estudios Marítimos del País Vasco* 8 (2016): 611–23.
10. Fernando Fernández González, "Castilla, Sevilla y el País Vasco en la segunda mitad del siglo XVIII," *Itsas Memoria: Revista de Estudios Marítimos del País Vasco* 4 (2003): 287–95.
11. Álvaro Aragón Ruano, "La evolución de la economía guipuzcoana en tiempos de Urdaneta: un período de desarrollo y expansión entre supuestas crisis," in *Andrés de Urdaneta: Un hombre moderno*, ed. Susana Truchuelo García (Ordizia, Spain: Ordiziako Udala, 2009), 119–44; José Antonio Azpiazu Elorza, "Los guipuzcoanos y Sevilla en la Alta Edad Moderna," *Itsas Memoria: Revista de Estudios Marítimos del País Vasco* 4 (2003): 207–13; Lutgardo García Fuentes, "Los vascos en la Carrera de Indias en la Edad Moderna: una minoría dominante," *Temas Americanistas* 16 (2003): 33–40.
12. Álvaro Aragón Ruano, "Euskal Herria 'itsastarra' lehen mundubiraren testuinguruan," in *Elkano eta lehen mundubira: 500 urte geroago* (Getaria, Spain: Mundubira 500 Elkano Fundazioa, 2020), 75–102; Estíbaliz González Dios, "Gipuzkoa en la primera globalización (ss. XVI–XVIII)," in Aragón Ruano, *Síntesis de la Historia de Gipuzkoa*, 299–302.
13. Alberto Angulo Morales, "Información, negociación y defensa: Las fronteras en las provincias exentas (XVI–XVII)," in *Dinámica de las*

fronteras en periodos de conflict: El Imperio español (1640–1815), ed. Miguel Ángel Melón Jiménez, Miguel Rodríguez Cancho, and Isabel Testón Núñez (Cáceres, Spain: Universidad de Extremadura, 2019), 154–67; Álvaro Aragón Ruano, "'... Faltar y ausentarse con esto los naturales de esta provinçia y quedar despoblada y hierma, sin defensa alguna...,' Discursos de frontera en Gipuzkoa durante la Edad Moderna," in *Naciones en el Estado-Nación: La formación cultural y política de naciones en la Europa contemporánea*, ed. Joseba Agirreazkuenaga Zigorraga and Eduardo J. Alonso Olea (Barcelona: Editorial Base, 2014), 404–5; González Dios, "Gipuzkoa," 291–92; *Notitia Vasconiae: Historiadores, juristas y pensadores políticos de Vasconia. Antigüedad, Edad Media y Moderna* (Madrid: Fundación Iura Vasconiae, Marcial Pons, 2019).

14. José Ramón Díaz de Durana, "La hidalguía universal en el País Vasco: Tópicos sobre sus orígenes y causas de su desigual generalización," *Cuadernos de Alzate* 31 (2004): 55–57.

15. Álvaro Aragón Ruano, "Discursos de frontera en el Pirineo occidental durante la Edad Moderna," in *Una década prodigiosa: Beligerancia y negociación entre la Corona y las provincias vascas (1717–1728)*, ed. Álvaro Aragón Ruano and Alberto Angulo Morales (Bilbao: UPV/EHU, 2019), 155–74.

16. Daniel Baldellou Monclús, "Idiosincrasia del modelo de transmisión de la propiedad en el Antiguo Régimen: El modelo de las familias del Pirineo," *Actas del I Congreso Internacional Jóvenes Investigadores Siglo de Oro*, 2012, 11–21; Daniel Baldellou Monclús and José Antonio Salas Auséns, "Noviazgo y matrimonio en Aragón: Casarse en la Europa del Antiguo Régimen," *Revista de Historia Moderna: Anales de la Universidad de Alicante* 34 (2016): 85; Pilar Erdozain Azpilikueta and Fernando Mikelarena Peña, "Algunas consideraciones en torno a la investigación del régimen de herencia troncal en la Euskal Herria tradicional," *Vasconia* 28 (1991): 71–91; José Antonio Moreno Almárcegui and Ana Zabalza Seguín, *El origen histórico de un sistema de heredero único: El prepirineo navarro, 1540–1739* (Pamplona, Spain: Rialp, 1999); Ana Zabalza Seguín, "El heredero ideal: Prácticas sucesorias en la Navarra pirenaica durante la Edad Moderna (1550–1725)," in *Actas del Congreso Internacional de la Población: V Congreso de la ADEH*, ed. David Sven Reher Sullivan (Logroño: 1999), 239–50.

17. Óscar Álvarez Gila and Alberto Angulo Morales, *Las migraciones vascas en perspectiva histórica (siglos XVI–XX)* (Bilbao: UPV/EHU, 2002); Alberto Angulo Morales and Álvaro Aragón Ruano, eds., *Recuperando el Norte: Empresas, capitales y proyectos atlánticos en la economía imperial hispánica* (Bilbao: UPV/EHU, 2016); Alberto Angulo Morales, "Los frutos de la movilidad: La emigración norteña peninsular en Madrid y el Imperio (siglos XVII y XVIII)," *Obradoiro de Historia Moderna* 24 (2015): 113–39; Alberto Angulo Morales, "Migration, Mobility and Voyages: A Case Study on the Use of Private Sources for the Understanding of Basque Migration in the Eighteenth Century," in *From the Records of my Deepest Memory: Personal Sources and the Study of European Migration, 18th–20th centuries*, ed. Óscar Álvarez Gila and Alberto Angulo Morales (Bilbao: UPV/EHU, 2016) 13–40; Alberto Angulo Morales, *De Cameros a Bilbao: Negocios, familia y nobleza en tiempos de crisis (1770–1834)* (Bilbao: UPV/EHU, 2007) 89–95; José Miguel Aramburu-Zudaire, "América y los vascos en la Edad Moderna: Una perspectiva historiográfica," *Vasconia* 34 (2005): 249–74; Juan Aranzadi, *Milenarismo vasco: Edad de Oro, etnia y nativismo* (Madrid: Taurus, 2000) 535–45; Jesús Arpal Poblador, *La sociedad tradicional en el País Vasco: El estamento de los hidalgos en Guipúzcoa* (San Sebastián: Haranburu, 1979) 213–43; José Manuel Azcona Pastor, *Identidad y estructura de la emigración vasca y navarra hacia Iberoamérica (Siglos XVI–XXI)* (Madrid: Thomson Reuters-Aranzadi, 2015); José María Imízcoz Beunza, ed., *Casa, familia y sociedad (País Vasco, España y América, siglos XV–XIX)* (Leioa, Spain: UPV/EHU, 2004).

18. Alberto Angulo Morales, "El *institutional entangled global network* de navarros y vascongados en la defensa atlántica por la plata peruana del Seiscientos (Madrid, Potosí y Puno)," *Protohistoria* 35 (2021): 361–78; David A. Brading, *Mineros y comerciantes en el México borbónico (1763–1810)* (Mexico City: Fondo de Cultura Económica, 2015); Clara García-Ayluardo, "El milagro de la Virgen: El desarrollo de los vascos como grupo de poder en la Nueva España," in *IV Seminario de Historia de la Real Sociedad Bascongada de los Amigos del País. "La RSBAP y Méjico"* (Donostia-San Sebastián: RSBAP, Tomo I, 1993) 439–57; Doris M. Ladd, *La nobleza mexicana en la época de la independencia, 1780–1826* (Mexico City: Fondo de Cultura Económica, 1984).

19. Álvarez Gila and Angulo Morales, *Las migraciones vascas*, 94, 107–8.
20. Álvaro Aragón Ruano and Alberto Angulo Morales, "Spanish Basque Country in Global Trade Networks in the Eighteenth Century," *International Journal of Maritime History* 25 (2013): 149–72; Lutgardo García Fuentes, *Los peruleros y el comercio de Sevilla con las Indias, 1580–1630* (Seville, Spain: Universidad de Sevilla, 1997); García Fuentes, "Los vascos," 29–49; Lutgardo García Fuentes, "La crisis del siglo XVII y las remesas de caudales indianos desde Sevilla para el País Vasco," *Archivo hispalense: Revista histórica, literaria y artística* 84, no. 255 (2001): 27–42; José Garmendia Arruebarrena, *Cádiz, los vascos y la carrera de Indias* (San Sebastián: Eusko Ikaskuntza, 1989); Jesús Turiso Sebastián, "Emigración, comerciantes y comercio en la región de Veracruz entre 1778–1822," *Naveg@mérica* 22 (2019): 11.
21. Alberto Angulo Morales, "Otro 'imposible vencido': hombres, provincias y reinos en la Corte en tiempos de Carlos II," in *Volver a la 'hora navarra': La contribución navarra a la construcción de la monarquía española en el siglo XVIII*, ed. Rafael Torres Sánchez (Pamplona, Spain: Universidad de Navarra, 2010), 33–72; Alberto Angulo Morales, "De la congregación de Cantabria o San Ignacio al proyecto de la Bascongada: El grupo de presión vasco en la Villa y Corte de Madrid (1713–1775)," in *Devoción, paisanaje e identidad: Las cofradías y congregaciones de naturales en España y en América (siglos XVI–XIX)*, ed. Óscar Álvarez Gila, Alberto Angulo Morales, and Jon Ander Ramos Martínez (Bilbao: UPV/EHU, 2014), 199–226; Angulo Morales and Aragón Ruano, *Recuperando el Norte*.
22. Alejandro Cardozo Uzcátegui, "El lobby cisatlántico del cacao: La Real Compañía Guipuzcoana de Caracas y el poder vasco en la provincia de Venezuela," in Angulo Morales and Aragón Ruano, *Recuperando el Norte*, 195–216; Irene Fattaccia, "The Resilience and Boomerang Effect of Chocolate: A Product's Globalization and Commodification," in *Global Goods and the Spanish Empire, 1492–1824: Circulation, Resistance and Diversity*, ed. Bethany Aram and Bartolomé Yun-Casalilla (London: Palgrave Macmillan, 2014), 255–73; Montserrat Gárate Ojanguren, *La Real Compañía Guipuzcoana de Caracas* (San Sebastián: Sociedad Guipuzcoana de Ediciones y Publicaciones,

1990), 519–84; José Garmendia Arruebarrena, "La Real Compañía Guipuzcoana de Caracas y su contribución en Sevilla," *Cuadernos de Sección, Eusko Ikaskuntza, Sociedad de Estudios Vascos* 8 (1986): 48–58; *Los vascos y América: Actas de las Jornadas sobre el comercio vasco con América en el siglo XVIII y la Real Compañía Guipuzcoana de Caracas en el II centenario de Carlos II* (Bilbao: Fundación Banco de Vizcaya, 1980); Adelina Rodríguez Mirabal, "La España reformista de comienzos del siglo XVIII y la nueva orientación del comercio ultramarino (El caso de la Compañía Guipuzcoana de Caracas)," *Ensayos Históricos: Anuario del Instituto de Estudios Hispánicos* 13 (2001): 39–54; Gerardo Vivas Pineda, *La aventura naval de la Compañía Guipuzcoana de Caracas* (Caracas: Fundación Polar, 1998); Gerardo Vivas Pineda, "La Compañía Guipuzcoana de Caracas: Los buques y sus hombres," in *Los vascos y América: Actas de las Jornadas sobre el comercio vasco con América en el siglo XVIII y la Real Compañía Guipuzcoana de Caracas en el II centenario de Carlos II* (Bilbao: Fundación Banco de Vizcaya, 1980), 313–17.

23. Alberto Angulo Morales, "Los hidalgos norteños en el centro de un Imperio: Madrid (1638–1850): Negocios, política e identidad," in Angulo Morales and Aragón Ruano, *Recuperando el Norte*, 261–96; Alfonso de Otazu and José Ramón Díaz de Durana, *El espíritu emprendedor de los vascos* (Madrid: Sílex, 2008), 246–58; Tamar Herzog, "Private Organizations as Global Networks in Early Modern Spain and Spanish America," in *The Collective and the Public in Latin America: Cultural Identities and Political Order*, ed. Luis Roniger and Tamar Herzog (Brighton, UK: Sussex Academic Press, 2000), 117–33.

24. Fernando Fernández González, *Comerciantes vascos en Sevilla, 1650–1700* (Vitoria-Gasteiz, Spain: Diputación de Sevilla/Gobierno Vasco, 2000), 277–84; Alberto Angulo Morales, "Mercados y financieros vascos: El circuito de la plata y su control en el Seiscientos," in *Tesoreros, "arrendadores" y financieros en los reinos hispánicos: La Corona de Castilla y el Reino de Navarra (Siglos XIV–XVII)*, ed. Ernesto García Fernández (Madrid: Ministerio de Economía y Hacienda, Instituto de Estudios Fiscales, 2012), 241–56; García Fuentes, "La crisis del siglo XVII," 27–42; Jesús María Usunáriz Garayoa, "Un aspecto de la emigración navarra al Nuevo Mundo durante el

siglo XVIII: Las remesas indianas," *Príncipe de Viana* 13 (1991): 383–92.
25. Xabier Alberdi Lonbide, *Conflictos de intereses en la economía marítima guipuzcoana. Siglos XVI–XVIII* (PhD diss., UPV/EHU, Vitoria-Gasteiz, 2012), 749–95.
26. Renato Barahona Arévalo, "A Seventeenth Century Vizcayan Sociopolitical Movement: The Salt-Tax Revolt (1631–1634)," *Euskal Herriaren historiari buruzko biltzarra* 3 (1988): 317–27.
27. J. C. Areizaga, A. Iturbe, and I. Llano, "Los agavillados de 1607: Sobre los antecedentes urbanos de la Matxinada de la Sal," in *II Congreso de Historia de Euskal Herria* (San Sebastián: Txertoa, 1988), 314.
28. José Carlos Enríquez Fernández and Javier Enríquez Fernández, "Comportamientos populares durante las machinadas vascas: Moral patibular y orden tradicional," *II Congreso de Historia de Euskal Herria* (San Sebastián: Txertoa, 1988), 345.
29. Eva Mendieta Garrote and Isabel Molina Martos, "Revuelta social en la Edad Moderna europea: Participación y discurso de las mujeres en la Matxinada de la sal de Bilbao (1631–1634), *Vasconia* 42 (2018): 7.
30. Mendieta Garrote and Molina Martos, "Revuelta social," 21; Angulo Morales and Echeberria Ayllón, "Furias de consumidores," 353–57.
31. Mendieta Garrote and Molina Martos, "Revuelta social," 22–23.
32. Mendieta Garrote and Molina Martos, "Revuelta social," 21.
33. Eva Mendieta Garrote, "Del silencio al alboroto: El control del lenguaje de la mujer en la Edad Moderna," *Memoria y Civilización* 18 (2015): 134–51.
34. María Antonia Bel Bravo, *Mujer y cambio social en la Edad Moderna* (Madrid: Encuentro, 2008), 96–97; Tomás Antonio Mantecón Movellán, "El peso de la infrajudicialidad en el control del crimen durante la Edad Moderna," *Estudis. Revista de historia moderna* 28 (2002): 73–74.
35. Jean-Jacques Rousseau, *Emilio o de la educación* (Barcelona: Fontanella, 1973): 249.
36. Steve Hidle, "The Shaming of Margaret Knowley: Gossip, Gender and the Experience of Authority in Early Modern England," *Continuity and Change* 9, no. 3 (1994): 395–96; Mendieta Garrote, "Del silencio al alboroto," 158.

37. Margarita Ortega López, "Estrategias de defensa de las mujeres de la sociedad popular española del siglo XVIII," *Arenal* 5, no. 2 (1998): 286.
38. Marcela Aguirrezabala and Marcela V. Tejerina, "Entre quejas confiadas y súplicas de amparo: Una aproximación a la condición de las mujeres en el Río de la Plata a fines del siglo XVIII," *Palobra* 13 (2013): 18–29.
39. Laura Oliván Santaliestra, "Por una historia diplomática de las mujeres en la Edad Moderna," in *Autoridad, poder e influencia: Mujeres que hacen historia*, ed. H. Gallego Franco and M. C. García Herrero (Baracelona: Icaria, 2017), 63–69.
40. Mendieta Garrote and Molina Martos, "Revuelta social," 22.
41. Charo Porres Marijuán, "El poder y los conflictos sociales," in *Historia del País Vasco: Edad Moderna (Siglos XVI–XVIII)*, ed. A. Angulo Morales, C. Porres Marijuán, and I. Reguera (Donostia: Hiria, 2004), 237–89; Mikel Zabala Montoya, "La rebelión del Estanco de la Sal (Bizkaia, 1631/34): Una revisión," *Boletín de la Real Academia de la Historia* 204, no. 1 (2007): 45–128.
42. Luis M. Bernal Serna, "Responsabilidades y conflictividad de las mujeres en las localidades portuarias (Vizcaya, 1550–1808)," *Itsas Memoria. Revista de Estudios Marítimos del País Vasco* 7 (2012): 199–200.
43. Maya González, "La gabelle en Basse-Navarre: La saline d'Ugarre à l'époque de Louis XIV (1683–1692)," *Euskonews* 338 (2016); Maite Lafourcade, "L'autonomie administrative du Pays Basque de France sous l'Ancien Regime," *Boletín JADO* 19 (2010): 135.
44. Álvaro Aragón Ruano, "Discrepancias en el seno de la burguesía guipuzcoana en torno a la libertad de comercio y el traslado de aduanas durante los siglos XVIII y XIX," *Hispania: Revista Española de Historia* 73, no. 245 (2013): 761–88; José María Iñurrategui Rodríguez, "Matxinada: El fuero y sus lecturas en la Guipúzcoa del Setecientos," in *El mundo hispánico en el Siglo de las Luces*, vol. 2 (Madrid: Universidad Complutense, 1996), 805–16; Xabier Lamikiz, "La matxinada de 1718 y su trasfondo socioeconómico," in Aragón Ruano and Angulo Morales, *Una década prodigiosa*, 95–123; Rosario Porres Marijuán, "Elites, poder provincial y reformismo borbónico en el País Vasco del siglo XVIII," in *Élites y poder en*

las monarquías ibéricas. Del siglo XVIII al primer liberalismo, ed. María López Díaz (Madrid: Biblioteca Nueva, 2013), 129–154.

45. Xabier Alberdi Lonbide, "Reforma de la administración de los recursos navales de Gipuzkoa a principios del siglo XVIII: La búsqueda de un nuevo equilibrio entre la política naval y económica de la Monarquía y las actividades de los principales hombres de negocios de la provincia," in Aragón Ruano and Angulo Morales, *Una década prodigiosa*, 86; Ricardo Cierbide Martinena, "La Compañía Guipuzcoana de Caracas y los vascos en Venezuela durante el siglo XVIII," *Revista Internacional de Estudios Vascos* 42, no. 1 (1997): 63–75; Montserrat Gárate Ojanguren, "Las cuentas de la Real Compañía Guipuzcoana de Caracas," *Moneda y Crédito* 153 (1980): 49–75.

46. Xabier Alberdi Lonbide, *Conflictos de intereses en la economía marítima guipuzcoana: Siglos XVI–XVIII* (PhD diss., UPV/EHU, Vitoria-Gasteiz, 2012), 1072–73; Cayetano Manrique and Amalio Marichalar, *Historia de la legislación y recitaciones del Derecho Civil de España* (Madrid: Imprenta Nacional, Tomo VIII, 1865), 305–6.

47. Biblioteca del Parlamento Vasco, Manuscritos, Patrimonio Bibliográfico Digitalizado; Angulo Morales and Echeberria Ayllón, "Furias de consumidores," 357.

48. Biblioteca del Parlamento Vasco, Manuscritos, Patrimonio Bibliográfico Digitalizado; Angulo Morales and Echeberria Ayllón, "Furias de consumidores," 357.

49. Aleix Romero Peña, "Mariano Luis de Urquijo, testigo y protagonista involuntario del motín de la Zamacolada (1804)," *Brocar* 33 (2009): 124.

50. Pierre Dop, "Une émeute de femmes à St-Jean-de-Luz en 1726," *Gure herria* 12 (1932): 268–69; Jean Nicolas, *La rébellion française: Mouvements populaires et conscience sociale* (Paris: Gallimard, 2008) 44, 86.

51. Jean-Luc Laffont, "Les femmes dans les revoltes populaires en France a l'époque moderne," *Memoires de l'Académie des sciences, inscriptions et belles lettres de Toulouse* 177 (2016): 172–73.

52. Mendieta Garrote, "Del silencio al alboroto," 151.

53. José Madariaga Orbea, *Sociedad y Lengua Vasca en los siglos XVII y XVIII* (Bilbao: Euskailtzaindia, 2014), 103; Philippe Veyrin, *Les*

Basques: de Labourd, de Soule et de la Basse Navarre, leur histoire et leurs traditions (Grenoble, France: Arthaud, 1947), 179.

54. Angulo Morales and Echeberria Ayllón, "Furias de consumidores," 346; Christian Desplat, "Fiscalité et sédition à Bayonne et en Labourd," *Bulletin de la Société Sciences, Lettres et Arts de Bayonne* 132 (1976): 147; Nicolas, *La rébellion*, 139–44; Pierre Yturbide, "Una émeute des femmes d'Hasparren en 1784," *Revista Internacional de Estudios Vascos* 1 (1908): 201.

55. Archivo Histórico del Santuario de Loyola, Historia, Legs. 17.144 y 15.154; Archivo Histórico de Euskadi, Archivo de la Casa Zabala, 84.17; Archivo Histórico Nacional, Consejos, Leg. 7145, Exp. 47; Archivo Histórico Foral de Bizkaia (AHFB), Gobierno y Asuntos Eclesiásticos, AJ00600/134; Porres Marijuán, "El poder," 271; Zabala Montoya, "La rebelión," 108.

56. Ruiz Astiz, "Herramientas," 92; Ruiz Astiz, "La participación," 119–33; Ruiz Astiz, "Cencerradas," 349.

57. Ana Isabel Ugalde, Pilar Aristizabal, Pablo Lekue, and María Teresa Vizcarra, "Mujeres vascas improvisadoras: Las *bertsolaris* del mundo tradicional (Siglos XV–XIX)," *Arenal* 27, no. 1 (2020): 147.

58. Madariaga Orbea, *Sociedad*, 632–34.

59. Alberto Angulo Morales and Álvaro Aragón Ruano, "No sólo pescado y harina a cambio de oro: Vascos en el comercio con los Estados Unidos durante el siglo XVIII," *Boletín americanista* 77 (2019): 147–66; Alberto Angulo Morales, "El clero y los productos coloniales en la España septentrional: Consumo, contrabando e inmunidad eclesiástica (Siglos XVII–XVIII)," in *Entre el fervor y la violencia: Estudios sobre los vascos y la Iglesia (Siglos XVI–XVIII)*, ed. Mª Rosario Porres (Bilbao: UPV/EHU, 2015), 187–216; Alberto Angulo Morales, "Estanco y contrabando de tabaco en el País Vasco (1684–1876)," in *Tabaco y economía en el siglo XVIII*, ed. A. González Enciso and R. Torres Sánchez (Pamplona, Spain: Eunsa, 1999), 195–237; Lafourcade, "L'autonomie," 129–35; Koldo Larrañaga, "Oihenart y el tema de los orígenes vascos," *Vasconia* 14 (1996): 115–43; Angulo Morales and Echeberria Ayllón, "Furias de consumidores," 341–49.

60. Anne Verju and Catherine Dhaussy, "De l'action féminine en période de révolte(s) etrévolution(s), 1770–1802," in *Révoltes et révolu-*

tions en Europe (Russie incluse) et aux Amériques de 1773 à 1802 en dissertations corrigées, ed. A. Jollet (Paris: Ellipses, 2005), 56–71.
61. Desplat, "Fiscalité," 140–46.
62. Dop, "Une émeute," 270; Nicolas, La rébellion, 35; Élie Pélaquier, "Les mouvements anti-fiscaux en Languedoc d'après les archives de la Cour des Comptes, Aides et Finances de Montpellier (1660–1789)," Annales du Midi 111, no. 125 (1999): 13.
63. Angulo Morales and Echeberria Ayllón, "Furias de consumidores," 345–46; Jean-Luc Laffont, "Les femmes dans les revoltes populaires en France a l'époque moderne," Memoires de l'Académie des sciences, inscriptions et belles lettres de Toulouse 177 (2016): 165.
64. Alberto Angulo Morales, Las puertas de la vida y la muerte. La administración aduanera en las provincias vascas (1690–1780) (Bilbao: UPV/EHU, 1994), 203–204.
65. Claire Brewster, "Women and the Spanish-American Wars of Independence: An overview," Feminist Review 79 (2005): 22–23.
66. Evelyn Cherpak, "The Participation of Women in the Wars for Independence in Northern South America 1810–1824," Minerva 11, no. 3 (1993): 2.
67. Cherpak, "Participation," 2.
68. Brewster, "Women," 23–25; Alejandra Ciriza, "Pensar el bicentenario: Una lectura feminista sobre colonialidad, mujeres y emancipación," Kairos: Revista de temas sociales 38 (2016): 122–23.
69. Cherpak, "Participation," 3.
70. Brewster, "Women," 22.
71. Bernal Serna, "Responsabilidades," 201; Ruiz Astiz, "La participación," 16–17.
72. Bernal Serna, "Responsabilidades," 201.
73. Alberto Angulo Morales and Iker Echeberria Ayllón, "Viviendo en la raya: Las mujeres y el mundo fronterizo en los Pirineos occidentales durante el Setecientos," Príncipe de Viana 272 (2018): 1191; Amélia Polónia, "El rostro oculto de la aventura de Magalhaes/Elcano: El protagonismo femenino en sociedades marítimas portuguesas en el siglo XVI," in Más allá del mito y la epopeya: El País Vasco y la expedición Magallanes-Elcano en el contexto de la primera globalización, ed. Ó. A. Angulo, Álvarez, Á. Aragón, and A. Zaballa (Madrid: Dykinson, 2022), 99–127.

CHAPTER TWO

The Female Preeminence of the Basque Coast

The coastal towns of the Basque Country had a higher female than male population, a difference that influenced the cultural, social, and business dynamics of the area. One of the main reasons for the disproportion was male emigration: in the sixteenth century, 36.9 percent of men died far from their towns because they emigrated either seasonally or permanently, as had also happened in Mexico in the eighteenth century.[1] The Juntas Generales de Guipúzcoa protested against "the loss of their sailors and the distressing situation in which the levies of sailors left the fishing fleet and, above all, their families."[2] This situation of absence and emptiness increased with the success of immigration to America.[3]

The formation of the RCGC in 1728 with capital from Basque trade began a new stage in the history of Basque-American relations, one that furthered male emigration. Furthermore, there are documented cases of men who used company ships to escape to Venezuela, leaving their fiancées. These crimes may have amplified the male vacuum,[4] building an Atlantic wall.[5] As Merry E. Wiesner-Hanks notes, in addition to geographical borders, there are other types of dividing lines, such as gender or sex.[6]

The contribution of women on the Basque coast in activities traditionally linked to men is based on a complex structural need. As a result, we see them benefiting from smuggling, one of the most important economic activities in the region. The maritime Euskal Herria is a multiborder, feminized space, with territories that have a certain legal autonomy and without customs on the coast. Thanks to this, women participated in fraud, often with products from the Atlantic world; for example, women from Álava trafficked tobacco in the dry ports of the interior.[7]

One nineteenth-century North American traveler, a woman referred to as Mrs. Bates, was surprised by the *bateleras* of Pasajes (woman steering a boat) in charge of transporting people and goods. With great insight, she describes the following: "We discovered the nook when the old woman with iron arms was taking us in her boat, rowing through a narrow passage (hence the name) between rock walls whose cracks and crevices make even the most respectable tourist shudder, making him want to become a smuggler."[8] The truth is a century earlier, the bateleras contributed to the fraud practiced by the RCGC, since "it was no secret that the company's ships transferred smuggled goods when they approached two or three leagues from the coast, that was when the *bateleras* of Pasajes appeared."[9] In 1790, the antismuggling judge of San Sebastián reported that "women used the excuse of shortages to extract gold coins and introduce billon, transport cotton, snuff and Brazilian tobacco and bring in revolutionary prints and stamps."[10] The permeable Basque border witnessed daily fraud.

This situation conditioned its inhabitants economically as well as socially and politically. The militarization of strategic enclaves such as San Sebastián or Fuenterrabía, close to the border with France, caused complex social dynamics.[11] The absence of local men often meant local women had more contact with the troops. The director of the RCGC himself, head of the commercial oligarchy of San Sebastián, had to face these "inconveniences." His daughter, Magdalena de Claessens, offered herself in marriage to a captain of the Vizcaya regiment, a union the head of the family would not allow. When he discovered her plans, he took her to a small boat, a ship that he used to cross the border, and interned her in the convent of the Clarisas of Bayona, a punishment to which she submitted.[12]

In the city of San Sebastián, meanwhile, the troops were protected by military jurisdiction, not the ordinary courts.[13] The guarantees that the military courts offered to the soldiers—or the idea that they had about such protection whether or not it was true—made them take refuge in their jurisdiction. The crown was interested in protecting its troops, a legislative action that, in the midst of the Guerra de la Convención, aimed to strengthen the jurisdiction of the military; however, shortly after, the king ruled in favor of the ordinary jurisdiction in lawsuits for marital disagreements—that is, the "classic" conflict resulting from this contact between civilians and military.[14]

In fact, the usual "absence of men and the greater influence of women in the economic, social and cultural structures and relations of these border areas,"[15] with troops occupying part of this vacuum, could have motivated a greater acceptance of illegitimate children in the north of the peninsula. Compared to abandonment, a mechanism used to protect female and family honor, acceptance rates were higher in the northern territories of the Spanish crown.[16]

Fish sellers, women from the countryside, boatmen, barmaids, smugglers, and many others portray daily life in these places: "the foul language and the noise of the fishmongers in the London market is nothing compared to that of the fishermen and apple-sellers in San Sebastián. They are always at each other's throats; they slap each other silly and they don't become friends again for a week."[17] This scene belongs to the English trade consul William Frankland, one of many who pointed out the virile qualities of Basque women.

Indeed, there are several authors who, throughout the modern centuries, highlight the masculine attributes of women, especially those who lived on the coast. The impact of these women on the socioeconomic structures thanks to the vacuum left by men is reflected in their chronicles. It is, in fact, an important phenomenon, a set of references, descriptions, archetypes, and speeches that show part of the image of Basque femininity.

One of the most significant chroniclers of Gipuzkoa in the seventeenth century describes the women who lived there as "good-looking and naturally serious, honest, very clean, manly and capable of many things, particularly those who live near the sea,"[18] a fact endorsed by the historian Juan Ramón de Iturriza when he pointed out that the women of Lequeitio were hardworking and manly.[19] The famous Alexander von Humboldt notes that this absence of men helped "forge a strong Basque woman, with temperament and initiative."[20] Furthermore, the Irish naturalist Guillermo Bowles noted:

> In other places women can hardly endure a moderate fatigue: and in Bilbao the lowest plebs work harder than if they were men. They are the village's laborers and porters, who load and unload the ships. The forced workers of Cartagena and Almadén are lazy compared to them. They go barefoot on both feet and legs, and undressed arms; and from the robustness of the muscles that can be seen on them, one can guess the strength they attain. In particular, their necks are similar to those of bulls, since they hold and carry on their heads such heavy loads that two regular men are needed to put them on them. The woman does not yield in strength to her husband, nor the sister to her brother; and well drunk and loaded with weight, they run freely and firmly, which is a pleasure to see.[21]

The renowned writer Victor Hugo also had the opportunity to visit the Basque Country, a "little resplendent Eden where I arrived by chance." His chronicle focuses on the "sexual division of social and work space"; without realizing it, he pointed out this male preference for sailing and the consequent female reality of staying on land:

> The population of that town [Pasajes] has only one industry, work on the water. The two genders have divided the work according to their strength. The man has the ship, the woman has

the boat; the man has the sea, the woman has the bay; the man goes fishing and leaves the gulf, the woman stays in the gulf and "passes" all those whom a business or an interest leads there from San Sebastián. Hence the boatwomen.[22]

The Guipuzcoan Jesuit Manuel de Larramendi was the one who most successfully propagated the virile attributes of the Basque woman. Part of the generation called *novatores*—person belonging to a movement of renewal of Spanish science and culture between the seventeenth and eighteenth centuries—he stands out in the first half of the eighteenth century for being the confessor of Queen Mariana of Neuburg during her exile in Bayonne.[23] Father Larramendi describes the Guipuzcoan woman as manly, with the aim of underlining his community project: in the context of the War of the Spanish Succession, the privileges of the province seemed to be in question.[24] According to him, the hardest-working women, those of low economic background, deserved to be highlighted for being virile as an attribute of their excellence: "he wanted to project an image of femininity that would be a bearer of the values of the province, the nobility of blood and primitive Christianity."[25]

"Of superior value than their sex," the best of them is in their extraordinary Guipuzcoan and masculine gifts: "the importance of provincial particularism prevailed over the rest of the variables, showing that sex has not always been the fundamental element in the construction of women's identity."[26] "The feminization of the coast and its integration into the working world opens the doors to a perspective of the phenomenon in territorial terms, the importance of which is confirmed by the need and capacity to create discourses such as Larramendi's."[27]

Within the framework of these discourses and of a particular social, economic, and cultural reality, the role of Basque women seems singular; in moments of social tension, they have made significant contributions. There were compelling reasons for calling these movements "émotions des ces femmes."

Because the term *emotion* has a negative connotation, however, its assimilation into the concept of revolt in a feminine sense deserves another interpretation. In modern centuries, emotions have been identified as passions of the soul in its most negative sense, inappropriate alterations that should be directed toward a greater purpose. The Catholic and Stoic traditions consider emotions as disturbances or illnesses of the soul and opposed to reason.[28] In contrast to women, slaves of their passions, men are related with reason. The aforementioned Father Larramendi supported educating the youngest by "pulling out from their souls the weeds, the vice, the bad inclination for a perfect self-denial and overcoming of their passions."[29] They needed to know "what passions are in order to overcome them."[30]

Women, as we see, were judged as irrational beings, incapable of controlling their emotions and tongues. Women, unable to control their passions, started the riots. For this reason, *emotion* became tied to revolt, both for its meanings of irrationality and spontaneous explosion and for its close link to femininity. Understood as evil, emotions clashed with the social, family, evangelical, and community order.[31]

Provoked by the emotional and irrational speech and actions of women, the rebellions of the period were identified as having been caused by emotions of a collective nature. Despite the prevailing models of femininity, the truth is that the androcentric society of the time relied on the voices of its women. However, did women also participate in the most violent, traumatic, and disruptive conflicts in an active way?

NOTES

1. Santiago Piquero Zarauz, "El siglo XVI, época dorada de los movimientos migratorios guipuzcoanos de media y larga distancia durante la Edad Moderna," in *La lucha de bandos en el País Vasco, de los Parientes Mayores a la Hidalguía Universal*, ed. José Ramón Díaz de Durana Ortiz de Urbina (Bilbao: UPV/EHU, 1998), 406.

2. D. Abreu Ferreira, "Fishmongers and Shipowners: Women in Maritime Communities of Early Modern Portugal," *Sixteenth Century Journal* 31, no. 1 (2000): 7–23; José Antonio Azpiazu Elorza, *Mujeres vascas, sumisión y poder: La condición femenina en la Alta Edad Moderna* (San Sebastián: R&B, 1995), 209; José Antonio Azpiazu Elorza, "Las mujeres vascas y el mar," *Itsas Memoria: Revista de Estudios Marítimos del País Vasco* 8 (2016): 811–29; Allyson M. Poska, *Women and Authority in Early Modern Spain: The Peasants of Galicia* (Oxford: Oxford University Press, 2005).

3. Azpiazu Elorza, *Mujeres vascas*, 209; María José de la Pascua Sánchez, "Vivir en soledad, vivir en compañía: Las mujeres y el mundo familiar en el siglo XVIII hispánico," in *El siglo XVIII en femenino: Las mujeres en el Siglo de las Luces*, ed. Manuel-Reyes García Hurtado (Madrid: Síntesis, 2016), 151–90.

4. Archivo Diocesano de Pamplona (ADP), Secretario Ollo, C/1682, No. 13; ADP, Secretario Almándoz, C/1926, No. 6; ADP, Secretario Almándoz, C/1997, No. 36; ADP, Secretario Almándoz, C/2068, No. 8.

5. Angulo Morales and Echeberria Ayllón, "Viviendo," 1189–90; María del Carmen Martínez Martínez, "Cartas privadas de emigrantes en pleitos civiles," in *Cinco Siglos de Cartas. Historia y prácticas epistolares en las épocas moderna y contemporánea*, ed. Antonio Castillo Gómez and Verónica Sierra Blas (Huelva, Spain: Universidad de Huelva, 2014) 187–202; María Rosario Roquero Ussía, "La Real Compañía Guipuzcoana de Caracas: La mujer donostiarra y la emigración a Ultramar (Siglo XVIII)," *Boletín de Estudios Históricos de San Sebastián* 48 (2015): 138–47; Jesús María Usunáriz Garayoa, "Cartas de amor y cartas de emigrantes como prueba judicial en España (Siglos XVI–XVIII)," *Hispanic Research Journal. Iberian and Latin American Studies* 16, no. 14 (2015): 296–310; Jesús María Usunáriz Garayoa, "'Nere Andrea, beti memorien daukedana': Amores y desamores de ultramar en el siglo XVIII," in *Navarra y el nuevo mundo*, ed. María del Mar Larraza Micheltorena (Pamplona, Spain: Mintzoa, 2016), 77–96.

6. Merry E. Wiesner-Hanks, "Crossing Borders in Transnational Gender History," *Journal of Global History* 6 (2011): 359.

7. Angulo Morales and Echeberria Ayllón, "Viviendo," 1183–85.

8. Beatriz Monreal Huegun, *Guipúzcoa en escritores y viajeros* (San Sebastián: Caja de Ahorros de Guipúzcoa, 1983), 53.
9. Roquero Ussía, "La Real Compañía," 113.
10. Archivo General de Simancas, Secretaría y Superintendencia de Hacienda, 1207; Angulo Morales and Echeberria Ayllón, "Viviendo," 1183.
11. Miguel Ángel Melón Jiménez, *Los tentáculos de la Hidra: Contrabando y militarización del orden público en España (1784-1800)* (Madrid: Sílex, 2009) 259-90; Susana Truchuelo García, "Fronteras marítimas en la Monarquía de los Habsburgo: El control de la costa cantábrica," *Manuscrits. Revista d'història moderna* 32 (2014): 33-60; Susana Truchuelo García, "'Junta de la frontera y junta de la tierra': Una propuesta reformista de Guipúzcoa ante las dificultades del último cuarto del siglo XVI," *Obradoiro de Historia Moderna* 16 (2007): 161-185.
12. ADP, Secretario Ollo, C/1475, No. 11; ADP, Secretario Ollo, C/1679, No. 4; Angulo Morales and Echeberria Ayllón, "Viviendo," 1186-87; Daniel Baldellou Monclús, "Transgresión y legalidad en el cortejo del siglo XVIII: El secuestro de mujeres en la diócesis de Zaragoza," *Studia histórica, Historia moderna* 38, no. 1 (2016): 155-92; María Rosario Roquero Ussía, "El convento y la política matrimonial de la burguesía donostiarra," *Boletín de Estudios Históricos de San Sebastián* 47 (2014): 129-33.
13. ADP, Secretario Ollo, C/1597, No. 11; ADP, Secretario Echalecu, C/1398, No. 24; ADP, Secretario Echalecu, C/1417, No. 4.
14. Archivo Municipal de Hernani–Hernaniko Udal Artxiboa, Fondo Histórico, E-3-I-3/1.
15. Angulo Morales and Echeberria Ayllón, "Viviendo," 1191.
16. Lola Valverde Lamsfús, *Entre el deshonor y la miseria: Infancia abandonada en Guipúzcoa y Navarra. Siglos XVIII y XIX* (Bilbao: Universidad del País Vasco, 1994), 46-55.
17. Pablo Gorosabel, *Noticias de las cosas memorables de Guipúzcoa* (Bilbao: La Gran Enciclopedia Vasca, 1972), 284-89; anon. [William Frankland], *Una descripción de San Sebastián relativa a su gobierno, costumbres y comercio* (San Sebastián: Librería Internacional, 1985), 42-43.

18. Lope Martínez de Isasti, *Compendio historial de Guipúzcoa* (Bilbao: La Gran Enciclopedia Vasca, 1972), 149.
19. María Jesús Fernández Fonseca and Ana Isabel Prado Antúnez, "Roles femeninos en la Bizkaia del siglo XIX: Aproximación a la situación de la mujer en el mundo laboral en ámbitos pesqueros urbanos," *Itsas Memoria* 3 (2000): 277.
20. Azpiazu Elorza, *Mujeres vascas*, 209.
21. Guillermo Bowles, *Introducción a la historia natural y a la geografía física de España* (Madrid: Imprenta de Francisco Manuel de Mena, 1775), 307–8.
22. Aguado, Ana María [et al.], *Textos para la historia de las mujeres en España* (Barcelona: Cátedra, 1994), 351–52.
23. Roquero Ussía, "El convento," 133; José Ignacio Tellechea Idígoras, "El padre Larramendi, S. J., confesor de Mariana de Neoburgo," *Hispania* 28 (1969): 627–70.
24. Bakarne Altonaga Begoña, "Mujeres viriles en el siglo XVIII: La construcción de la feminidad por el discurso foralista de Manuel de Larramendi," *Historia Contemporánea* 52 (2016): 9–42; Bakarne Altonaga Begoña, "Generoa Antzinako Erregimenean: Manuel Larramendiren ikuspuntua eta bere itzala," *Sancho el Sabio* 2, número extraordinario (2018): 107–27.
25. Altonaga Begoña, "Mujeres viriles," 41.
26. Altonaga Begoña, "Mujeres viriles," 41–42.
27. Angulo Morales and Echeberria Ayllón, "Viviendo," 1192.
28. Carmen Iglesias, *Razón, sentimiento y utopía* (Barcelona: Galaxia Gutenberg, 2006): 354.
29. María Rosa Ayerbe Iribar, "Manuel de Larramendi y la enseñanza femenina en el siglo XVIII: Constituciones del Seminario de niñas 'Nuestra Señora de la Soledad,' de Bergara (1741)," *Boletín de la Real Sociedad Bascongada de los Amigos del País* 64, no. 2 (2008): 801–2.
30. Ayerbe Iribar, "Manuel de Larramendi," 807.
31. Iker Echeberria Ayllón, *La plata embustera: Emociones y divorcio en la Guipúzcoa del siglo XVIII* (Bilbao: UPV/EHU, 2017), 229–30.

CHAPTER THREE

A Lady on the Military Front

"Try to have a good time, to live a holy life, to please your husband and your mother, to have no quarrels with anyone, to act in all your actions with judgment and calm, and do not let the goods of this world make you proud, and thank His Divine Majesty for it; show yourself affable and courteous to everyone, especially to the poor, for this does not lead to the loss of esteem, and honor everyone, and do not whisper against anyone."[1]

"Be careful with my orders to get along with all the Relatives, and generally with everyone . . . for your part win the will of everyone and do not lose it or spoil it because of some sour little temper that you have, which is necessary to put aside, if you have it, do not become hateful, or spiteful; do not be haughty, arrogant, or vain . . . do not want to compete with others who want to excel over you, but treat yourself with a moderate decency, that this will seem good to everyone and you will get rid of many spiritual worries, and above all obey your husband, who will not want anything that opposes this, and with that you comply by pleasing him, and loving him, that is what you are obliged to do."[2]

These are the words dedicated to his daughter by General Manuel Joaquín de Montiano, the governor of St. Augustine, the oldest European settlement in the United States, during the Guerra del Asiento, known in the English-speaking world as the War of Jenkins' Ear.

The volatile international politics after Utrecht remained fragile despite the years of peace between 1728 and 1738. Except for the War of the Polish Succession and some fights to control Florida, international military conflicts barely disturbed the coexistence of the Atlantic powers until 1739, when Great Britain declared war on Spain.[3] When a Florida coast guard sailor named Juan León de Fandiño captured the ship *Rebecca* and cut off the ear of its captain, the Englishman Robert Jenkins, everyone's life changed forever.[4] From that point on, Governor Manuel Joaquín de Montiano was involved in an endless war. Although he described his subordinate's attitude with statements such as "our Corsair Fandiño . . . Great Corsair, and the one whom the English, without naming him, mention in the *Mercurios*, cut off the ears of their nation,"[5] the war would end up devouring him.[6]

Meanwhile, the governor and captain general of St. Augustine explained to his daughter the role of a good wife. With all the pedagogical and moralistic literature of the period, his speech shows how individuals of the time merged these discourses. We often forget that, outside of wars or other long-term processes of undoubted academic value, the people who starred in these events had regular lives.[7] Individuals like the general not only participated in great performances but also had more ordinary concerns—in this specific case, to show his daughter the way of a good wife.

During these years, did the Basque Enlightenment defend some kind of feminine canon? Certainly, yes. Gender archetypes and roles permeate eighteenth-century Basque society. Women from low socioeconomic backgrounds were protagonists in the riots that swept through the Basque geography during the modern centuries. Meanwhile, the model of the submissive woman previously mentioned was imposed among the elites as one more ingredient in their personal development. Ladies in the eighteenth century were conditioned by the model of the perfect married woman, a modest and humble wife with the responsibility of taking care of the family under the shadow of the paterfamilias.[8] It is difficult to see women's prominence in moments of contention, since the stereotypical constructs of the female gender distanced them from such events. This is due to several factors, such as their economic and social status, their belonging to the hegemonic class, their education, and their own significance as women—conditioned by discourses like that of the general. However, a multitude of female experiences, rather than a singular, common one, ran through the century.

We have a unique example of a noble lady in a military environment in the Basque Country, the only one documented to date, which offers an interesting picture. Before its publication in 2023,[9] women were considered "silent witness[es], because we lack direct first-person testimonies of real life in the camps, of the expeditions."[10] In addition to providing such a first-person account, this woman's journey allows us to outline, in a schematic way, the Basque female elite of the time.

Let's jump to the year 1805. This is a critical time for the Spanish monarchy, which is close to collapse. Four years earlier, with the Treaty of Aranjuez of 1801, Napoleon Bonaparte granted the recently created satellite state of Etruria, the former Grand Duchy of Tuscany in Italy, to the House of Bourbon. In exchange, Spain renounced the Duchy of Parma and granted Louisiana to the French Empire. The importance of the treaty, however, lies in the Spanish-French alliance to combat their common enemy: Great Britain.

It was during this time that the wife of Joaquín José de Vera, a midranking officer of the Guadalajara regiment, decided to follow her husband. In the eighteenth century, civility manuals recommended that soldiers travel free of wives (although prostitutes were accepted despite being seen as lascivious threats to the troops).[11] While in earlier times the accompaniment of wives had been common, this trend declined during the Enlightenment and until at least the French Revolution, when the female presence increased again in the form of midwives, water carriers, cooks, prostitutes, nurses, and general "camp followers."[12]

Without the work carried out by these women, several military campaigns would have failed. Although these women served in positions that were considered more acceptable for women and not as soldiers, "they were exposed to the same conditions as the soldiers." In Ecuador, the *guarichas* "followed the soldiers during all the campaigns for Independence. In 1817 and 1819, Generals Pablo Morillo and Francisco Santander forbade women from marching with the troops."[13] The future second president of the Republic of Colombia, Francisco Santander, did not hide his displeasure: "twenty-five recruits come and thirty women surround me, forty little children crying for their husbands and fathers."[14]

A few decades earlier, the *Gaceta de México* (the first newspaper printed in New Spain) pointed out that female camp followers were an interference to armies: "One of the many abuses that exist in the armies is that which results from the license given to soldiers to marry without the consent of their Chiefs. The number of women who follow the troops is so large that they greatly delay their march, consume a large amount of food, and occupy the wagons destined for the transport of provisions and baggage."[15]

Despite the attempts by military commanders to limit or forbid the presence of women in camps and expeditions, they continued to be part of the armies. Margarita de Urrea, an Antioquia native with Basque ancestors, followed her husband for four long years, as did the Venezuelan aristocrat of Basque origin Josefa Aristiguieta, married to the British general Gregor McGregor.[16] In fact, women composed 3 percent of the British navy expedition that joined the "rebel" army during the wars of independence. One of them, Mary English, became the center of social interaction between English officers.[17]

If an officer's wife was to join him, she was required to fill her role exquisitely: "the military does not demand the virtue of courage, but rather that she have the courage of virtue."[18] And this was precisely what María Teresa de Olazabal y Veroiz achieved over the year, fulfilling the expectations placed on her.

At the start of her journey, she was in the town of Tolosa, Gipuzkoa. She was not in the best mood, frustrated at starting a long journey without a destination, nor in the best condition: "I don't know how my head is today." After a sad letter, she said goodbye to her friends and colleagues.[19]

Their first significant stop was outside of Pamplona, in the pre-Pyrenean town of Ororbia, where, despite the cold January weather, she and her husband stayed comfortably at the home of a doctor who was a friend of the family. During the first stage of their adventure, the couple frequently had relatives write to friends along their route who might be able to host them. This doctor wrote to María Teresa's influential uncle to tell him about her state of mind: "that poor girl is recovering somewhat from the anger of being separate from your kind company."

Before reaching Zaragoza, their next stop, María Teresa shows another of the great concerns of a wife: the price of food. As the person responsible for the family's care, nutrition, and health, she is aware of the high prices: "There is no money to go on like this, a pound of lamb costs 8 *reales*, a pound of bread costs 9 *cuartos*, and in light of all this, I assure you that I am eager to reach our destination." They were healthy, "but very cold."[20]

The army was quartered in the capital of the Kingdom of Aragon, a city where María Teresa could stay with relatives, until the following summer. She was delighted to have the company of other women, whom she had missed so much during the march.[21] The weeks passed comfortably, with María Teresa sending gifts, requesting favors,[22] and asking for various clothes, although, she noted, "it is not my nature to cause trouble to others."[23] This break allowed her to recover part of her life, a routine focused on the management of the house, family affairs, walks, masses, and gatherings.

María Teresa admitted that she was not made for that kind of military life: "Every day it becomes harder for me, especially considering how far away we are."[24] Continuing on her husband's march, obeying him in everything under all circumstances, was complicated and exhausting, although she was not inclined to separate from him. This was verified when part of the regiment was sent to Teruel as part of a sanitary quarantine: "although my cousins have urged me to stay here, I have not agreed, because now that I have left my house, I am determined not to abandon him as long as they allow me and my health allows me, I assure you that I am very sorry, but it is necessary to obey and keep quiet."[25]

This attitude corresponds to the feminine canons of the period,[26] particularly those associated with officers' wives. Days in Teruel were very hard—"bad, very expensive and cold,"[27] while the troops were moved like "dogs."[28] Then her husband stole from the *caja*—the common fund of the troops. The debt was considerable, which pushed her to request family help: "I do not doubt that he will feel sorry for my misfortunes and give me some relief, because if Joaquín had not had this misappropriation of the Caja when he was Captain of the Caja, we would not be deducted as we are and for that reason we do not receive more than 612 reales per month and we still have to pay 3,000 reales, which just considering that this has to be paid, does not cease to give me very bad times and contributes to my poor health."[29]

María Teresa had a melancholic, obedient, and resigned personality. According to one of her cousins, she lacked the necessary personality to face a military expedition: "Let them leave the march soon, because it is not for her temperament, nor will it ever be done, as many others do: her temperament is extremely melancholic and she does little or nothing to distract herself and adapt herself as best as possible to the circumstances. She has a very bad time this way, and so bad that no one has it worse."[30]

Financial problems were not helping either, as before traveling to Barcelona she had to fire her maid. From then on, she would have to manage on her own as the executor of household tasks, missing her "beloved homeland."[31]

"We have arrived at this [Barcelona] exhausted and I am very damaged.... This life is to end life, because there is no one who can take so many marches."[32] However, the most "painful" of her days would take place later, on the way to the Kingdom of Etruria. Such was the refuge she experienced crossing France that if on some other occasion the French needed the same accommodation in her house—as would happen just two years later, after the Treaty of Fontainebleau—she noted that would not hesitate to treat them the same: "I would take revenge because these unworthy people have managed to sacrifice us."[33] After several walks along narrow, pre-Alpine trails between Nice and Genoa, she finally reached her destination: Florence.

More than a year had passed since her departure. At this point, her return was impossible. The tenor of her correspondence was melancholic, full of complaints about her delicate health and financial collapse—"we have been ruined for life. . . . Only God knows how we arrived here."[34] Amid requests for help, María Teresa was forgotten by her relatives, a situation aggravated by distance. However, the little correspondence she sent to her family from then on reveals her desires and concerns as the woman of the Basque elite that she was.

Florence impressed her. She describes in detail the city's carnivals, theaters, dances, and richness of its costumes. Although complaining about high prices, her economic situation, and the lack of news, she writes admiringly about the queen regent Maria Luisa, daughter of Carlos IV, Infanta of Spain, and mother of Louis II, heir to the throne of Etruria.[35] Without a doubt, it was the dances and events hosted by the sovereign that she most wanted to highlight in her letters. Upon the regiment's arrival, for example, the queen went out onto the balcony to receive the troops, inviting the high command and offering ten reales to each soldier.[36] Being in the presence of a queen was an act of the greatest magnitude for a woman of the period: "On Saint Louis' Day there was a hand-kissing, I could not go, and the Queen asked Joaquín when he kissed her hand, 'and your wife?' He said that I was ill and for this reason I had not been able to go and kiss Her Majesty's hand, she said, 'Poor thing, I am sorry.'"[37] That a sovereign was concerned about her—surely a mere formality—deserved to be announced to her relatives.

Six months later, María Teresa, despite some health problems, wanted to join a party organized by the queen. Her wish was to dance with her, as she danced with the ladies, or to "copy something."[38] She was interested in fashion, dance, botany, and music, as befit a woman of her status.[39] She demonstrated these interests by sending a series of arias and seeds to her relatives.[40]

The Florentine year ended when Napoleon Bonaparte ordered the regiment to join the expedition commanded by the Marquis of la Romana in Hamburg, Germany.[41] These were moments of panic and doubt.[42] The fear of being left alone in a foreign country with no one to look after her and no money pushed María Teresa to consider traveling to Madrid, where "I will be able to carry out my demands and see if I can get [her husband] out of this march."[43] Like many women of the time, her intention was to go to the court and arbitrate in the name of her husband, although she had no money to aid her cause.

As María Teresa's comment highlights, one of the most important social roles of women at this time was their capacity for mediation and agency. As we have seen, in the riots that swept through the Basque Country, women arbitrated with royal officials. They raised their voices, even negotiating with the authorities. This capacity for arbitration is connected to the previously mentioned attribute, the plea. Agency and plea are not the same thing, but they seem to be related, as they are part of the strategic use of gender. In this regard, in his analysis of the Colombian wars of independence, Matthew Brown points out the following: "It was more common, however, that the women themselves petitioned the authorities. In Hispanic America, these petitions were consistent with a cultural tradition of middle- and high-status women who persistently applied to public authorities, who in turn often responded to such representations out of fear of shame."[44]

Such was the impact of women's agency capacity that in the unstable beginning of the nineteenth century, political power took action. A year earlier, in 1804, the crown prohibited women from residing at court in their efforts to obtain a position or promotion for their husbands or relatives—that is, the authorities attempted limiting women's negotiating capacity. Their "unfair or inappropriate claims" were restricted by a Royal Order that eventually reached New Spain, affecting the framework of Atlantic relations.[45]

Mediation is also related to the "persuasive power" that some writers of the time assigned to women. There are documented cases from Colombia.[46] During the Mexican War of Independence, the Marquise of San Miguel de Aguayo, belonging to one of the most powerful Basque lineages of the viceroyalty, received requests from her brother to interfere on his behalf. He had been accused of participating in the famous landing of the Navarrese Xabier Mina, and although he was later absolved, he had been unable to erase this "stain" on his reputation and continued to be defamed. For this reason, he wrote to his sister begging her and his "little mother" to intercede for him: "to agree on the actions to free me from harassment, because due to Cancelada's slander and lies I must have many enemies."[47]

Although she had planned to travel to Madrid, María Teresa de Olazabal achieved her mission by writing letters without leaving her husband. In the first days of the trip, she wrote to her uncle asking him to take them "out of this mess" to a new position that would allow them to enjoy a more peaceful life.

In Florence, María Teresa became so depressed that she imagined herself alone, going to a hospital and dying of grief.[48] For this reason, she decided to stay with her husband, from whom she did not want to separate—"it does not seem to me that anyone is capable of feeling more strongly than I, the departure of my beloved Joaquín."[49] Thus, she heads to Germany.

After months without any news, she wrote from Hamburg at the end of the summer of 1807. The regiment had participated in the siege of Stralsund, where everything seemed to go well. However, in this correspondence she narrated something exceptional. And it is unusual for two reasons. First, because it is written in Basque, a language that everyone spoke in Euskal Herria and the nobility did not use in their correspondence. Having letters written in this language from a woman is rare. Second, because of the nature of the message, as it narrates certain events that happened during the siege that she tries to hide by using Basque, specifically, the damage produced by the troops:

> The entire Spanish mission was ordered to come to this city and on the second day after the Spanish troops left, the town of Stralsund was surrendered [au jaquingo suten eta argatic agindu suten erretiraseco guriac, bada claro da isandudata misiva onetan, en fin guriac ondo irten dira eta gaungoicoari emandisascagun grasiac, bada iraun basuten gueiasan (¿?) posible birisia, eta ain inposible da arsia plasa ura iran gabe, beste, isiliaco composisio gabe nola dioten gureco usquietan parasen diot au; goguac emango dio].... We are here all the Spanish troops and it is said that we will be here until winter.[50]

From then on, the luck of María Teresa, her husband, and the regiment was confusing, even tragic. At the beginning of 1808, they were in the small town of Bilderberg of the Elbe, where they were accommodated in "unhappy cottages" with thatched roofs. The weather conditions, cold and humid, made them ill. The general of their division, the Prince of Pontecorvo, had just died. However, things were about to get worse: the future of the Guadalajara regiment would be dramatic.[51]

After more than 2,600 kilometers of marching across western Europe, the squadron took part in the Expedition to Denmark, a campaign designed by Napoleon Bonaparte to try to block the landing of British troops on the continent. Then the May 2 uprising took place in Madrid, the first event of a Spanish War of Independence destined to change the course of the Hispanic world.

The "damned war" of Spain, as the French emperor called it, resonated across the Atlantic Ocean to the American colonies, where independence movements were on the historical horizon. Despite French attempts to isolate the Spanish troops on Danish soil, news of the Aranjuez mutiny and the uprising of May 2, 1808, reached Spanish ears, starting the uprising against the French command and the resulting boarding for the Iberian Peninsula.[52] The regiments of Asturias and Guadalajara, however, were not so lucky, having to join José Bonaparte's unit, which fought in Italy, France, and Russia.[53] Despite everything, it seems that María Teresa was able to escape: her correspondence places her back in San Sebastián in 1810.[54] Three years later, the city was razed by British and French troops.[55]

NOTES

1. Manuel Joaquín de Montiano to Teresa de Montiano, St. Augustine, FL, March 4, 1749, AHFB, Fondo Gortázar, 2456/013.
2. Manuel Joaquín de Montiano to Teresa de Montiano, St. Augustine, FL, March 30, 1749. AHFB, Fondo Gortázar, 2456/013.
3. Sylvia Lyn Hilton Stow, "El conflicto anglo-español en Florida: Utopía y realismo en la política española, 1732–39," *Quinto centenario* 5 (1983): 97–130.
4. María Baudot Monroy, "Asientos y política naval: El suministro de víveres a la Armada al inicio de la guerra contra Gran Bretaña, 1739–1741," *Estudia Histórica: Historia Moderna* 35 (2013): 127–58; Jorge Cerdá Crespo, *Conflictos coloniales: La Guerra de los Nueve Años 1739–1748* (Alicante, Spain: Universidad de Alicante, 2010); Manuel Gracia Rivas, "En torno a la biografía de Blas de Lezo," *Itsas Memoria: Revista de Estudios Marítimos del País Vasco* 7 (2012): 508; Adrian J. Pearce, *El comercio británico con Hispanoamérica* (Mexico City: Colegio de México, 2017).
5. Manuel Joaquín de Montiano to his brothers, St. Augustine, FL, December 28, 1740, AHFB, Fondo Gortázar, 2456/010.
6. AHFB, Fondo Gortázar, 2439/026; AHFB, Fondo Gortázar, 2456/009; AHFB, Fondo Gortázar, 2436/006; AHFB, Fondo Gor-

tázar, 2456/010; AHFB, Fondo Gortázar, 2456/011; AHFB, Fondo Gortázar, 2456/012; AHFB, Fondo Gortázar, 2456/015; AHFB, Fondo Gortázar, 2446/016; AHFB, Fondo Gortázar, 2486/025; AHFB, Fondo Gortázar, 2456/013; *Relación del ingreso de las tropas inglesas en los territorios de La Florida, mandados por el general Don Diego Ogletorpe, comandante de las fuerzas de tierras de S.M.B. y defensa que hizo de aquella plaza su Gobernador, Don Manuel de Montiano*, AHFB, Fondo Gortázar, 2456/009; Archivo Familiar Montiano (AFM), FIL20100017128; Hilton Stow, "El conflicto," 112; *Agustín de Montiano y Luyando, primer Director de la Real Academia de la Historia* (Madrid: Real Academia de la Historia, 1926); Víctor Peralta Ruiz, *Patrones clientes y amigos: El poder burocrático indiano en la España del siglo XVIII* (Madrid: CSIC, 2006), 106 and 216.

7. AHFB, Fondo Gortázar, 2456/013; AFM, FIL20100017128; David Mateos Varona, *Cartas desde Florida: Manuel Joaquín de Montiano, bilbaíno y gobernador de Florida (1739–1749) y de Panamá (1749–1759)* (Bilbao: Universidad de Deusto, Manuscrito, 2009).

8. María Ángeles Cantero Rosales, "De 'perfecta casada' a 'ángel del hogar' o la construcción del arquetipo femenino en el XIX," *Revista Electrónica de Estudios Filológicos* 14 (2007); Fray Luis de León, *La perfecta casada* (Salamanca, Spain: Tomás de Alva librero, 1603).

9. Alberto Angulo Morales and Iker Echeberria Ayllón, "Herederas de la Ilustración vasca: El papel femenino en tiempos de revoluciones," in *Las mujeres en las revoluciones liberales atlánticas: Roles entre lealtades, independencias y patrias (1780–1873)*, ed. Alejandro Cardozo Uzcátegui (Bogotá: Universidad Sergio Arboleda, 2023), 195–227.

10. M. García Hurtado, "Mujeres y militares en el siglo XVIII: De discursos teóricos y realidad práctica," in *El siglo XVIII en femenino: Las mujeres en el Siglo de las Luces*, ed. M. García Hurtado (Madrid: Síntesis, 2016), 328.

11. García Hurtado, "Mujeres," 328–65.

12. García Hurtado, "Mujeres," 373; N. Rivera de Jesús, "La participación de las mujeres en la Guerra de Independencia de las Trece Colonias," in *X Congreso Virtual sobre Historia de las Mujeres* (Jaén, Spain: Archivo Histórico Diocesano de Jaén, 2018), 744.

13. Amy Taxin, "La participación de la mujer en la Independencia: el caso de Manuela Sáenz," *Procesos: Revista Ecuatoriana de Historia* 14 (1999): 94.
14. Roger Pita Pico, "Resistencia y reivindicaciones de las mujeres en las guerras de independencia de Colombia: una aproximación a través de sus cartas y reclamaciones," *Arenal* 26, no. 2 (2019): 617; Daniel Morán and Montserratt Rivera, "Libertadoras en tiempos de Revolución: La participación de las mujeres en la Independencia del Perú y América Latina," *Desde el Sur* 13, no. 1 (2021): 16.
15. *Gaceta de México*, July 13, 1793.
16. Cherpak, "The Participation," 5.
17. Matthew Brown, "Adventures, Foreign Women and Masculinity in the Colombian Wars of Independence," *Feminist Review* 79 (2005): 37–42; Cherpak, "The Participation," 5.
18. García Hurtado, "Mujeres," 415.
19. Archivo de la Casa de Olazabal (ACO), 001905, secc. 11, leg. 27, núm. 1.
20. María Teresa de Olazabal y Veroiz to Joaquín José de Vera a José Francisco de Veroiz, Caparroso, January 12, 1805, ACO, 001905, secc. 11, leg. 27, núm. 1.
21. María Teresa de Olazabal y Veroiz to José Francisco de Veroiz, Zaragoza, January 19, 1805, ACO, 001905, secc. 11, leg. 27, núm. 1.
22. Manuela de Salcedo to José Francisco de Veroiz, Bilbao, May 22, 1805, ACO, 001905, secc. 11, leg. 27, núm. 1.
23. María Teresa de Olazabal y Veroiz to José Francisco de Veroiz, Zaragoza, January 22, 1805, ACO, 001905, secc. 11, leg. 27, núm. 1.
24. María Teresa de Olazabal y Veroiz to José Francisco de Veroiz, Zaragoza, January 22, 1805, ACO, 001905, secc. 11, leg. 27, núm. 1.
25. Villafranca del Campo, Teruel and Cariñana, February 1, 1805–February 17, 1805, ACO, 001905, secc. 11, leg. 27, núm. 1; María Teresa de Olazabal y Veroiz to José Francisco de Veroiz, Zaragoza, January 24, 1805, ACO, 001905, secc. 11, leg. 27, núm. 1.
26. James S. Amelang and Mary Nash, *Historia y género: Las mujeres en la Europa Moderna y Contemporánea* (Valencia, Spain: Edicions Alfons el Magnànim, 1990); Rosa María Capel and Margarita Ortega, "La familia en la Edad Moderna," *Arenal: Revista de historia de las mujeres* 13, no. 1 (2006); *Balance y Perspectivas de los Estudios de las Mujeres y del Género* (Madrid: Instituto de la Mujer, 2002).

27. María Teresa de Olazabal y Veroiz to José Francisco de Veroiz, Villafranca del Campo, February 1, 1805, ACO, 001905, secc. 11, leg. 27, núm. 1.
28. María Teresa de Olazabal y Veroiz to José Francisco de Veroiz, Teruel, February 7, 1805, ACO, 001905, secc. 11, leg. 27, núm. 1.
29. María Teresa de Olazabal y Veroiz to José Francisco de Veroiz, Zaragoza, June 11, 1805, ACO, 001905, secc. 11, leg. 27, núm. 1.
30. Concepción to José Francisco de Veroiz, Zaragoza, May 1805, ACO, 001905, secc. 11, leg. 27, núm. 1.
31. María Teresa de Olazabal y Veroiz to José Francisco de Veroiz, Zaragoza, February 26, 1805, ACO, 001905, secc. 11, leg. 27, núm. 1.
32. María Teresa de Olazabal y Veroiz to José Francisco de Veroiz, Barcelona, June 29, 1805, ACO, 001905, secc. 11, leg. 27, núm. 1.
33. María Teresa de Olazabal y Veroiz to her brothers Juan, Antonio and Antoni, Genoa, February 20, 1806, ACO, 001905, secc. 11, leg. 27, núm. 1.
34. Florence, August 16, 1806, ACO, 001905, secc. 11, leg. 27, núm. 1.
35. C. Robles Do Campo, "Los infantes de España bajo la Ley Sálica," *Anales de la Real Academia Matritense de Heráldica y Genealogía* 10 (2007): 331.
36. Florence, March 14, 1806, ACO, 001905, secc. 11, leg. 27, núm. 1.
37. Florence, September 2, 1806, ACO, 001905, secc. 11, leg. 27, núm. 1.
38. Florence, September 2, 1806 and 02/02/1807, ACO, 001905, secc. 11, leg. 27, núm. 1.
39. Rosa María Capel, "Mujer y educación en el Antiguo Régimen," *Historia de la Educación. Revista interuniversitaria* 26 (2007): 85–110; Pilar Gonzalbo Aizpuru, "La educación colonial. Una mirada reflexiva," *Revista Historia de la Educación Latinoamericana* 2 (2000): 180–88; Isabel Morant Deusa, "Mujeres ilustradas en el debate de la educación: Francia y España," *Cuadernos de Historia Moderna*, anejo 3 (2004): 59–84; Antonio Viñao Frago, "La influencia de Campomanes, Olavide y Cabarrús en la educación," in *Historia de la educación en España y América*, ed. B. Delgado Criado (Madrid: Morata, 1993), 657–68.
40. Florence, September 2, 1806, ACO, 001905, secc. 11, leg. 27, núm. 1.
41. José María Bueno Carrera, *La expedición española a Dinamarca, 1807–1808* (Madrid: Agualarga, 2000).
42. Florence, April 1 & 17, 1807, ACO, 001905, secc. 11, leg. 27, núm. 1.

43. María Teresa de Olazabal y Veroiz to Antoni, Florence, March 31, 1807, ACO, 001905, secc. 11, leg. 27, núm. 1; Joaquín José de Vera to José Francisco de Veroiz, Florence, April 1, 1807, ACO, 001905, secc. 11, leg. 27, núm. 1.
44. Brown, "Adventures," 43.
45. Archivo General de la Nación (México) (AGN), Indiferente virreinal, Volumen 2732, Expediente 016; AGN, Bandos, Volumen 23, Expediente 78.
46. Pita Pico, "Resistencia," 612–16.
47. AGN, Colección de Documentos para la Historia de la Guerra de Independencia, Tomo VI, Volumen V, Documento 1024.
48. Florence, April 17, 1807, ACO, 001905, secc. 11, leg. 27, núm. 1.
49. María Teresa de Olazabal y Veroiz to Antoni, Florencia, March 31, 1807, ACO, 001905, secc. 11, leg. 27, núm. 1.
50. María Teresa de Olazabal y Veroiz to José Francisco de Veroiz, Hamburgo, September 11, 1807, ACO, 001905, secc. 11, leg. 27, núm. 1.
51. María Teresa de Olazabal y Veroiz to José Francisco de Veroiz, Bilberder del Elba, January 12, 1808, ACO, 001905, secc. 11, leg. 27, núm. 1.
52. José Manuel Guerrero Acosta, *Memorias de soldados españoles durante la Guerra de la Independencia (1806–1815)* (Madrid: Ministerio de Defensa, Subdirección General de Documentación y Publicaciones, 2009).
53. Juan Corbalán De Celis y Durán, "Sobre la Expedición del marqués de la Romana y otros hechos de armas" (undated): 1–16.
54. San Sebastián, April 24, 1810, ACO, 001905, secc. 11, leg. 27, núm. 1.
55. Jean-Marc Lafon, "San Sebastián (1813): Bloqueos, sitios y destrucción," in *Los sitios en la Guerra de la Independencia: La lucha en las ciudades*, ed. Gonzalo Butrón Prida and Pedro Víctor Rújula López (Madrid: Sílex, 2012), 335–56; Carlos Larrinaga Rodríguez, *San Sebastián, 1813: Historia y memoria* (Donostia: Hiria Liburuak, 2013); Luis Murugarrren Zamora, *1813, San Sebastián incendiada: Británicos y portugueses* (San Sebastián: Sociedad Guipuzcoana de Ediciones y Publicaciones, 1993).

CHAPTER FOUR

On Some Female Canons

Letter correspondence opens up a new field of research: "It is one of the forms of expression especially chosen by women, so it is a basic instrument for collecting their impressions."[1] The experiences of women who participated in military expeditions within the context of the Atlantic Revolutions, at least for the Hispanic world, are not, however, part of our memory. On the other hand, we will always have the account given by María Teresa de Olazabal y Veroiz, who shared her desires, fears, impressions, and experiences.

"I see, my uncle, what you are telling me is to take care of myself and take charge. I am a soldier, and to stick to what is most necessary. We are already doing it like that."[2] This is what she writes at the beginning of her odyssey. Her relatives called her, perhaps with affection, "the soldier." However, María Teresa de Olazabal y Veroiz represents much more than that. She is a woman educated and socialized in the most elitist structures of the time, a woman removed from her existential universe and forced to play the role of the "female soldier."

Identity and gender are historical architectures that change over time, and female standards mutated over the course of the eighteenth century. At the beginning of the century, the model of the perfect married woman portrayed by authors such as Fray Luis de León—an archetype linked, in part, to socioeconomic privilege—may have been one of the most popular.[3] None of its characteristics were lost with the change of the era, although new elements did emerge throughout the eighteenth century. Femininity, in some way, was reformed.

With the European Enlightenment, new archetypes of femininity emerged to add to the previous ones. They gave women new devices, aspirations, and meanings. Starting from a pedagogical turn that changed their education, the path drawn by the enlightened elites was imposed among the most privileged. And within the Hispanic world, the social environment of María Teresa, those of Basque origin were some of the most prominent reformers.[4]

When, at the beginning of the Atlantic Revolutions in 1765, the first enlightened society in the history of the Spanish monarchy was established in the Basque Country, the RSBAP, one of its opening speeches focused on women.[5] According to the Marquis of Montehermoso, the author of the speech, there were differences between sexes. Based on these differences, there were also distinct social functions. The original problem, however, lay in women's education, which had to be improved so that they could emerge from their traditional intellectual limitation, fulfill their roles as wives and mothers, and live content within the limits that "nature prescribed" for them.[6]

This speech, "Philosophical-Moral Discourse: Women,"[7] belongs to a very common current of thought within the RSBAP in those years according to which women should fulfill the essential task of educating the future members of the nation. Pablo de Olavide, a member of the society born in Lima, successfully outlined this utilitarian and naturalist vision around 1768.[8]

According to Olavide's writings,[9] women of the elite would be destined to "play a more brilliant role in the world later on." The nation needed mothers to educate future citizens, a central idea for national interests that represents the best way to achieve universal education, especially for the nobility. For this reason, their education should be granted by the state, although the RSBAP also made its own attempts.[10]

Utilitarian thought recognized that well-educated women, due to the "terrible influence and powerful effect" they exercised over men, would end up forcing change in the opposite sex.[11] The literature of the period emphasizes "their beneficial influence on man, guiding his passionate excesses and turning him into a responsible subject in his public and private obligations."[12] These messages that underline their importance when it comes to "educating masculine feelings to build a civilized society"[13] were shared by Olavide and his Basque colleagues.[14]

The ideal of "domesticated femininity" was not, of course, original.[15] It was inspired by the model of femininity imagined by Jean-Jacques Rousseau, the Smolny Institute created by Catherine the Great in 1764,[16] and the contributions of Olavide himself. The construction of eighteenth-century femininity is, in the Basque case, a flexible phenomenon, basically subscribed to the nobility and with a transnational nature. The Hispanic-American elites also had their own model, very similar to that developed in Europe, a standard that echoed in the "republican mother" of the United States of America.[17] In short, a shared ideal established throughout the Atlantic world.

In the viceroyalty of New Spain, a similar process happened, developing this model of domestic femininity supported by the reformist elites. A woman is understood as "mother, support for her husband, comfort for her family and guide for her children."[18] This role worked as a reference for "social motherhood," practiced during the most belligerent years of the Atlantic Revolutions, both in Spain and America.

As we see for the Basque Country, these canons were spread in the private sphere, among the reformers who read pedagogical treatises and literature of the time, attended social gatherings, or read newspapers. Many of them, despite the distance, were linked to the RSBAP. The circulation of ideas, books, newspapers, and the new sociability played important roles within the Atlantic framework: "The enlightened thought deployed mainly in the emerging modern press allowed the opening of a circulation of ideas and scientific, political and economic content, settling new platforms of sociability in which women would become subjects of controversy."[19]

The press became one of the most important tools for the transmission of the new feminine canon. In these publications, the New Spaniards of Basque origin knew how to stand out:[20] "The press is established as a device that has a clear pedagogical orientation within which differentiated practices for women and men are conceptualized in a multiracial and culturally heterogeneous society."[21]

Creoles of Basque origin played a central role in the emergence of the New Spanish press from Juan Ignacio María de Castorena Ursúa y Goyeneche, creator of the *Gaceta de México* in 1722 and considered the first journalist in the history of Hispanic America,[22] to José Antonio de Alzate y Ramírez, creator of the *Diario Literario de México*, member of the RSBAP,[23] and "symbol of Mexican enlightenment."[24] The responsibility of this group for the diffusion of new feminine canons was fundamental.

This female role was to have a public utility and political virtuosity. In their role as mothers transmitting civic, religious, and national values, women were meant to find a new existential dimension: "the significant sociopolitical and public function attributed to motherhood offers the idea of the mother-educator an innovative role."[25]

In addition to individual proposals, the RSBAP attempted to put this ideal of female education into practice on three occasions.[26] Based on educating "young maidens in the maxims of Christianity and virtue," its main objective was to raise "good mothers and women of the home" because "women, by general consent and acceptance, have the power to demand gifts from men in civil dealings, to participate with them in the cares and delights of domestic life, and to have a great influence on the greatest revolutions and political events."[27] We are seeing the beginning of that nineteenth-century model known as the "angel of the home."

Thus, women like María Teresa de Olazabal y Veroiz are constructed, at least in part, in terms of social treatment. The importance of representing the family on walks, at social gatherings, during visits, when attending masses, or at public events[28] and transmitting a perfect image to the rest of the community is one of women's great attributes.[29]

In her letters, María Teresa remembered socialites, wrote about dances, and showed her taste for music. The "external qualities" of her sex were concentrated on aspects such as good manners, speech, singing, or music,[30] all for the pleasure of her peers and to allow her to shine socially.

Within critical and reforming discourses, the Spanish Enlightenment developed its own contributions. José Clavijo y Fajardo would demand, from 1762, a female education focused on the formation of good mothers. In this way, women would be freed from the tyranny of beauty—expensive and ridiculous fashions were a serious detriment to the family economy. These ideas—*costumbristas*—were refuted by a Cádiz-based author writing under the pseudonym Beatriz Cienfuegos who openly criticized the objectification of ladies as social objects.[31] Constrained to ignorance, women remained vulgar objects of desire.[32] These criticisms of bad habits, fashions, and luxury led to pedagogical demands and even the questioning of the inequality between genders. Discourses on femininity are therefore included within concerns about society, its customs, its relationships, and its harmony.[33]

Father Larramendi also criticized the fact that the noble ladies of Gipuzkoa liked Castilian fashion. This interest contrasted with the virile women of low socioeconomic status that he admired.[34] And it is here, in fact, where one of the most interesting elements emerges: the etymological difference between the virile (*viril*) woman and the manly (*hombruna*) one. The word *virile* was understood as "that which belongs to the male"; in contrast, *manly* meant "that which belongs to the man. In a joking voice."[35]

"When a woman acts as a scholar, she loses the most beautiful part of her graces; but this does not mean that she should be condemned to the center of ignorance, and to the need to remain silent or to not be able to speak about anything but useless or even worse things, such as gossip."[36] These words from the Marquis of

Montehermoso, author of the aforementioned speech, placed women between absolute ignorance and erudition, both criticized by personalities of the period. "A good Mother, an excellent Mistress" should be exempt from physical and philosophical tasks.[37] In this way, he proposes to reach the middle point between the illiterate and the learned-manly,[38] a woman who, limited by a nature that embraces, escapes from old archetypes. The speech of José María Aguirre Ortés de Velasco bases the gender differences on new naturalistic conceptions.[39]

Larramendi's virile woman thus found an alternative construction.[40] If the Jesuit from Gipuzkoa praised the hard-working and humble woman, granting her the category of manly, the enlightened Basques associated the manly woman with the learned one. The Jesuit Francisco de Isla also expressed identical ideas speaking about his friend Teresa de Montiano, that daughter who never got to know her father, General Montiano: "she is a very manly Mother, and she will subject the dictates or tenderness of love to reason, exchanging the liquid for the solid,"[41] i.e., as a rational being, she was a manly mother. Now, while the Jesuits did so in a flattering sense, the circle of enlightened Basques used it to criticize the most wise.[42]

This problem, with complementary discourses, would spread throughout the entire Hispanic world in the eighteenth and nineteenth centuries, from the Iberian Peninsula to America. The failures of the RSBAP to establish a center to educate daughters of the elite turned out to be successful for men, thanks to the support offered by the Basque community settled in Mexico. And it is here that we see one of the great economic and cultural events that happened on an international scale during the Atlantic Revolutions, events led by Basques from both shores that connect with the later processes of independence. I am talking about the great Atlantic project known as the RSBAP and its links with the Brotherhood of Aránzazu in Mexico City.

NOTES

1. Gloria Espigado Tocino, "Las mujeres y la política durante la Guerra de la Independencia," *Ayer* 86, no. 2 (2012): 80.
2. María Teresa de Olazabal y Veroiz to José Francisco de Veroiz, Teruel, February 6, 1805, ACO, 001905, secc. 11, leg. 27, núm. 1.
3. María Luisa Candau Chacón, "Literatura, género y moral en el Barroco hispano: Pedro de Jesús y sus consejos a "señoras y demás mujeres"," *Hispania Sacra* 127 (2011): 103–31; Juan Gomis Coloma, "Romances conyugales: Buenas y malas esposas en la literatura popular del siglo XVIII," *Tiempos Modernos* 18, no. 1 (2009): 1–26; Oihane Oliveri Korta, "El gran gobierno de la dicha señora: Economía doméstica y mujer en el estamento hidalgo guipuzcoano," in *Economía doméstica y redes sociales en el Antiguo Régimen*, ed. José María Imízcoz Beunza and Oihane Oliveri Korta (Madrid: Sílex, 2010), 89–118.
4. Iker Echeberria Ayllón, *Basque Women's Education in the 18th Century. An Atlantic Issue* (Reno: Center for Basque Studies, University of Nevada, 2023).
5. Maite Recarte Barriola, "Ideario pedagógico de la Real Sociedad Bascongada de los Amigos del País, según los discursos de sus Juntas Generales," in *I Seminario de historia de la Real Sociedad Bascongada de los Amigos del País* (San Sebastián: RSBAP, 1986), 319.
6. Emilio Palacios Fernández, *La mujer y las letras en la España del siglo XVIII* (Madrid: Laberinto, 2002), 76–77.
7. Xabier María de Munibe, "Historia de la Real Sociedad Bascongada," *Revista Internacional de Estudios Vascos* 22 (1931): 450–53.
8. María José Alonso Seoane, "El último sueño de Pablo de Olavide," *Cuadernos Dieciochistas* 4 (2003): 47–65; Luis Perdices de Blas, *Pablo de Olavide (1725–1803), el ilustrado* (Madrid: Universidad Complutense, 1993); Pablo Ortega del Cerro, "Forging Social Links through the Navy: Elite Family Connections across the Spanish Atlantic, 1750–1810," *Atlantic Studies* 17, no. 2 (2020): 215; Luis Perdices de Blas, "Mujer, educación y mercado de trabajo en el proyecto reformista de Pablo de Olavide," *ICE: Revista de Economía* 852 (2010): 99–111; Viñao Frago, "La influencia," 657–68.

9. Letter from Pedro Jacinto de Álava to Pablo de Olavide, Vitoria, September 1, 1774, Archivo del Territorio Histórico de Álava (ATHA), Fondo Prestamero, caja 31, N° 70.
10. Biblioteca Nacional de España, MSS/22012/2; Archivo Municipal de Bergara [AMB], 03-C/123-006.
11. *Idea abreviada se un Seminario o Casa de educación que se intenta establecer en la Ciudad de Vitoria bajo la dirección de la R. S. B. de los Amigos del País*, APV, Fondo Álava, legajo 3; Mónica Bolufer Peruga, *Arte y artificio de la vida en común. Los modelos de comportamiento y sus tensiones en el siglo de las Luces* (Madrid: Marcial Pons, 2019), 213.
12. Mónica Bolufer Peruga, "Afectos razonables: Equilibrios de la sensibilidad dieciochesca," in *La cultura de las emociones y las emociones en la cultura española contemporánea (siglos XVIII–XXI)*, ed. Luisa Elena Delgado, Pura Fernández, and Jo Labanyi (Madrid: Cátedra, 2018), 47.
13. Bolufer Peruga, "Afectos razonables," 47.
14. AMB, 03-C/123-006.
15. Mónica Bolufer Peruga, "Modelar conductas y sensibilidades: Un campo abierto de indagación histórica," in *Educar los sentimientos y las costumbres: Una mirada desde la historia*, ed. Mónica Bolufer, Carolina Blutrach, and Juan Gomis (Zaragoza, Spain: Institución Fernando el Católico, CSIC, 2014), 7–9; Mónica Bolufer Peruga, "En torno a la sensibilidad dieciochesca: Discursos, prácticas, paradojas," in *Las mujeres y las emociones en Europa y América. Siglos XVII–XIX*, ed. María Luisa Candau Chacón (Santander, Spain: Universidad de Cantabria, 2016), 35; Isabel Morant Deusa, "¿Qué es una mujer? O la condición sentimental de la mujer," in *Mujeres en la historia del pensamiento*, ed. Rosa María Rodríguez Magda (Barcelona: Anthropos, 1997), 147–52; Isabel Morant Deusa, "El hombre y la mujer en el matrimonio: Moral y sentimientos familiares," in *Familia y organización social en Europa y América, siglos XV–XX*, ed. Francisco Chacón Jiménez, Juan Hernández Franco, and Francisco García González (Murcia, Spain: Universidad de Murcia, 2007), 204; María José de la Pascua Sánchez, "Una aproximación a la Historia de la familia como espacio de afectos y desafectos: El mundo hispánico del Setecientos," *Chronica Nova* 27 (2000): 136–37.

16. Robin Bisha, Jehanne M. Gheith, Christine Holden, and William G. Wagner, *Russian Women. Experience & Expression: An Anthology of Sources* (Bloomington: Indiana University Press, 2002), 163; Carolyn C. Lougee, "'Its Frequent Visitor': Death at Boarding School in Early Modern Europe," in *Women's Education in Early Modern Europe. A History, 1500–1800*, ed. Barbara J. Whitehead (New York: Garland Publishing, 1999), 204.
17. Averil E. McClelland, *The Education of Women in the United States* (New York: Garland Publishing, 1992), 123; Margaret A. Nash, "Young Ladies' Academy of Philadelphia," in *Historical Dictionary of Women's Education in the United States*, ed. Linda Eisenmann (Westport, CT: Greenwood Press, 1998), 498; Margaret A. Nash, *Women's Education in the United States: 1780–1840* (New York: Palgrave Macmillan, 2005), 35–37.
18. María Cristina Mata Montes de Oca, "Mujeres en el límite del periodo virreinal," in *Historia de las mujeres en México* (Mexico City: Instituto Nacional de Estudios Históricos de las Revoluciones de México, 2015), 47.
19. Carol Arcos Herrera, "Sujetos de controversia: Aportes para una bibliografía sobre las mujeres en el siglo XVIII y la Ilustración," *Revista de Crítica Literaria Latinoamericana* 67 (2008): 113.
20. Yelopattli Hernández Torres, "Melindrosas, bárbaras y maternales: El oficio de las parteras en la discusión periodística de la 'Gaceta de México' y el "Diario de México," *Letras Femeninas* 40, no. 2 (2014): 63–77; Yelopattli Hernández Torres, "Entre mesura y coquetería: Ilustración, prensa y maternidad en la Nueva España," *Forma: Revista d'estudis comparatius; Art, literatura, pensament* 12 (2015): 53–66; Alberto Saladino García, "La Real Sociedad Bascongada de los Amigos del País y las publicaciones periódicas del siglo XVIII en Nueva España," in *IV Seminario de Historia de la Real Sociedad Bascongada de los Amigos del País. "La RSBAP y Méjico,"* tomo 2 (Donostia–San Sebastián: RSBAP, 1993), 729–36; José Santos Hernández Pérez, "La manifestación de la Ilustración a través de los 'prospectos' de la prensa hispanoamericana," *El Argonauta español* 14 (2017); Yelopattli Hernández Torres, "Melindrosas, bárbaras y maternales: El oficio de las parteras en la discusión periodística de la 'Gaceta de México' y el "Diario de México," *Letras Femeninas* 40, no. 2 (2014): 63–77; Yelopattli Hernández Torres, "Entre mesura y coquetería: Ilustración,

prensa y maternidad en la Nueva España," *Forma. Revista d'estudis comparatius. Art, literatura, pensament* 12 (2015): 53–66.
21. Arcos Herrera, "Sujetos de controversia," 115.
22. Isabel Arenas Frutos, "Entre la mitra y la pluma: El sacerdote ilustrado Castorena y Ursúa (México, 1668–1733)," in *El Humanismo Español, su proyección en América y Canarias en la época del Humanismo*, ed. A. Martín Rodríguez and G. Santana Henríquez (Las Palmas de Gran Canaria, Spain: Universidad de Las Palmas de Gran Canaria, 2006), 273–86; Isabel Arenas Frutos, "La Ilustración y el nuevo universo cultural de México en la época del arzobispo Lorenzana," in *Humanismo y tradición clásica en España y América*, ed. J. M. Nieto Ibáñez (León, Spain: Universidad de León, 2002), 463–90; Víctor J. Cid Carmona, "La Gaceta de México y la promoción de impresos españoles durante la primera mitad del siglo XVIII," *Titivillus* 1 (2015): 422.
23. María Justina Sarabia Viejo, "Humanismo y Ciencia: José Antonio de Alzate y las 'Gacetas de Literatura de México' (1788–1795)," in *El Humanismo Español, su proyección en América y Canarias en la época del Humanismo*, ed. A. Martín Rodríguez and G. Santana Henríquez (Las Palmas de Gran Canaria, Spain: Universidad de Las Palmas de Gran Canaria, 2006), 287–300.
24. Saladino García, "La Real Sociedad," 734.
25. Mónica Bolufer Peruga, "Josefa Amar e Inés Joyes: Dos perspectivas femeninas sobre el matrimonio en el siglo XVIII," in *Historia de la mujer e historia del matrimonio*, ed. María Victoria López-Cordón and Montserrat Carbonell Esteller (Murcia, Spain: Universidad de Murcia, 1997), 203–17; María Victoria López-Cordón, *Condición femenina y razón ilustrada: Josefa Amar y Borbón* (Zaragoza, Spain: Universidad de Zaragoza, 2006); Constance A. Sullivan, "Las escritoras del siglo XVIII," in *Breve historia feminista de la literatura española (en lengua castellana)*, tomo 4, ed. Iris M. Zavala (Barcelona: Anthropos, 1997), 325–30; Rosa María Capel Martínez, "Preludio de una emancipación: la emergencia de la mujer ciudadana," *Cuadernos de Historia Moderna* 6 (2007): 172–79.
26. Echeberria Ayllón, *Basque Women's*; Manuel José de Lara Ródenas, "Un modelo ilustrado de educación para la mujer: José Isidoro Morales y la hija de José de Mazarredo," in *Las mujeres y el honor en la Europa Moderna*, ed. María Luisa Candau Chacón (Huelva, Spain:

Universidad de Huelva, 2014), 139–61; José Isidoro Morales, *Comentarios de Don José Isidoro Morales al excelentísimo señor Don José de Mazarredo sobre la enseñanza de su hija* (Madrid: Imprenta de Don Gabriel de Sacha, 1796).

27. ATHA, Fondo Prestamero, caja 8, N° 18; *Copia del plan y Ordenanzas de un seminario o casa de educación para señoritas que se intenta establecer en la Ciudad de Vitoria*, ATHA, December 3, 1784.

28. Joaquín Álvarez Barrientos, "Reunirse y conversar: las tertulias del siglo XVIII," *Ínsula* 738 (2008): 1; Fernando Ampudia de Haro, "Cortesía y prudencia: Una gestión civilizada del comportamiento y de las emociones," in *Accidentes del alma: Las emociones en la Edad Moderna*, ed. María Tausiet and James S. Amelang (Madrid: Abada Editores, 2009), 123–43; Jesús Astigarraga, *Los ilustrados vascos: Ideas, instituciones y reformas económicas en España* (Barcelona: Crítica, 2003); Mónica Bolufer Peruga, *Mujeres e Ilustración: La construcción de la feminidad en la Ilustración española* (Valencia, Spain: Institució Alfons el Magnánim, 1998); Mónica Bolufer Peruga, "Sociabilidad mixta y civilización: Miradas desde España," in *Educar los sentimientos y las costumbres: Una mirada desde la historia*, ed. Mónica Bolufer, Carolina Blutrach, and Juan Gomis (Zaragoza, Spain: Institución Fernando el Católico, CSIC, 2014), 149–73; Díaz de Durana and Otazu, *El espíritu*; Luis Miguel Enciso Recio, *Las Sociedades Económicas en el Siglo de las Luces* (Madrid: Real Academia de la Historia, 2010), 119–25; Gaspar Melchor de Jovellanos, *Diarios*, ed. Julio Somoza (Oviedo, Spain: Instituto de Estudios Asturianos, 1955); Robert Johnson and Maite Zubiaurre, *Antropología del pensamiento feminista español* (Madrid: Cátedra, 2012), 45–51; McClelland, *The Education*, 23; Paloma Manzanos Arreal and Francisca Vives Casas, *La vida cotidiana de las mujeres en la Vitoria de los siglos XVIII y XIX* (Vitoria-Gasteiz, Spain: Ayuntamiento de Vitoria-Gasteiz, 2005), 91–107; María de los Ángeles Pérez Samper, "Espacios y prácticas de sociabilidad en el siglo XVIII: Tertulias, refrescos y cafés de Barcelona," *Cuadernos de Historia Moderna* 26 (2001): 11–55; Jean Sarrailh, *La España ilustrada de la segunda mitad del siglo XVIII* (Mexico City: Fondo de Cultura Económica, 1957); Manuela Urra Olazabal, *La Compañía de María en Bergara: Dos siglos de Historia* (Vitoria-Gasteiz, Spain: Gobierno Vasco, 1999), 185.

29. Oihane Oliveri Korta, "Mujer, casa y familia en el estamento hidalgo guipuzcoano del siglo XVI." *Arenal* 13, no. 1 (2006): 39–59.
30. Jon Bagües i Erriondo, "El conde de Peñaflorida, impulsor de la Ilustración musical en el País Vasco," *Musiker, Cuadernos de Música* 4 (1988): 106–48; Ana Vega Toscano, "La música en el espacio femenino del siglo XVIII español," in *El siglo XVIII en femenino: Las mujeres en el Siglo de las Luces,* ed. Manuel-Reyes García Hurtado (Madrid: Síntesis, 2016), 293–304.
31. Constance Sullivan, "Gender, Text, and Cross-Dressing: The Case of 'Beatriz Cienfuegos' and La Pensadora Gaditana," *Dieciocho* 18, no. 1 (1995): 27–47.
32. Palacios Fernández, *La mujer,* 29–38.
33. Mónica Bolufer Peruga and Isabel Morant Deusa, "Sobre la razón, la educación y el amor de las mujeres: Mujeres y hombres en la España y en la Francia de las Luces," *Studia Historica. Historia Moderna* 15 (1996): 184.
34. Altonaga Begoña, "Mujeres viriles," 41–42.
35. *Diccionario de Autoridades,* Real Academia Española, 1726–1739.
36. Munibe, "Historia," 452.
37. Munibe, "Historia," 452–53.
38. Recarte Barriola, "Ideario pedagógico," 320.
39. Palacios Fernández, *La mujer,* 76–77; Maite Recarte Barriola, *Ilustración vasca y renovación educativa: La Real Sociedad Bascongada de los Amigos del País* (Salamanca, Spain: Universidad Pontificia de Salamanca, RSBAP, 1990), 113–14; Recarte Barriola, "Ideario pedagógico," 319–20.
40. Altonaga Begoña, "Mujeres viriles," 41–42.
41. Francisco de Isla to José Domingo Gortázar, Pontevedra, June 15, 1761, AHFB, Gortázar, 2463/019.
42. See also Echeberria Ayllón, *Basque Women's.*

CHAPTER FIVE

Basques in Mexico

Like other communities of European origin, Basques immigrated to the New World using mechanisms of support between natives, links that united individuals, families, and institutions.[1] Whether through affiliation, trust, or friendship, these individuals created a network that helped everyone, although it was mostly men who benefited from it.

After almost three centuries of domination, the Basques of New Spain controlled strategic economic sectors, such as mining, agriculture, and commerce, with many of their number in high-ranking and intermediate institutional positions—viceroys, archbishops, and judges. The social, economic, and political influence achieved by this community placed its actors at the head of the colonial exploitation system, and all this despite being the fourth-largest peninsular group by population.

Following the corporatist system of the time, the most prestigious individuals represented the group. To cite one example, before the executive positions of the powerful Mexican Trade Consulate were voted for each year, these individuals met, "on their own behalf and in the name of the Basque nation," to hire the services of two agents to manage these nominations in their favor.[2] In this way, together with people from Cantabria, they managed to control the trade consulate responsible for connecting Asia and America with Europe.

During the early modern age, Basques attended the Spanish court to defend and represent their interests, a phenomenon reinforced with the foundation of brotherhoods in the main centers of the Hispanic monarchy: Seville in 1530; Cádiz in 1625; Lima in

1635;[3] Madrid in 1684, established by the Navarrese;[4] the one in 1715 with an "agent of the dependencies of the Indies" who had exclusive rights to represent American affairs in the court;[5] or the Brotherhood of Aránzazu in Manila in 1749.[6] This well-connected network has its epicenter in Madrid, where the Cofradía de San Ignacio (Brotherhood of Saint Ignatius), founded in 1715 with capital from America, stands out for operating "quid pro quo on an imperial and transatlantic scale."[7]

Because they were created under the protection of patron saints of Basque origin, such as Saint Ignatius of Loyola, Saint Francis Xavier, and the Virgin of Aránzazu, these organizations had strong identity connotations with which to promote their devotional missions. By celebrating the festivals of these saints, the Basque emigrants fortified their social and identity ties, distinguishing themselves from other migrants.[8] Furthermore, they developed solidarity among natives, economic and commercial transactions, and the defense of the interests expressed by Basque institutions. This "universal dimension"[9] helped create a Basque-Navarrese "institutional entangled global network" within the Spanish monarchy: "In essence, communication and collaboration between emigrants, native associations and territorial authorities explain the migration policy of the natives of the Pyrenean lands."[10] Taking advantage of this network, members of these groups, with the Madrid-based San Ignacio at the head, reached high levels of power.[11]

In New Spain, the Mexican Brotherhood of Aránzazu was the most important of all,[12] although it was also a growing phenomenon. Similar organizations began in Guadalajara, Zacatecas,[13] Veracruz, Puebla, and San Luis Potosí.[14]

The Basque brotherhood in Mexico City achieved significant success during the eighteenth century. It was established as an organization outside the ordinary jurisdiction of peninsular Spain, under the direct protection of the crown.[15] It founded the so-called Colegio de las Vizcaínas, an institution to educate daughters of Basque emigrants, and focused on investing capital among Basques.[16] Its economic importance was such that "it emerged, due to the amount of its investments, as the most important engine of the economy of New Spain."¹⁷ It is also connected to two of the most important Basque institutions of the period: the Brotherhood of San Ignacio of Madrid, fundamental to achieving the jurisdictional autonomy of the school,¹⁸ and the RSBAP, which established its headquarters in the Vizcaínas in New Spain. In this way, a triangular Atlantic framework was created.¹⁹

The brotherhood only accepted donations of Basque-Navarrese origin, just as the College of the Vizcaínas prioritized its daughters. This endogamous attitude was essential not only to safeguard its identity but also to protect its transactions, business that helped its members remain at the top of the Mexican economy.²⁰

One of its main purposes was to act as a group of influence on a global scale. This integral dimension, establishing relations between the Atlantic and Pacific worlds, can be seen in the foundation of the Vizcaínas and in its businesses. Until 1720, for example, the Basque group in Mexico carried out some dealings with the Philippines to support its activities.²¹

At the end of the eighteenth century, the brotherhood had 3,087 members, a significant number considering that in the middle of the century, the Basque-Navarrese colony in Mexico City had barely 400 families. The most remarkable thing is that at the end of the seventeenth century, 30.3 percent were women. In the middle of the eighteenth century, "women represented 52.45% of the members."²² Although management positions were always held by men, the fact that women of Basque origin constituted the majority in one of the most powerful institutions of the time is a noteworthy fact.

The most important members of the organization belong to the great New Spanish nobility, that "semi-hereditary and practically endogamous commercial and business elite" well portrayed by Brading.²³ They were, in fact, those who managed the destiny of Mexico. The Castañiza, Fagoaga,²⁴ Ycaza, Yraeta,²⁵ and Bassoco families and the marquises of San Miguel de Aguayo stand out above the rest. What was their behavior during the Atlantic Revolutions?

NOTES

1. Alberto Angulo Morales, "De la familia provincial a la atlántica: Hijos de las Provincias y Señorío; Reputación y éxito en la movilidad norteña (XVI–XIX)," in *Familias, trayectorias, desigualdades: Estudios de historia social en España y en Europa ss. XVI–XIX*, ed. Francisco García González (Madrid: Sílex, 2021), 179–200; Alberto Angulo Morales, "Embajadores, agentes, congregaciones y conferencias: La proyección exterior de las provincias vascas (Siglos XV–XIX)," in *Delegaciones de Euskadi (1936–1975): Antecedentes históricos de los siglos XVI al XIX, origen y desarrollo* (Vitoria-Gasteiz, Spain: Gobierno Vasco-Eusko Jaurlaritza, 2010), 23–98.
2. Archivo General de Notarías de la Ciudad de México, Escribano Félix Fernando Zamorano, Notaría 749, Volumen 5295.
3. Elisa Luque Alcaide, "Relaciones intercontinentales de la Cofradía de Aránzazu de México," in *IV Seminario de Historia de la Real Sociedad Bascongada de los Amigos del País: "La RSBAP y Méjico,"* tomo 1 (Donostia–San Sebastián: RSBAP, 1993), 463–65.
4. Elena Sánchez de Madariaga, "Caridad, devoción e identidad de origen: Las cofradías de naturales y nacionales en el Madrid de la Edad Moderna," in *Devoción, paisanaje e identidad: Las cofradías y congregaciones de naturales en España y en América (Siglos XVI–XIX)*, ed. Óscar Álvarez Gila, Alberto Angulo Morales, and Jon Ander Ramos Martínez (Bilbao: UPV/EHU, 2014), 25–26.
5. Luque Alcaide, "Relaciones intercontinentales," 463.
6. Antonio García-Abásolo, "Cofradías y hospitales de Filipinas (siglos XVI–XVIII)," in Devoción, paisanaje e identidad. Las cofradías y congregaciones de naturales en España y en América (siglos XVI–XIX), ed. Óscar Álvarez Gila, Alberto Angulo Morales and Jon Ander Ramos Martínez (Bilbao: UPV/EHU, 2014), 75–77.
7. Angulo Morales, "Los frutos," 126–128; Alberto Angulo Morales, "De la congregación," 199–226.
8. García-Ayluardo, "El milagro," 441–43.
9. Luque Alcaide, "Relaciones intercontinentales," 465.
10. Angulo Morales, "El institutional," 362.
11. Elisa Luque Alcaide, "Recursos de la Cofradía de Aránzazu de México ante la corona (1729–1763)," *Revista de Indias* 56, no. 206 (1996): 213–18.

12. Elisa Luque Alcaide, "La cofradía de Aránzazu de México (1681–1861): Continuidad de un proyecto," in *Devoción, paisanaje e identidad: Las cofradías y congregaciones de naturales en España y en América (Siglos XVI–XIX)*, ed. Óscar Álvarez Gila, Alberto Angulo Morales, and Jon Ander Ramos Martínez (Bilbao: UPV/EHU, 2014), 227–46.
13. Fréderique Langue, *Los señores de Zacatecas: Una aristocracia minera del siglo XVIII novohispano* (Mexico City: Fondo de Cultura Económica, 1999), 363–64.
14. María Cristina Torales Pacheco, *Ilustrados en la Nueva España: Los socios de la Real Sociedad Bascongada de los Amigos del País* (Mexico City: Universidad Iberoamericana, 2001), 30–31.
15. Archivo Histórico del Colegio de las Vizcaínas (AHCV), Estante 6, Tabla IV, Volumen 6; Luque Alcaide, "Recursos," 205–8; Pedro Ramos y Ramos and Magdalena Rius de la Pola, "Tres momentos en la vida del Colegio de las Vizcaínas," in *Los vascos en las regiones de México: Siglos XVI–XX*, tomo 4, ed. Amaya Garritz (Mexico City: UNAM, 1999), 103–4; José Ignacio Tellechea Idígoras, "La Cofradía de Nuestra Señora de Aránzazu en la ciudad de México (1681–1794)," in *Las huellas de Aránzazu en América*, ed. Óscar Álvarez Gila and Idoia Arrieta Elizalde (Donostia: Lankidetzan, 2004), 44–49; José Ignacio Tellechea Idígoras, *El Colegio de las Vizcaínas de México y el Real Seminario de Vergara* (Vitoria-Gasteiz, Spain: Eusko Jaurlaritza-Gobierno Vasco, 1992).
16. Echeberria Ayllón, *Basque Women's*.
17. Josefina Muriel, *La sociedad novohispana y sus colegios de niñas*, tomo 2, *Fundaciones del siglo XVII y XVIII* (Mexico City: UNAM, 2004), 188.
18. AHCV, Estante 4, Tabla V, Volumen 1.
19. Alberto Angulo Morales, "Las geografías epistolares de las élites vascongadas y la formación de comunidades ilustradas en el siglo XVIII: la Real Congregación de San Ignacio y la Real Sociedad Bascongada de los Amigos del País," in *"Las cartas las inventó el afecto": Ensayos sobre epistolografía en el Siglo de las Luces*, ed. Rafael Padrón Fernández (Santa Cruz de Tenerife, Spain: Ediciones Idea, 2013), 69; Angulo Morales, "De la familia," 149; Palacios Fernández, "Proyección de la ilustración vasca en América," *Revista Internacional de Estudios Vascos* 43 (1998): 33–60; Carmen María Panera Rico, "La edad de la Ilustración en España: Lazos de fortuna, devoción y saber entre el País Vasco y América,"

Itsas Memoria: Revista de Estudios Marítimos del País Vasco 3 (2000): 711–27; María Cristina Torales Pacheco, "Los socios de la Real Sociedad Bascongada de los Amigos del País en México," in *IV Seminario de Historia de la Real Sociedad Bascongada de los Amigos del País: "La RSBAP y Méjico,"* tomo 1 (Donostia–San Sebastián: RSBAP, 1993), 81–116; María Cristina Torales Pacheco, "Presencia en México de los socios europeos de la RSBAP," in *La Bascongada y Europa: Actas del V Seminario de Historia de la Real Sociedad Bascongada de los Amigos del País,* ed. Guadalupe Rubio de Urquía and María Montserrat Gárate Ojanguren (Donostia–San Sebastián: RSBAP, 1999), 441–62; *La Real Sociedad Bascongada y América* (Madrid: Fundación BBVA, 1992).

20. Muriel, *La sociedad,* 187.
21. Luque Alcaide, "Relaciones intercontinentales," 477–80; Elisa Luque Alcaide, "Asociacionismo vasco en la Nueva España: modelo étnico-cultural," in *Los vascos en las regiones de México. Siglos XVI–XX,* tomo 2, ed. Amaya Garritz (Mexico City: UNAM, 1996), 72.
22. Luque Alcaide, "Asociacionismo vasco," 70–71.
23. Leonor Ludlow Wiechers, "Los vascos-mexicanos ante los gobiernos independientes. Relaciones financieras y políticas," in *IV Seminario de Historia de la Real Sociedad Bascongada de los Amigos del País: "La RSBAP y Méjico,"* tomo 1 (Donostia–San Sebastián: RSBAP, 1993), 909; Brading, *Mineros y comerciantes;* María Pía Taracena, "La migración dorada: Una familia vizcaína encuentra fama y fortuna en la ciudad de México a finales del siglo XVIII y siglo XIX. El caso de los Bassoco," in *Los vascos en las regiones de México: Siglos XVI–XX,* tomo 4, ed. Amaya Garritz (Mexico City: UNAM, 1999), 220; Verónica Zárate Toscano, "Estrategias familiares de los nobles de origen vasco en la Nueva España," in *Los vascos en las regiones de México: Siglos XVI–XX,* tomo 2, ed. Amaya Garritz (Mexico City: UNAM, 1999), 226.
24. Juan Javier Pescador, "La familia Fagoaga y los matrimonios en la Ciudad de México en el siglo XVIII," in *Familias novohispanas, siglos XVI a XIX,* ed. Pilar Gonzalbo Aizpuru (Mexico City: Colegio de México, 199), 203–26.
25. Cristina Torales Pacheco, "La familia Yraeta, Yturbe e Ycaza," in *Familias novohispanas, siglos XVI al XIX,* ed. Pilar Gonzalbo Aizpuru (Mexico City: Colegio de México, 1991), 181–202.

CHAPTER SIX

Basque "Support" for the Crown

In general terms, at the end of the eighteenth century, the Basque colony in Mexico focused its efforts on helping the Spanish mainland. There were several political and military conflicts that worried these wealthy families. In the context of the Atlantic Revolutions, conflicts such as the War of Jenkins' Ear, the Seven Years' War, and the American War of Independence required their participation. After all, they were at the top of the system, having received countless benefits from the crown.

Without going into the matter in depth, I would like to underline the significant amount of capital sent by these families to the Crown, occasionally for negotiating purposes.[1] The substantial volume of documentation indicates this.[2] The course of events led several of these families to position themselves against the mainland.

Multiple transformations took place during the period, elements that converged in the Mexican Declaration of Independence in 1821: greater political influence of the military commands, crisis on the mainland, decline of silver capitalism, rise of political liberalism, and corrosion of the crop trade, among others. The rebellion of the Mexican Bajío (Lowlands) led by Miguel Hidalgo destroyed part of the farming sector, supporters of silver capitalism, which was essential for the economy of New Spain and its elites.[3] And the interesting thing about this episode is that women, once again, took part in the protests, fulfilling their traditional role. In 1820, a third of the land conquered by the rebellion was occupied by them.[4]

Hidalgo—whose mother was of Basque descent—was the protagonist of the Cry of Dolores alongside two characters of the same origin, Ignacio Allende and Juan Aldama, who joined the same gatherings. The first major conspiracy against the Spanish government, the Valladolid Plot of 1809, also involved the participation of Mexicans from Basque lands, such as José Mariano Michelena, José María Izazaga, and Manuel Iturriaga.[5] The fact that a good portion of the actors were descendants of Basque families is explained by their aforementioned migratory success and its importance in colonial society. This group was, throughout the eighteenth century, the most relevant in economic, political, and social terms.[6] It was, in the words of Ramírez Maya, the catalytic group.[7]

Meanwhile, the Aránzazu Brotherhood suffered significant transfers, being forced to lend funds.[8] Different loyalties arose within the organization. Many of its members, also linked to the RSBAP, supported independence—like the members of the nearby School of Mining. However, the Vizcaínas school remained loyal to the crown. In 1813, several students signed an ex-voto pronouncing themselves "faithful patriots" and servants of Nuestra Señora de los Remedios—Our Lady of Remedies, the standard of the royalists.[9]

However, the girls did not stay away from the rebel faction. They also had a great role model. A former classmate was responsible for lighting the spark of independence: Josefa Ortiz lived for eight months at the school.[10] With such a reference, in a meeting held in February 1813 the school principal denounced that among the students there was "the detestable system of insurrection in the expressions poured out against the European Spaniards." This "aggressive Mexicanist" consciousness, in the words of Josefina Muriel, was what led to the signing of the aforementioned ex-voto against independence.[11] Nevertheless, insurgent elements remained present in the Vizcaínas:

> America is by nature separated from Spain, and it must be so by Justice. None of the rights that Spain claims for its domination is legitimate . . . having deposed the barbarism that reigned in past centuries, it is well known by all men, even those of

mediocrity, that to conquer a kingdom is to usurp it, to steal it. Therefore, since America should not depend on Spain, those who unjustly and recklessly oppose its Independence cannot properly call themselves defenders of its integrity, and the title that corresponds to them is that of true enemies who try to tyrannize it . . . What! Is it not a just cause to free the Fatherland from the tyrannical oppression in which for the long space of 3 centuries it has been groaning under the Spanish yoke?[12]

Another educational institution linked to the Basque group was the Belén school. For years it served as a prison for women from the rebel side, where María Leona Vicario, another of the great female figures of the independence, was imprisoned.[13] Despite serving in this role, the school stands out for its loyalty to the emancipatory movement, perhaps due to its strong devotion to the Virgin of Guadalupe.

Decades before, piety was essential to form individual and group identities. The Basques expressed their identity with their continuous demonstrations, serving as elements of integration. And they were the main sponsors of the devotion to Guadalupe, a symbol of Mexican identity. Juan Antonio de Vizarrón y Eguiarreta, a bishop who promoted the construction of the Vizcaínas, swore loyalty to the Virgin of Guadalupe as the patron of New Spain in 1737.[14] The school of Belén, dependent on the archbishopric, developed a strong devotion to her from then on, an institution where a strong pro-independence feeling emerged over the years. After José María Morelos, another of the great promoters of independence, was shot, Belén's students performed with messages against royal authority, *In Praise of Our Lady of Guadalupe*.[15]

In this context, the anger of the Mexican elites increased, and so "the first plan for the independence of Mexico was conceived by the owners of the usurped capital."[16] Many of them, of course, were of Basque origin. As Lucas Alamán wrote, if falling into generalization slightly, in the nineteenth century, "all the conquerors of America and especially of New Spain, were natives of Badajoz and Medellín in Extremadura, and all those who caused the ruin of the Spanish empire established by them in the new world, came from the Basque provinces."[17] The children of that first independent Mexico observed it that way.

The Basque community was one of the main ones when it came to spreading this enlightened ideology essential to understanding emancipation. And many of these figures were, in one way or another, connected to these institutions. Likewise, the Society of Jesus, expelled in 1767, was one of those responsible for developing this Mexican identity, "an ideological movement that was expressed in the Independence."[18] The members of the RSBAP, some of them educated by the Society of Jesus, would serve as a bridge between them and the independence movement. Figures such as José Antonio de Alzate or Juan Ignacio María de Castorena Ursúa stand out above the rest. In this way, part of the Basque enlightened movement would achieve a transformative spirit, with great geopolitical consequences.

The influence of the successors of the RSBAP and the Brotherhood of Aránzazu in the independence movement was extraordinary. At least eighty-four individuals belonging to this enlightened elite were directly involved in the process, one of the most important in the history of the Atlantic Revolutions. Among them were the Navarrese bishop Juan Ruiz de Cabañas, who donated 25,000 pesos to the cause; Francisco de Gamboa, drafter of the constitutions of the Vizcaínas; the Navarrese José Joaquín Iturbide, the father of the future first Mexican emperor; and the Marquis of San Miguel de Aguayo, member of the Guadalupes.[19] In the Declaration of Independence of the Mexican Empire we find signatories of Basque origin such as Fagoaga, Azcárate, Iturbide, Guridi y Alcocer, Velasco, Jaúregui, Icaza, Horbegoso, and Echevers.[20]

After independence, "the Mexican Basques managed to preserve their former social status for several decades, staying within the networks of political and financial control and preserving their previous authority and social prestige."[21] The Brotherhood of

Aránzazu, which had not broken its economic ties with the Basque Country,[22] helped the new government in its fight against General Antonio López de Santa Anna.[23] What happened, meanwhile, to the women?

NOTES

1. Francisco Andújar Castillo, "Interpretar la corrupción: el marqués de Villarrocha, Capitán General de Panamá (1698–1717)," *Revista Complutense de Historia de América* 43 (2017): 77–78; Francisco Andújar Castillo, *El sonido del dinero: Monarquía, ejército y venalidad en la España del siglo XVIII* (Madrid: Marcial Pons Historia, 2004); Francisco Andújar Castillo, "Venalidad y gasto military: Sobre la financiación de la Guerra de los Nueve Años," in *Un Estado militar: España, 1650–1820*, ed. Agustín González Enciso (Madrid: Actas, 2012), 395–422; Manuel Ballesteros Gaibrois, "El vasco Diego de Gardoqui, primer embajador de España ante los Estados Unidos de América," in *Euskal Herria y el Nuevo Mundo: La contribución de los vascos a la formación de las Américas*, ed. Ronald Escobedo Mansilla, Ana de Zaballa Beascoechea, and Óscar Álvarez Gila (Bilbao: UPV/EHU, 1996), 305–18; Begoña Cava Mesa, "Enlightenment figure, trader and diplomat: The historical contribution of Diego de Gardoqui to the Independence of the United States," in *Recovered Memories: Spain, New Orleans and the Support for the American Revolution*, ed. José Manuel Guerrero Acosta (Madrid: Iberdrola, 2018), 119–30; Rafael Domínguez Martín, *Cántabros en México: Historia de un éxito colectivo* (Santander, Spain: Gobierno de Cantabria, 2005); Freddy Domínguez Nárez, "Nación, pensamiento e intelligentsia en el movimiento de independencia de 1810 en México," *América: Cahiers du CRICCAL* 41 (2012): 45; Montserrat Gárate Ojanguren, "Remesas de capitales mexicanos a Europa en el siglo XIX. La participación vasca," in *Los vascos en las regiones de México: Siglos XVI–XX*, tomo 1, ed. Amaya Garritz (Mexico City: UNAM, 1996), 286–88; Guadalupe Jiménez Codinach, "Algunos miembros de la Real Sociedad Bascongada y sus descendientes, amigos de la Independencia de la Nueva España," in *IV Seminario de Historia de la*

Real Sociedad Bascongada de los Amigos del País: "La RSBAP y Méjico," tomo 2 (Donostia–San Sebastián: RSBAP, 1993), 851; Dolores del Mar Sánchez González, "El virrey Miguel José de Azanza y la conspiración de los machetes ¿Primer intento de independencia mexicana?," in *Una crisis atlántica: España, América y los acontecimientos de 1808*, ed. Concepción Navarro Azcue, Arrigo Amadori, and Miguel Luque Talaván (Madrid: Universidad Complutense, 2010), 29–38; Salvador Méndez Reyes, "Los Fagoaga: Magnates de las minas zacatecanas y la independencia," in *Los vascos en las regiones de México, siglos XVI–XX*, tomo 5, ed. Amaya Garritz (Mexico City: UNAM, 1999), 297–302; Pedro Pérez Herrero, "Los beneficiarios del reformismo borbónico: Metrópoli versus élites novohispanas," *Historia Mexicana* 41, no. 2 (1991): 239; Tomás Pérez Vejo, "El retrato como arma de poder: La representación de vizcaínos y montañeses en la Nueva España del siglo XVIII," in *Devoción, paisanaje e identidad. Las cofradías y congregaciones de naturales en España y en América (siglos XVI–XIX)*, ed. Óscar Álvarez Gila, Alberto Angulo Morales, and Jon Ander Ramos Martínez (Bilbao: UPV/EHU, 2014), 289–316; Julio Juan Polo Sánchez, "Vascos y montañeses: Arte, poder e identidades nacionales en el virreinato de Nueva España," *Acta Artis. Estudis d'Art Modern* 3 (2015): 63–73; Carmina Ramírez Maya, "En el prisma de la Independencia: Los vascos en México," in *Los vascos en las Independencias Americanas*, ed. Óscar Álvarez Gila (Bogotá: Fundación Centro Vasco Euskal Etxea, 2010), 236; Von Wobeser "La Consolidación," 419–20; Jaime E. Rodríguez, "La Revolución Francesa y la Independencia de México," in *La Revolución Francesa en México*, ed. Solange Alberro, Alicia Hernández Chávez, and Elías Trabulse (Mexico City: Colegio de México, 1993), 139; Jesús Ruiz de Gordejuela Urquijo, "Los Voluntarios de Fernando VII de Ciudad de México: ¿Baluarte de la capital y confianza del reino?," *Revista de Indias* 262 (2014): 775–76; Luis Sazatornil Ruiz, ed., *Arte y mecenazgo indiano: Del Cantábrico al Caribe* (Gijón: Ediciones Trea, 2007); Taracena, "La migración dorada," 221; Gisela von Wobeser "La Consolidación de Vales Reales como factor determinante de la lucha de Independencia en México, 1804–1808," *HMex* 61, no. 2 (2006): 375.

2. AGN, Indiferente virreinal, Volumen 2375, Expediente 013; AGN, Gobierno Virreinal, Marina, Volumen 39, Expedientes 80, 81 y 82;

AGN, Indiferente virreinal, Volumen 0858, Expediente 004; AGN, Indiferente virreinal, Volumen 3598, Expediente 048; AGN, Indiferente virreinal, Volumen 3641, Expediente 001; AGN, Indiferente virreinal, Volumen 4787, Expediente 034; AGN, Correspondencia de virreyes, Volumen 180; AGN, Correspondencia de virreyes, Volumen 182; AGN, Reales Cédulas Originales, Volumen 161, Expediente 171; AGN, Reales Cédulas Originales, Volumen 163, Expediente 173; AGN, Reales Cédulas Originales, Volumen 165-A, Expediente 105; AGN, Reales Cédulas Originales, Volumen 172, Expediente 99; AGN, Reales Cédulas Originales, Volumen 172, Expediente 110; AGN, Reales Cédulas Originales, Volumen 173, Expediente 87; AGN, Marina, Volumen 79, Expediente 4; AGN, Indiferente virreinal, 2634, Expediente 013; AGN, Reales Cédulas Originales, Volumen 148, Expediente 151; AGN, Bandos 011, Volumen 24, Expediente 134; AGN, Reales Cédulas Originales, Volumen 207, Expediente 76; AGN, Reales Cédulas Originales, Volumen 207, Expediente 77; AGN, Reales Cédulas Originales, Volumen 207, Expediente 78; AGN, Real Audiencia, Infidencias 060, Volumen 6, Expediente 10; AGN, Indiferente Virreinal, Volumen 2231, Expediente 009; AGN, Indiferente Virreinal, Volumen 20, Expediente 028; AGN, Indiferente Virreinal, Volumen 1113, Expediente 011; AGN, Indiferente Virreinal, Volumen 4353, Expediente 012; AHCV, Estante 6, Tabla III, Volumen 10. AGN, Indiferente virreinal, Volumen 4787, Expediente 029.
3. John Tutino, "Breaking New Spain, 1808–1821: Remaking Power, Production and Patriarchy before Iguala," *Mexican Studies* 37, no. 3 (2021): 369.
4. Tutino, "Breaking New Spain," 384.
5. Ramírez Maya, "En el prisma," 227.
6. Jesús Ruiz de Gordejuela Urquijo, "Los vascos y navarros en México en el tránsito de colonia a nación," in *Del espacio cantábrico al mundo Americano: Perspectivas sobre migración, etnicidad y retorno*, ed. Óscar Álvarez Gila and Juan Bosco Amores Carredano (Bilbao: UPV/EHU, 2015), 250.
7. Ramírez Maya, "En el prisma," 221.
8. García-Ayluardo, "El milagro," 455–456.
9. Muriel, *La sociedad novohispana*, 257.
10. Muriel, *La sociedad novohispana*, 232.

11. Muriel, *La sociedad novohispana*, 257.
12. AHCV, Estante 6, Tabla 4, Volumen 2.
13. Ana Belén García López, "La participación de las mujeres en la independencia hispanoamericana a través de los medios de comunicación," *Historia y Comunicación Social* 16 (2011): 39; Muriel, *La sociedad novohispana*, 109-10.
14. Josefina Muriel, "Los arzobispos vascos y sus obras dedicadas a las mujeres novohispanas," in *Los vascos en las regiones de México: Siglos XVI-XX*, tomo 4, ed. Amaya Garritz (México: UNAM, 1999), 63-65.
15. Muriel, *La sociedad novohispana*, 112-13.
16. Jiménez Codinach, "Algunos miembros," 845.
17. Lucas Alamán, *Historia de Méjico* (Mexico City: Editorial Jus, Volumen 1, 1968), 229.
18. Torales Pacheco, *Ilustrados*, 188.
19. Muriel, "Los arzobispos vascos," 69-71; Jiménez Codinach, "Algunos miembros," 846-69; Von Wobeser "La Consolidación," 418-19.
20. Guadalupe Pérez San Vicente, *Análisis Paleográfico sobre el Acta de Independencia* (Mexico City: UNAM, 1961), 3-4.
21. Ludlow Wiechers, "Los vascos-mexicanos," 910.
22. Gárate Ojanguren, "Remesas," 288.
23. Minister of Finance Medina to José María de Echave. Mexico City, December 24, 1822, and January 14, 1823, AHCV, Estante 15, Tabla 2, Volumen 2.

CHAPTER SEVEN

(Basque) Women in the Atlantic Revolutions

In 1808, Napoleon's armies invaded the Iberian Peninsula, starting the Spanish War of Independence, a period of war that led to the definitive fracture between the Old and New Worlds. In August 1811, the Basque general Gabriel de Mendizábal e Iraeta sent a message of help to American women.[1] Using epic language, the man responsible for leading the northern army during the Spanish War of Independence exhorted the women of the New World to send their money:

> Which kingdom, city, town or village has not been marked by the fury of these murderers and the heroism of its inhabitants? But those bordering on the Pyrenees and its slopes and branches, a rugged and barren region, except for men, who fill the armies and fleets, and in happier times emigrated copiously to those countries to provide themselves with your favor the fortune that their own denied them, thus strengthening between the inhabitants of both hemispheres relations and fraternity more cordial and preferential than with the other Mediterranean people of the peninsula, it will be easy for you to form an idea of the misery and lack of means that afflicts them. . . . Lovable sex from overseas! . . . The Roman ladies, in the troubles of the republic due to shortage of cash and food, contributed to filling the coffers of the state with their savings and treasures; and those of Carthage in the Third Punic War, after having worked with men in the armament and fortification of their walls and arsenals night and day in the last disastrous times of that rival of Rome, they cut off their hair, the most necessary and precious adornment, to make cables and moorings to hold the relics of

their dying Navy. Will you be less, you above all, Mexicans and Limeans? Cooperate then, you, to whom nature gave such an active empire over men, to form under the direction and collection of so many gentlemen prelates, ecclesiastics and officials of all hierarchies, a patriotic donation box.[2]

Mendizábal's call is another example of the essential role that society at the time assigned to women. With the Iberian Peninsula invaded by Napoleon's armies, they had to participate in the war effort, although the way they did so would vary. Their attitudes and actions were linked to gender stereotypes and roles, in some cases respecting and in others transgressing them.

Women who support political causes by financing them—that is, by donating their wealth—fulfill the wishes of that androcentric and patriarchal society by embodying the most widespread archetype of femininity of the period. Contributing to the war by offering their money was within the canon attributed to femininity.

Reacting to the different calls, some powerful women of New Spain would join in the aid, such as the Countess of San Mateo de Valparaíso. Widow of Miguel de Berrio y Zaldívar, Marquis of Jaral de Berrio, this woman gave 6,000 pesos in exchange for certain favors—"once the Peace is concluded, her great-grandson Don José Joaquín Fernández de Córdoba y Moncada will be attended to."[3] The widowed Marquise of Apartado, for her part, arranged with Madrid the sending of 10,000 pesos as well as a loan worth 45,000 pesos in exchange for another favor. This demonstrates the management that these ladies had of their political and social environment, just as their male relatives did.[4] For her part, the widowed Marquise of Castañiza, Manuela de Fagoaga, was congratulated by the regency of the kingdom for the 2,000 pesos she donated,[5] an amount that rose to 3,090 pesos from the donation of the estate of her late husband.[6]

Sometimes, it was not a personal or individual decision: these women fulfilled the wishes of their deceased husbands.[7] The family macrocosm, the house or extended family, was imposed as one of the bases that most conditioned female action during the early modern centuries, since the sending of funds consisted of not only a patriotic duty but also a legal, family, and class-based one.

Even though they are humble, the donations made by women are indisputable. Due to their secondary role within the family, economic, and social orders, there were very few donations made, although as the century progressed these would increase, as did calls for their collaboration. As a hypothesis, it is possible that many of these women were widows in charge of their families, as in the cases previously mentioned, and the number of widows was significant. In the center of Mexico City, streets inhabited mostly by the elites, 30 percent of the households were governed by women,[8] and 14 percent of businesses were run by women, 66 percent of whom were widows.[9] In 1811, a third of adult women shared this status, a statistic that rose to 40 percent in 1848.[10]

As the request for voluntary donations spread throughout New Spain, women and men helped the mainland. Among the list of those individuals who decided to offer a certain amount to the crown, we generally find a significant number of people of Basque origin, including women.[11] Such would be the case of María Josefa Lazcano, from Ostoticpac; Doña Josefa, from the Las Papas ranch; and "the widow of Ayala" from Otumba. The reports highlight the town of San Nicolás Obispo Oltotupac, where a list was drawn up with all the widows who contributed to the cause: twenty-six in total. We know that there were four widowers and nineteen widows in Belén, four widowers and nine widows in San Francisco, three and five respectively in Santiago and only two widows, finally, in San Miguel.[12] As we can see, a good part of the women who sent their donations to the crown did so as widows, performing that family interregnum.[13]

In this context, one of the most unusual and atypical female donations took place: the wealthy widow of Basque origin, María Josefa Vergara, offered all her assets to the city council of Querétaro, governed at that time by Miguel Domínguez, one of the founding fathers of the Mexican nation. Her donation included precise instructions on economic operations, social reforms, and cultural integration.[14] It was the year 1809, one year before the outbreak of war.

Several years prior, in the United States, women from Philadelphia started a campaign to finance the Continental army, actions that place them within the feminine archetype of the period.[15] Taking up arms did not correspond to the ideal of modesty, prudence, and contemplation; however, sending funds was within the social norm, as it was for their New Spanish contemporaries.

Perhaps one of the most interesting cases happened in Mexico City. In 1809, female residents of the capital of New Spain held a fundraiser to help the mainland: 3,178 pesos were collected and deposited in the home of the Basque man Antonio Bassoco, known for his loyalty to the monarch. However, the amount seemed small to them. It was then that they wrote a letter addressed to all the women of the city and published in the *Gaceta de México*.[16] Among the seven signatories, all of them belonging to the capital elite, three were of Basque origin: Ana María Iraeta de Mier, María Josefa Yermo de Yermo, and Margarita Zúñiga de Amezola.

> Dear Lady: Never has Christian piety been presented with objects so worthy of its efforts as those offered by our unfortunate age. A holy and venerable Religion, a King who was once much loved, was tyrannically persecuted, and a Nation which, after having given us birth and its ancient honor, sees itself generously sacrificed to the defense of the law of its God, and the empire of its Sovereign, are today those who effectively demand from us the manifestation of the intimate sentiments of our hearts.
>
> Mexico will have seen, and the world will know, the charity, modesty, decorum, and fervor with which the ladies who inhabit this city requested and carried out a most solemn novena to the

Patriarch, St. Joseph, despite the delicacy of their sex for physical work, the blushing that their education inspired in them, and the criticism that their attempt aroused, to obtain at all possible cost from the Lord, the arbiter of our fate, the necessary aid.

But we are well aware that the compassion which your character produces is not yet satisfied, nor would we believe that we had fulfilled our desires, if our requests ceased here, when temporal aid to the needy should be added to the vows directed to heaven; when the word went out from [illegible mark]ua in another conversation, and even from the pulpit, that the Ladies, in addition to the amount they collect, should contribute from their own duties to provide for the widows and orphans of those who have died in the present war, some relief in their serious emergencies; and when even foreign Ladies have given us this kind of examples, which, if we do not imitate them, must fill us with confusion and shame.

The time has come. By prudently saving, more than half of what was collected for the Novena was left over for this purpose. Although it is a small amount for its purpose, it will be placed in the gazette as the first item, followed by a note from the Ladies who contribute, stating the amount that each one will give; and everything will be sent without delay to the Supreme Central Board through this superior authority, so that His Majesty may distribute it according to his intention, without it being our intention to curtail His sovereign powers, if the salvation of the country, which is the first and most urgent need, requires that our contributions be applied to it.

We do not doubt your disposition for this purpose, as the urging of some has determined us to this claim: and so we hope that, as unequivocal proof of your generous piety, you will be pleased to place the amount with which you contribute at the home of Mr. D. Antonio Bassoco, who has offered to be the Depositary, and will give the corresponding receipt. May God keep your life for many years. Mexico, June 10, 1809.[17]

Appealing to the heart, to their noblest feelings, to feminine virtues, to their patriotism, and to their duty to help, these women managed to raise 29,045 pesos from ladies in Mexico City, Sombrerete, and Guadalajara. Their purpose was to help other women, widows, and orphans affected by the war in Spain. Among the donors, 328 in total, around 60 had Basque ancestors, some as important as the viceroy Francisca Xaviera de Echegaray y Garibay. And although they represented only 20 percent of the total, their wealth amounted to at least 8,100 pesos, or 28 percent.

Women from other places followed their example. Residents from San Luis Potosí, Oaxaca, Veracruz, Durango, and Sinaloa sent their money. The ladies of Veracruz flooded the port with a proclamation full of epic language with references to the Spanish Reconquista and the patriotism of women, a document that evokes the call of General Mendizábal. Published in Veracruz on July 24, 1811, the text was signed by, among others, Ana Josefa Zabaleta de Panes and María Soledad Esain de Zabaleta:

> "Let the vile Corsican and his abominable satellites know that the weaker sex of this noble city of Veracruz opposes him and will strongly oppose him . . ."; "Perhaps we are not the first to think this, and hopefully it is so, because we do not aspire to achieve glory but to provide means to help our brothers . . ." and appealing to their "Spanish spirit" and referring to the "heroic" expulsion of the Moors by "our ancestors," they asked that "there be reborn, then, from among the Americans, new Amazons who will destroy with their donations, since they cannot do it with their hands, these abortions of nature."[18]

The importance of the fundraising carried out in Mexico City is measured, however, by the future of its protagonists. A year after the collection, these women founded the first women's society in the history of the Mexican capital, the "Marian Patriots." Organized to defend Spain from the Napoleonic invasion, their activities changed with the political drift of the viceroyalty, offering their support to the monarchy and serving as support for the royalist side. Ana María Iraeta, one of the most important ladies of the capital, was the main person responsible for this organization made up of more than 2,500 women. After independence, she was named principal lady to Empress Ana Huarte, wife of Agustín de Iturbide and daughter of a merchant born in Goizueta, Navarre.[19] The first emperors of independent Mexico were, in fact, born in the Mexican city of Valladolid, and both were sons of wealthy Navarrese merchants. Their connection is consistent, given the background, with the endogamous and group-based attitude practiced by the Basque-Navarrese elites.

The main symbol of the Marian Patriots was the Virgin of Los Remedios, a sign adopted by the royalists in 1811 as protector of weapons and "Generalissima" of New Spain.[20] Their actions included espionage, financing, and propaganda and were so important that, in 1820, they were rewarded by Ferdinand VII, king of Spain, with the Isabel la Católica Medal.[21]

Getting such public credit from the sovereign power also implies having fulfilled certain requirements associated with feminine canons. "The concepts of nation and religion come together and give form to patriotism . . . country, king and religion provide the symbolic excuse for the ladies to be able to show off their firm Spanishness, going out into the public arena without the risk of being denaturalized, making use of the powers associated with their condition as mothers of the citizen." The assimilation of the trinomial King, Religion, and Nation would have supposedly led them to be more active in conservative associations. The fact that this triad appears in the first lines of the text published in the *Gaceta de México* by the future Marian Patriots, with the lady of Basque origin Ana María de Iraeta at the head, explains itself.[22]

On the other hand, it is also worth remarking on the scant recognition that this group of women has received from a historiographical point of view. Chambers points out that while the memory of

American revolutionaries was manipulated and mythologized, women supporters of the royalists have been completely ignored.[23]

Social and economic realities, as well as racial and gender ones, play a fundamental role when it comes to defining the action of these women. With all the possible exceptions and nuances that history always offers us, those who participated in the conflicts from a privileged socioeconomic position did so by complying with the enlightened canons of femininity, so-called domesticated femininity. Elitist, after all. Their incursion into the public arena can be classified as an extension of their duty as mothers, as devout and pious women, and as protagonists of the social gathering, that dual space between public and private life. The action of poor women, although not exclusively, seems different and can be considered, in certain cases, transgressive.

Some ladies of high Spanish society, in Spain and America, belong to the informal spheres of political power thanks, in part, to the recognition of their enlightened relatives: "women, by general consent and acceptance, have the power to demand . . . a great influence in the greatest revolutions and political events."[24] This was recognized, on paper, by the enlightened men of the Basque Country. At the same time, the Spanish female nobility managed to make their social capital profitable by intervening directly in the game of partisan alliances.[25]

Broadly speaking, from 1808 the Spanish political scene was divided between the supporters of the Napoleonic regime of Joseph I, Napoleon's brother, and those opposed to it, who took up arms in defense of the future king Ferdinand VII. Within this faction, liberal and conservative positions emerged, giving rise to the first constitution in the history of Spain, the Constitution of Cadiz of 1812.[26]

"Whether they were pro-French or not, supporters of the Josephine party out of ideological conviction or conditioned to it by family ties and economic interests, the truth is that the very broad spectrum represented by the women of the Basque nobility during that period leads us to recognize a heterogeneous panorama."²⁷ We know the experience lived by María Teresa de Olazábal y Veróiz, whose antipathy for the French will be beyond any doubt. On the other hand, there is the figure of María Pilar Acedo y Sarria, Marquise of Montehermoso.

Born in the Guipuzcoan town of Tolosa, this lady was part of the court during the War of Independence. Married to Ortuño de Aguirre, Marquis of Montehermoso and a prominent enlightened man from Álava, she met Joseph Bonaparte in 1808 when he was staying at the family palace on his way to Madrid, where he would take possession of the Spanish throne, and became the official mistress of the king. Her Frenchified husband was named Knight of the Chamber, Grandee of Spain, and Knight of the Order of Spain, although the greatest favor he could receive consisted of the exchange of his palace for 300,000 francs. Napoleon Bonaparte once observed that the palace was not worth that amount even with the marquise inside.²⁸

In the words of Abel Hugo, brother of the famous author Victor Hugo, María Pilar was "very proud and very involved in her role as official mistress, to the point that she used her status as royal favorite to give orders to the local governors"—that is to say, she really did exercise a position of power during the brief period she was in Madrid, until Joseph Bonaparte was expelled from Spain and she with him.²⁹ From then on, her fate was exile, a space she shared with other ladies of Basque high society accused of Frenchification.

One of these was María Antonia de Moyúa, wife of the well-known minister of the navy and member of the RSBAP José de Mazarredo. After a brief exile in Paris, María Antonia returned to Bilbao, where she was subjected to a trial or purification process in order to receive her widow's pension.³⁰ Other notable examples were Manuela de Salazar, second Marquise of La Alameda, and María Águeda de Valencegui, personal friends of María del Pilar Acedo y Sarria. Furthermore, thanks to this friendship, the Marquise of Montehermoso was able to help María Águeda de Valencegui "when she was arrested by the French because two of her ten children, Juan and Luis, were declared anti-French."[31] Years later, the three friends met again in a shared exile with numerous pro-French women of Spanish origin.[32]

Some of the gatherings at the end of the eighteenth century began to deal with political matters,[33] meetings that on some occasions ended with the imprisonment of those attending. This climate had severe consequences for a resident well known to the above, the Marquise of Legarda, who in 1814 was imprisoned for being pro-French along with the rest of her fellow members.[34]

The conflict-ridden and repressive atmosphere would directly affect women in Basque high society. The reasons that led them to participate in the events surrounding the conflict could have been different, from personal ideological conviction to the role played by their relatives, which led them, in some way, to place themselves on one side or to be perceived by the authorities as collaborators. A good part of the ministers chosen by Joseph Bonaparte were of Basque-Navarrese origin, an aspect that reveals the impact that the enlightened Basque elites had within the Spanish monarchy. José de Mazarredo was named minister of the navy, Mariano Luis de Urquijo was secretary of state, the Navarrese Manuel Romero Echalecu and Miguel José de Azanza the portfolios of Interior and Ecclesiastical Affairs and the Basque-French Francisco Cabarrús, the Ministry of Finance.

Within the Spanish context, the so-called *afrancesadas* (Frenchified women) were the objects of brutal criticism, such as that of the friar Manuel Martínez, who referred to "my ladies, the traitors." The pro-French ideological and cultural movement seems connected to the Enlightenment, certainly linked to the most privileged class, although not exclusively. However, I argue their political positioning could have been due to a multitude of factors, such as personal ideological conviction, economic interest, fear of losing personal assets, various loyalties, or family conditioning.[35] These positions, moreover, changed over time.

The aforementioned case of María Antonia de Moyúa from Bilbao is not the only one. Born in New Spain and of Navarrese origin, María Josefa Alegría married the viceroy, the Navarrese Miguel José Azanza. Professedly pro-French during the Josephine regime, she likely coincided with the Marquise of Montehermoso on her visits to the court, where her husband held important political positions. In the end, of course, she ended up exiled.[36] And on the opposite side we have the remarkable Rosario Cepeda, wife of the Biscayan military man and future governor of Veracruz, Pedro Miguel de Gorostiza. Born in Cádiz, she stood out in the famous organization Junta de Damas de Honor y Mérito, although throughout the conflict she had to, in some way, distance herself from the political positions defended by several of her children, who were declared anti-French.[37] The plurality of experiences, as we see, was important.

The simultaneous participation of women from different social classes also represents one of the great changes compared to previous periods: a national conflict that more or less frequently challenged all of them and for which they participated actively in the public arena. In previous periods, women from low social classes fought against economic injustice, within the class logic of the Ancient Régime. The nobility focused on its own political fights. The Spanish War of Independence, however, consists of a scenario of generalized political and military conflict that applied to all of them. If we add to this the transformation observed in the mandates and discourses of gender, with greater prominence or visibility within political events, we can better understand the change.

Some writers will call for female mobilization, but this must be done in accordance with their social position and without crossing the boundaries imposed by nature. The words of Frasquita Larrea, daughter of a prosperous merchant from Álava, apply precisely to this.[38] Referring to the explosion of periodicals that occurred during those years, Espigado Tocino explains, "What this press comes to optimize is a discourse of female excellence compatible with the express formulation of the complementarity of the sexes and the separation of spheres."[39]

Another example is that of the anonymous L.M.P., who invited women to create a women's society to serve "as mothers and wives of soldiers... respecting the limits of feminine action."[40] However, perhaps the most prolific author was Manuela López de Ulloa, the standard-bearer of a generation that managed to open a "channel of participation" in the public debate.[41] Among others, Beatriz Cienfuegos and her publication *La Pensadora Gaditana* and María del Carmen Silva and her *Robespierre Español* stand out.[42]

More examples of this female intervention can be found, once again, in Cadiz, besieged by Bonapartist troops. The ladies of Puerto de Santa María were asked by residents of Cádiz to collaborate in the organization of a fundraiser, a proclamation signed, among others, by women with surnames of Basque origin such as María del Carmen Uriarte or Josefa Luisa de Vicuña y Echave.[43] It is a phenomenon that runs through the entire Atlantic world, from Philadelphia to Cadiz.

A similar action carried out by the Spanish female nobility, very active in these years, consists of the call made by the Society of Ladies of Ferdinand VII to collect funds in the city of Seville. This call, in fact, extends to the rest of the capitals of the kingdom.[44] In the city of Seville, the *Real Hermandad Patriótica de Señoras* is also founded.[45] There are clear parallels with what happened in Mexico City.

Caring for people is another of the gender roles most saddled onto women of the time, which stimulates their action. In Zaragoza, besieged by Napoleonic troops, Josefa de Azlor y Villavicencio, the widowed Marquise of Ayerbe, improvised a field hospital in her palace; the possibility that she was related to Ignacia de Azlor y Echeverz, founder of *Enseñanza de México*—educational institution for Mexican women—and of Basque origin is pending prosopographical analysis. Josefa's sister organized a company of women to resist the siege, a group in charge of assisting the troops by carrying water, ammunition, and the injured.[46]

This besieged Spain offers examples of all kinds. The *Atalaya de la Mancha* published an extraordinary session that took place on April 3, 1814, in the Cortes Generales, where the case of Francisca Esteban, a native of Segovia, was presented. According to the parliamentary debate, this heroine had managed to free a total of 1,800 prisoners, "curing the sick in her own home," for which she deserved a pension.[47] In Madrid, another anonymous woman earned the nickname Mother of Prisoners and was known throughout Spain and France.[48] Eventually, her name reached the public, since the press of the time did not hesitate to give the necessary publicity to this kind of figure, spreading her fame as a role model:

> Soon the hospitals of St. Francis and Hospice were filled with wretches covered in dust, with wounds, or burning with fever. Teresa Calvo went to these mansions of pain and tears, in a state of exhaustion; at the same time, she performed the duties of mother, doctor, and minister of the altar: with one hand she applied the lint to the wound, with the other she showed the dying man on the divine Crucifix the end and crown of Christian hope. In vain did the cruel enemy oppose this intrepid charity with the grossest insults, the most humiliating treatment, and even the error of bayonets; the Castilian heroine, the more firm in her purpose the more she was opposed, aroused the compassion of her fellow citizens, invoked their generosity, returned and turned with all kinds of help and assistance, appeared and reappeared like the sun surrounded by black clouds in the hospitals, in the center of the Retiro, to meet the prisoners who were being taken to France; She facilitates the escape of some, provides shoes and food for others, leaving engraved in the hearts of all the sweet memory of a tender and generous mother who, to the admiration and amazement of the French themselves, knew how to overcome all dangers, attack and smooth out the greatest obstacles to make the fate of her sons less harsh.[49]

And the case of the Baroness of Beniparell is very similar:

> Impelled by the noble feelings that characterize a Spanish heroine, she dedicated herself with the greatest efforts and troubles to providing all the assistance that was possible for her assets to the Spanish prisoners, not only by herself, but also through her daughters and servants; also inspiring other ladies of her class to accompany her and contribute to her beneficial designs. In her house, the stews were cooked for the Spanish wounded who were sent to that hospital, where she herself and her daughters supplied the food . . . suffering for these important events the hatred, oppression and vengeance of the French, who ironically gave her the name of guardian of the Spanish prisoners.[50]

Another similar example is that of Angela Nabio. Her exceptional performance supplying the guerrillas of the famous Empecinado (Undaunted) earned her praise from the Madrid press, although the risks assumed distanced her from the female stereotype: "this figure, rising above the nature of her own sex and indifferent to its existence, was assigned three years ago to provide all kinds of weapons to the brave soldiers in the province of Guadalajara who were enlisting under the heroic leader Don Juan Martín El Empecinado."[51]

In this way, Spanish women achieve a certain significance or recognition by exercising "social motherhood" by making use of "forms of collective and philanthropic sociability," an aspect that leads them to perform tasks of mobilization or transmission of patriotic feelings. This was, at least, the purpose of some proclamations, which in a certain sense are elitist—these speeches on femininity are based on these schemes, in addition to the fact that the authors themselves had to belong, almost by force, to the most privileged class, since they had access to an advantageous culture and education. In other words, the messages are aimed at women who participate in the fight by transmitting national sentiment, raising funds, mobilizing volunteers, and caring for the injured, the so-called social motherhood.[52] Spanish women had to contribute to the war efforts while respecting gender rules, something similar to what was observed among their American contemporaries. Faced with the myth of female passivity and women's role as victim in a context of war,[53] we therefore observe different realities.

Spying is another of the areas where they stand out the most.[54] This activity, persecuted and punished, fell within the margins of female action because it was linked to rumor and the passive role of women. "Women used their influence in the domestic sphere to gain access to private information. . . . They were less suspicious than their husbands, brothers and sons."[55] In this respect, figures such as the Colombian of Basque origin Policarpa Salavarrieta stand out. The "main agent of the clandestine network of information and mail that fed the patriotic army," Policarpa distributed revolutionary messages hidden in oranges.[56] Another example is the anonymous informant who exposed the plot against the life of Simón Bolívar on the famous "September night." Manuela Sáenz de Vergara y Aizpuru, another of the heroes of the American independence with Basque origins, will go down in history for saving the Liberator's life after she informed him of a threat to his life.[57]

Meanwhile, in Mexico, Josefa Ortiz operated in a similar way, giving rise to the Cry of Dolores. In New Granada, women like Mercedes Loaiza or Eugenia Arrazola were sentenced to death for spying.[58] And on the other side of the coin, the Chilean woman of Basque origin Carmen Ureta received "lands held from a royal official for her work as a spy."[59]

The figure of the seductress is very controversial. "Many women from the lower classes served the insurgent cause as couriers and troop seductresses, even going so far as to prostitute themselves in order to gain followers for the cause."[60] When discussing the power of queens, Crawford reflects on "sexual power" and its relationship with their ability to manipulate gender expectations to produce political benefits in their favor.[61] The stereotypical image that is built around them is evident, "a superficial description of how a woman could contribute to a cause by using her physical beauty, since this only contributes to the stereotype of the femme fatale of spies and downplays their cunning and bravery."[62] The enlightened Basques also speak of this "atrocious feminine influence" exercised on men.[63]

These informants were motivated by political and personal purposes, greatly risking their lives. That is the reality. The Friné Mexicana (Mexican Phryne) named Maria Tomasa Álvarez "was commissioned to seduce Iturbide's troops" and executed in 1814. Carmen Camacho was hanged. The seductresses of Tula were also sentenced to death. And in the Llanos de Apan, Mexico, the so-called Eleven Thousand Virgins acted.[64] These actions were never recognized as patriotic acts "but rather as the attitude of an immoral woman or a being with the 'weaknesses of her sex.'"[65]

One framework or space in which they were respected and valued was the salon. The social gathering can be measured by its importance in understanding the social dimension of power. Ladies participate in this sociability that articulates social networks and power, while civility is assumed as a tool or strategy of power, allowing them to attract clients or come into contact with spheres of political power.[66] "This new domestic functionality requires enhancing the spaces where these practices are carried out, which is in line with an enlightened vision that assigns women a positive influence on social development, as civilizers and moderators of customs."[67]

This salon culture established a link between their domestic function and public and political space, "a space from which the women of the pro-independence elite had to radiate their influence towards the public stage... the domestic sphere began to function as a politicized terrain."[68] And in the meetings organized throughout the American continent, women were able to exercise their political activism by debating,[69] designing alliances, or recruiting allies.

"The plots to rebel against the Spanish yoke were born from these political meetings ... women attended the gatherings and just as frequently sponsored them."⁷⁰ The Mexican Mariana de Toro de Lazarín represents one of the most extreme cases, as she planned, together with her fellow members, a conspiracy to arrest and hang the viceroy Francisco Xavier Venegas. When the plot was discovered, she was imprisoned until 1820.⁷¹

"Mariquita Sánchez de Thompson organized secret meetings in her house with an independence spirit," as did Juana Ramírez or Josefa Palacios, in Venezuela.⁷² In 1809, "the rebels met in the house of Manuela Cañizares.... In Colombia, Joaquina Aroca offered her house for the meeting of indigenous people who rose up against the Spaniards in Natagaima.... She was shot on September 5, 1816."⁷³ The famous Juana de Azurduy from a young age "organized secret meetings related to the uprising of Túpac Amaru II. While married, she continued to organize gatherings to discuss politics. Figures such as Matías Monteagudo, Juan José Castelli, and Mariano Moreno participated in these meetings, who would later become important figures in the May Revolution."⁷⁴ Manuela Sanz de Santamaría, from Bogotá, hosted the Buen Gusto gathering, where revolutionary plans were discussed.⁷⁵

Ladies of American high society organized banquets, soirées, and patriotic parties, becoming directly involved in "national construction, bringing together and smoothing out differences between the leaders called to build the new nation, and eventually, imprinting their own visions through the influence they exert on members of their family networks."⁷⁶ Not all female contribution to war efforts were as entertaining, however. There were women whose participation was much more painful. Camp followers are a good example of this.

The tasks carried out by these women also fell within the socially accepted, without breaking gender norms. They contributed to the fight while still respecting society's normative framework, but some women did choose to break with these structures.

Some of the protagonists of the revolutionary period took advantage of the fight "to intercede in public life and transgress social barriers."[77] The change from previous periods seems evident, since until then, women's actions had generally been carried out in accordance with gender archetypes. In the different conflicts, whether they were represented by women of the nobility or the low estate, they complied with gender expectations, without going beyond the normative framework. During the Atlantic Revolutions, however, we observe a proliferation of cases that went beyond these limits, female experiences that previously could be considered exceptional. And one of the most interesting aspects of this change is its transnational character, since it shook the entire Atlantic world, from America to Europe.

It should be noted that women were already participating in armed combat as early as the fifteenth century.[78] Although this was not something new for Europeans and Americans, the transformation that took place during the decades of the Atlantic Revolutions suggests an explosion of cases that may have generated a series of political, cultural, and social consequences. The numerous actions that occurred during the revolutionary period may have caused medium- and long-term changes, including in gender relations.

In the case of the Spanish War of Independence, "the various female practices ... involved ... different degrees of transgression of the ideal of femininity of the time." Understood as the action that broke with gender roles, exceeding its limits, this transgressive attitude does not have the intention of achieving political rights, although it does create a precedent for the future.[79] The difference between transgressing and questioning the norm is an interesting topic of analysis. The former is linked to the recognition of the norm, its noncompliance, and subsequent maintenance by those in power, without structural changes. The latter, on the contrary, rejects the agreed norm and fights against it. Such questioning can force, in the long term, the modification of said norm.[80] I point this out because of the doubts and reflections that arise from the analysis of this type of female action in context of the Atlantic Revolutions, especially with regard to its consequences.

In Mexico, many women fought in combat. Antonia Nava, nicknamed La Generala, took part "in the siege suffered by Nicolás Bravo's troops." There were others, such as Manuela Medina, also known as La Capitana;[81] María Fermina Rivera, La Marina; La Fina; La Barragana; and María Josefa Martínez, who commanded troops dressed as a soldier. The anonymous Guanajuateña led a contingent of women,[82] just as Gertrudis Bocanegra did in 1810.[83] As we can see, many women took part in the battles.

In Cochabamba, women refused to surrender their weapons to General José Manuel Goyeneche: "When they were all asked if they wanted to surrender, they said no, that they would rather have the glory of dying fighting, and the ambassador who came from Cochabamba died at the hands of the women. After a short while, the enemy army was seen to be formed and the women immediately opened fire with their shawls tied to their waists, shooting for three hours."[84]

Perhaps the most famous of those who fought to liberate America was the Bolivian woman of Basque ancestry Juana de Azurduy, who was named lieutenant colonel and took part in many military actions.[85] She fought in sixteen battles commanding her own battalion, which was made up of women and indigenous people,[86] among others. In fact, she had a personal guard made up of twenty-five "Amazons."[87] The famous Manuela Sáenz, also of Basque origin, participated in the final battle of Ayacucho. According to the French scientist Jean-Baptiste Boussingault, "she had given proof of her military value, alongside General Sucre, she attended the battle of Ayacucho, lance in hand, the last encounter that took place between Americans and Spaniards."[88] Another who stands out, Juana Ramírez, organized a battalion of women to defend Maturín.[89]

Josefa Camejo, a Venezuelan, nicknamed the Joan of Arc of the independence movement, was part of the group of women who volunteered for the battle.[90] In the "representation made by the fair sex to the government of Barinas" from 1811, a total of twenty-one women reject the fragility ascribed to their sex for combat:

> Armed with a firm character and putting aside the weakness that is attributed to us, we are fully aware of the dangers the country faces. . . . As members of the female sex, sir, we do not fear the horrors of war: the explosion of the cannon will only encourage us: its fire will light our desire for the freedom that we will sustain at any price in honor of the Fatherland. By virtue of this and wishing to enlist in the service to replace the soldiers who have left for San Fernando, we beseech you to bear us in mind and send us wherever is convenient.[91]

Finally, another who stands out is María de Larraín, head of a group of women from the Quito neighborhoods of San Roque and San Blás, who confronted the royalists. Accused of having thrown rocks at the president of the Court, Count Ruiz de Castilla, they participated in his downfall and death.[92]

In the Basque Country, meanwhile, many women distinguished themselves by using weapons. Circumstances also favored the most combative, because although it was unthinkable that they would be admitted into a regular army, the guerrilla phenomenon was able to offer them a space in which to fight. Juana Ruiz, from Álava—born in Samaniego—became famous after having participated "in several guerrilla actions with the group commanded by Peña."[93] She was seventeen years old. Meanwhile, in Vizcaya and Álava, one of the best-known guerrilla fighters, Martina de Ibaibarriaga, also known as La Vizcaína, operated.

Born in Bérriz, her many actions brought her to lead in the valleys of Basque Country a group of fifty horsemen, a guerrilla group accused and tried for banditry. In a letter written to French general Doumonstier, the police commissioner of Vitoria said that "La Martina, a second Amazon, has made all the towns of Vizcaya and Álava tremble with twenty villains; she has committed countless robberies and murders." Captured by Mina's guerrillas, eight of its members were shot, although Martina's female condition seems to have saved her. Later, although it is not entirely corroborated, it seems that she participated in the famous Battle of Vitoria, where it is believed that the Basque general Francisco de Longa y Anchía played a joke on the Duke of Wellington himself, telling him about the bravery that Martina had shown in the fight and then revealing to him, to the surprise of the British, that she was a woman. In fact, one of the most controversial elements of her biography is that she dressed as a man in order to recruit and fight, exploits that led her to obtain the rank of captain.[94]

These two female figures represent the tip of the iceberg. To the experiences of women like María Ángela de Tellería, who orchestrated the ingenious escape of several prisoners from the Durango town jail and was awarded a lifetime salary of 4,000 reales by the Prizes Commission of the Cortes of Cádiz we should add countless cases: female collaborators, *guerrilleras*—a women who fight in a paramilitary group, spies, and so on. The Extraordinary Criminal Courts created by the Josephine regime judged a total of 268 Spanish women, almost 20 percent in Vizcaya.[95] Such is the magnitude of the role played by Basque women in the context of the Spanish War of Independence.

At the same time, the Spanish press reported the great achievements of female guerrilla fighters such as Manuela Sancho, Casta Álvarez, and Agustina de Aragón, portrayed as Amazons driven by their emotions and patriotic ardor.[96] An interesting example can be found in the letters of a French commander published in *El Conciso gaditano*:

> On the 16th, a woman who had been captured near the village with her weapons in her hands was shot. This unfortunate woman flattered herself that she had killed 14 Frenchmen and wounded more men. She was of average height; two saber blows she had received in the face disfigured her face, and the scars

gave her a manly countenance that commanded respect. She heard her death sentence with courage and left the court martial, saying out loud: "Oh, dogs! May I not tear out their souls!" Why should the name of this heroine not be discovered and published?[97]

The most combative, however, were generally part of the lower class. "This active participation of women in the conflict represented a breach of the enlightened norms of gender behavior,"[98] since a large part of public opinion believed the feminine archetype did not align with war.[99] Spanish society in those years moved between varied discourses, accepting and recognizing the role played by these "Amazons" and rejecting their emotional disorder, transgression of gender norms, and use of masculine clothing. These women were far removed from the feminine roles and archetypes of motherhood, gentleness, and decorum.

An example of this generalized criticism can be found in the viceroyalty of New Spain, as these criticisms are found throughout the Hispanic sphere. In 1793, the *Gaceta de México* published news criticizing the presence in armies of women dressed as men.

In an attitude that was certainly neutral or uncritical—perhaps because at that time these acts were disqualified by themselves in the eyes of the reader, the participation of women in battle dressed as men is published: "According to the *Gazette* of the city itself [Frankfurt] there are more than 10 women in Custine's army who serve dressed as Soldiers. Indeed, among the prisoners taken to Cologne after the action of Duren, one of them was found who had received three wounds; and among the number of those taken to Frankfurt by the Prussians there was another who served as an Officer."[100] Perhaps this news brought to the reader's memory the figure of Catalina de Erauso, a native of San Sebastián.[101]

Is this a significant or anecdotal phenomenon? According to the *Gaceta*, French women actively participated in the battlefield:

"The most veteran generals confess that they have never seen such tenacious ferocity, nor such a formal disdain for risks, and even for death.... Among their dead were found many women dressed as soldiers."[102] Simón Bolívar himself thanked these Amazons for their participation in the liberation of the province of Trujillo:

> Even the fair sex, the delights of the human race, our Amazons have fought against the tyrants of San Carlos with divine courage.... The monsters and tigers of Spain have filled the measure of their nation's cowardice, they have turned their infamous weapons against the candid and feminine breasts of our beauties; they have shed their blood; they have made many of them expire, and they have loaded them with chains, because they conceived the sublime design of liberating their beloved homeland.[103]

Women of North American and Haitian origins also participated directly in the Atlantic revolutionary cycle. The winds of change had been blowing through the New World for years, spreading these images and news.

Haitian women, for example, participated in the rebellion in an irregular way, where ethnoracial and socioeconomic components played a fundamental role. In general terms, it was the Afro-descendant women who fought for the rebel side, exercising a certain political influence using informal methods, carrying out espionage work or fighting.[104] The interesting thing about these events was in the racial division of the conflict, since while women of French descent maintained a distance from it, Afro-descendants were more active participants in the fight, being in addition, the slandered group in all kinds of pejorative speeches. The argument of the depraved, libertine, indomitable, and lascivious mulatto woman served as an element of attraction for the French troops, at least from the rhetorical level. A speech that objectified Afro-descendants as mere trophies to conquer.[105] The question here, due to chronological and spatial proximity, is to find out whether similar positions existed in the subsequent Spanish-American independence uprisings—that is, whether Creoles, mestizos, mulattoes, Native Americans, and Spaniards (Basques in this case) positioned themselves in the conflict based on their ethnoracial conditions, their socioeconomic conditions, a mixture of both, or neither.

NOTES

1. Carlos Rilova Jericó, "Vida de un general de las Guerras Napoleónicas, Gabriel de Mendizábal e Iraeta (1764–1838)," *Boletín de Estudios Históricos de San Sebastián* 45 (2012): 199–248.
2. AHCV, Estante 6, Tabla 4, Vol. 2.
3. AGN, Reales Cédulas Originales, Volumen 173, Expediente 105.
4. AGN, Reales Cédulas Originales, Volumen 172, Expediente 98.
5. AGN, Reales Cédulas Originales, Volumen 207, Expediente 79.
6. AGN, Reales Cédulas Originales, Volumen 207, Expediente 83.
7. Margarita Birriel Salcedo, "Sobrevivir al cónyuge: Viudas y viudedad en la España Moderna," *Chronica Nova* 34 (2008): 7–12; McCaa, "La viuda," 299–324; Beatrice Moring and Richard Wall, *Widows in European Economy and Society, 1600–1920* (Woodbridge, UK: Boydell Press, 2017); Amaia Nausia Primoulier, "Las viudas y las segundas nupcias en la Europa moderna: últimas aportaciones," *Memoria y Civilización* 9 (2006): 233–60; Scarlett O'Phelan Godoy, "Las viudas de empresarios mineros en el Perú borbónico," *Histórica* 27, no 2 (2003): 357–81; Ofelia Rey Castelao, "Las viudas de Galicia a finales del Antiguo Régimen," *Chronica Nova* 34 (2008): 91–122.
8. Pilar Gonzalbo Aizpuru, "Por decisión o necesidad: La jefatura femenina en los hogares de México virreinal," *Revista de Historiografía* 26 (2017): 57.
9. Gonzalbo Aizpuru, "Por decisión," 63; Josefina Muriel, "La transmisión cultural en la familia criolla novohispana," in *Familias novohispanas, siglos XVI al XIX*, ed. Pilar Gonzalbo Aizpuru (Mexico City: Colegio de México, 1991) 119–20.

10. Robert McCaa, "La viuda viva del México borbónico: Sus voces, variedades y vejaciones," in *Familias novohispanas, siglos XVI al XIX*, ed. Pilar Gonzalbo Aizpuru (Mexico City: Colegio de México, 1991), 302.
11. AGN, Indiferente virreinal, Volumen 2974, Expediente 008; AGN, Indiferente virreinal, Volumen 3039, Expediente 008; AGN, Indiferente virreinal, Volumen 3082, Expediente 010.
12. AGN, Indiferente virreinal, Volumen 2021, Expediente 007.
13. Katherine Clark, "Visible Negotiations: Widowhood as a Category for Assessing Women's Lives and Work in Early Modern Europe," *Gender & History* 21, no. 1 (2009): 190–95; Elisa García-Prieto, "La gestión femenina del patrimonio nobiliar: Doña Teresa de Saavedra y Zúñiga, condesa de Villalonso: una aristócrata en los reinados de Felipe II y Felipe III," *Cuadernos de Historia Moderna* 41, no. 1 (2016): 112–17.
14. Tutino, "Breaking," 383–385.
15. Francis D. Cogliano and Kirsten E. Phimister, *Revolutionary America, 1763–1815: A Source book* (London: Taylor & Francis Group, 2010): 189–90.
16. Marco Antonio Landavazo, "La fidelidad al rey: Donativos y préstamos novohispanos para la guerra contra Napoleón," *HMex* 48-3 (1999): 510–11.
17. *Gaceta de México*, November 13, 1809.
18. Landavazo, "La fidelidad," 512.
19. María Cristina Torales Pacheco, *La Compañía de Comercio de Francisco Ignacio de Yraeta (1767–1797)* (Mexico City: IMCE, 1985); María Cristina Torales Pacheco, "Tres viudas de la elite novohispana en el siglo XVIII," in *Viudas en la Historia* (Mexico City: CONDUMEX, 2002), 205–27.
20. AGN, Impresos Oficiales, Vol. 30, Exp. 10; AGN, Impresos Oficiales, Vol. 31, Exp. 32.
21. Brewster, "Women," 28; Ivana Frasquet, "Actrices en la independencia de México: Buscando su lugar en la Historia," in *Jamás ha llovido reyes del cielo: De independencias, revoluciones y liberalismos en Iberoamérica*, ed. Ivana Frasquet (Quito: Corporación Editorial Nacional, 2013), 218; María Ángeles Gálvez Ruiz, "La construcción del nuevo Estado y la cuestión de las mujeres en México," *Chronica*

Nova 38 (2012): 138; Muriel, "La sociedad novohispana," 257; Celia del Palacio Montiel, "La participación femenina en la Independencia de México," in *Historia de las mujeres en México* (Mexico City: Instituto Nacional de Estudios Históricos de las Revoluciones de México, 2015), 87.

22. Gloria Espigado Tocino, "Mujeres y ciudadanía: Del Antiguo Régimen a la Revolución Liberal," *Revista HMiC* 1 (2003): 182–83.
23. Sarah C. Chambers, "¿Actoras políticas o ayudantes abnegadas? Repensando las actitudes hacia las mujeres durante las guerras de independencia hispanoamericana," in *L'Atlantique Révolutionnaire*, ed. Clément Thibaud, Gabriel Entin, Alejandro Gómez, and Federica Morelli (Bécherel, France: Les Perséides Editions, 2013), 301.
24. ATHA, Fondo Prestamero, caja 8, Nº 18; *Copia del plan y Ordenanzas de un seminario o casa de educación para señoritas que se intenta establecer en la Ciudad de Vitoria*, ATHA, March 12, 1784.
25. María Victoria López-Cordón, "El espejo palatino o la malla de las damas: ¿sociabilidad cortesana o cultura política?," in *El siglo XVIII en femenino: Las mujeres en el Siglo de las Luces*, ed. Manuel García Hurtado (Madrid: Síntesis, 2016) 86.
26. Ronald Fraser, *La maldita guerra de España: Historia social de la Guerra de la Independencia, 1808–1814* (Barcelona: Crítica, 2006).
27. Angulo Morales and Echeberria Ayllón, "Herederas de la Ilustración," 202.
28. Juan Vidal-Abarca López, "Linajes alaveses: Los Aguirre; Marqueses de Montehermoso," *Boletín de la Institución Sancho el Sabio* 19 (1975): 181–244.
29. Elisa Martín-Valdepeñas Yagüe, "'Mis señoras traidoras': Las afrancesadas, una historia olvidada," *Revista HMiC* 8 (2010): 86.
30. Martín-Valdepeñas Yagüe, "'Mis señoras traidoras,'" 95.
31. AMA, VELASCO, C.144, N.6; AMA, URBINA, C.25, N.5; Paloma Manzanos Arreal and Francisca Vives Casas, *Las mujeres en Vitoria-Gasteiz a lo largo de los siglos: Recorridos y biografías* (Vitoria-Gasteiz, Spain: Ayuntamiento de Vitoria-Gasteiz, 2001) 189.
32. Martín-Valdepeñas Yagüe, "'Mis señoras traidoras,'" 83.
33. Gloria Franco Rubio, "El ejercicio del poder en la España del siglo XVIII," *Mélanges de la Casa de Velázquez* 35, no. 1 (2005): 5.

34. Paloma Manzanos Arreal and Francisca Vives Casas, *La vida cotidiana de las mujeres en la Vitoria de los siglos XVIII y XIX* (Vitoria-Gasteiz, Spain: Ayuntamiento de Vitoria-Gasteiz, 2005), 106.
35. Martín-Valdepeñas Yagüe, "'Mis señoras traidoras,'" 80–104.
36. Martín-Valdepeñas Yagüe, "'Mis señoras traidoras,'" 92–93.
37. Martín-Valdepeñas Yagüe, "'Mis señoras traidoras,'" 95; Alfonso Saura Sánchez, "Acercamiento literario y biográfico a Pedro Ángel de Gorostiza y Cepeda: Documentos y pistas sueltas," *Literatura Mexicana* 18, no. 2 (2007): 104–8.
38. María Cruz Romeo Mateo, "Españolas en la guerra de 1808: Heroínas recordadas," in *Heterodoxas, guerrilleras y ciudadanas: Resistencias femeninas en la España moderna y contemporánea*, ed. Mercedes Yusta and Ignacio Peiró (Zaragoza, Spain: IFC/CSIC, 2015), 78–79. See also Marieta Cantos Casenave, "Entre la tertulia y la imprenta, la palabra encendida de una patriota andaluza, Frasquita Larrea (1775–1838)," in *Heroínas y patriotas: Mujeres de 1808*, ed. Irene Castells Oliván, Gloria Espigado Tocino, and María Cruz Romeo Mateo (Madrid: Cátedra, 2009), 269–94; Gloria Espigado Tocino, "Europeas y españolas contra Napoleón: Un estudio comparado," *Revista HMiC* 8 (2010): 59–60.
39. Espigado Tocino, "Mujeres y ciudadanía," 179.
40. Espigado Tocino, "Europeas y españolas," 60.
41. Marieta Cantos Casenave, "La Literatura femenina en la Guerra de Independencia: A la ciudadanía por el patriotismo," *Revista HMiC* 8 (2010): 33–42.
42. Espigado Tocino, "Mujeres y ciudadanía," 179.
43. Marieta Cantos Casenave, "Mujeres en el Primer Liberalismo," in *La Constitución de 1812. Clave del liberalismo en Andalucía*, ed. Alberto Ramos Santana (Seville, Spain: FPACEA, Junta de Andalucía, 2012), 93; Cantos Casenave, "La Literatura femenina," 35–36.
44. Cantos Casenave, "La Literatura femenina," 36.
45. Espigado Tocino, "Mujeres y ciudadanía," 180.
46. Elena Fernández García, "Transgresión total y transgresión parcial en las defensoras de la patria," *Mélanges de la Casa de Velázquez* 38 (2008): 138–39.
47. *Atalaya de la Mancha*, April 4, 1814.

48. Atalaya de la Mancha, June 13, 1814.
49. El Procurador General del Rey y de la Nación, August 5, 1814.
50. Diario de Madrid, July 7, 1814.
51. Diario de Madrid, June 10, 1813.
52. Romeo Mateo, "Españolas en la guerra," 81; Espigado Tocino, "Las mujeres," 70.
53. Espigado Tocino, "Europeas y españolas," 51.
54. Morán and Rivera, "Libertadoras," 9–10; María José Vilalta, "Historia de las mujeres y memoria histórica: Manuela Sáenz interpela a Simón Bolívar (1822–1830)," *European Review of Latin American and Caribbean Studies* 93 (2012): 64.
55. Taxin, "La participación," 90.
56. Sarah de Mojica, "La leyenda de Policarpa Salavarrieta," in *Entre el olvido y el recuerdo: iconos, lugares de memoria y cánones de la historia y la literatura en Colombia*, ed. Carlos Rincón, Sarah de Mojica, and Liliana Gómez (Bogotá: Editorial Pontificia Universidad Javeriana, 2010), 143; Carmen de Mora Valcárcel, "Una mujer de armas tomar: La coronel Juan de Azurduy," in *Milicia y sociedad ilustrada en España y América*, actas 1 (2003): 507.
57. Taxin, "La participación," 91.
58. Cherpak, "The Participation," 5.
59. Chambers, "¿Actoras políticas," 312.
60. Palacio Montiel, "La participación," 82–83.
61. Katherine Crawford, "Revisiting Monarchy: Women and the Prospects for Power," *Journal of Women's History* 24, no. 1 (2012): 166.
62. Morán and Rivera, "Libertadoras," 8.
63. APV, Fondo Álava, legajo 3.
64. Palacio Montiel, "La participación," 83.
65. Morán and Rivera, "Libertadoras," 8.
66. Franco Rubio, "El ejercicio," 55–56.
67. Carol Arcos and Alicia Salomone, "Mujeres e Independencia en Chile: La cultura del trato y la escritura de cartas," *Teresa: Revista de Literatura Brasileira* 12, no. 13 (2013): 210.
68. Arcos and Salomone, "Mujeres," 208.
69. Vilalta, "Historia," 64.
70. Taxin, "La participación," 89.

71. Barry Matthew Robinson, "La reclusión de mujeres rebeldes: el recogimiento en la guerra de independencia mexicana, 1810–1819," *Fronteras de la Historia* 15, no. 2 (2010): 238–39.
72. Mora Valcárcel, "Una mujer," 507; Taxin, "La participación," 89.
73. Cherpak, "The Participation," 2; Taxin, "La participación," 89.
74. Morán and Rivera, "Libertadoras," 11.
75. Cherpak, "The Participation," 2.
76. Arcos and Salomone, "Mujeres," 213.
77. Morán and Rivera, "Libertadoras," 3.
78. Brewster, "Women," 22.
79. Fernández García, "Transgresión total," 136–37.
80. Dolores Juliano, *Excluidas y marginales* (Madrid: Cátedra, 2004).
81. Brewster, "Women," 30.
82. Palacio Montiel, "La participación," 79–82.
83. Mora Valcárcel, "Una mujer," 507.
84. Alejandra Ciriza Jofré, "Genealogías feministas: sobre mujeres, revoluciones e Ilustración. Una mirada desde el Sur," *Estudios Feministas* 20, no. 3 (2012): 621.
85. Mora Valcárcel, "Una mujer," 504–7.
86. Morán and Rivera, "Libertadoras," 11–12.
87. Brewster, "Women," 30.
88. Taxin, "La participación," 102.
89. Brewster, "Women," 30.
90. Cherpak, "The Participation," 7.
91. Brewster, "Women," 29.
92. Taxin, "La participación," 93.
93. Fernández García, "Transgresión total," 145.
94. Fernández García, "Transgresión total," 145–46; Juan José Sánchez Arreseigor, *Vascos contra Napoleón* (Madrid: Editorial Actas, 2010), 183–85.
95. Fernández García, "Transgresión total," 143–44; Sánchez Arreseigor, *Vascos contra Napoleón*, 175–87.
96. Espigado Tocino, "Mujeres y ciudadanía," 178; Romeo Mateo, "Españolas en la guerra," 69–73; Enric Ucelay Da Cal, "Agustina, la dama del cañón: El topos de la heroína fálica y el invento del patriotismo," in *Heroínas y patriotas. Mujeres de 1808*, ed. Irene Castells Oliván,

Gloria Espigado Tocino, and María Cruz Romeo Mateo (Madrid: Cátedra, 2009), 193–268.
97. El Conciso, October 19, 1812.
98. Fernández García, "Transgresión total," 147.
99. Romeo Mateo, "Españolas en la guerra," 73.
100. *Gaceta de México*, May 14, 1793.
101. Eva Mendieta Garrote, *In Search of Catalina de Erauso: The National and Sexual Identity of the Lieutenant Nun* (Reno: Center for Basque Studies, University of Nevada, 2019).
102. *Gaceta de México*, May 24, 1794.
103. Taxin, "La participación," 95.
104. Philippe Girard, "Rebels with a Cause: Women in the Haitian War of Independence, 1802–04," *Gender & History* 21, no. 1 (2009): 62–72.
105. Girard, "Rebels with a Cause," 62–66.

CHAPTER EIGHT

Building Heroines for the Nation

One of the great historical consequences of the Spanish War of Independence is the political constitution of nations such as Spain, Mexico, Venezuela, and other American countries. From 1808 onward, this great Atlantic empire known as the Hispanic monarchy collapsed. And in the specific case of Spain, the new political forms, in such complex and extreme circumstances, were loaded with nationalist speeches containing a gender prism: that is, rhetoric shaped or fueled by discursive elements based on gender and in defense of the new nation.

"Populist or national exaltation required the symbolic visibility of women," a nonlinear process of glorification "subject to the prevailing gender discourses" that "constituted one of the aspects of the creation of the nation-state."[1] In this way, the Spanish-French conflict witnessed the spread of the myth of the heroine as a symbol of the new nation that had taken up arms: "heroines have been essential pieces in the construction of the national myth of the people in arms."[2]

What is the meaning of this representation? In my view, it could be said that it is based on several interconnected elements. On the one hand, it is a recent myth, since the female figure that embodies "the expression of the feeling and identity of the nation" arose in the French Revolution, a time when "female allegories... replaced the image of the king in the representation of the nation-state"— although such representations had already existed since the seventeenth century.[3] On the other hand, Gloria Espigado rightly asserts, "There is a clear division between the symbolic woman, the allegory, and real women, susceptible to rights. It is, once again, a reflection of a division of roles: for women, the representation, the allegory, the symbol; for men, the effective exercise of citizenship, political rights."[4]

It could be argued that from a symbolic and discursive perspective, although supported by tangible facts, the female figure of power was perceived for her capacity for mediation or agency.[5] The image of the queen was recognized in the past for her ability to mediate between vassals and the king,[6] a link that could well be useful when representing the new national feeling, helping as a bridge, in some way, between the state/power and the nation as a whole. In other words, the use of female figures to represent national feeling and identity could help the nation identify with it thanks to the arbitrating role between the people and political power exemplified by femininity.

Added to this was the link or relationship that society established between femininity and emotion. Women, as a general rule, were identified as passionate beings, holders of these sensitive qualities, and weak for surrendering to their emotions. All this in contrast to masculinity, capable of controlling its feelings and being "naturally" endowed with rationality and the exercise of political power.

Since the Enlightenment, however, affections began to be perceived as useful for social development. Although René Descartes offers a useful view of them due to their natural quality, it was David Hume's empiricism that managed to reverse "the subordination of emotions by stating that reason is and must be the slave of passions."[7] For Jean-Jacques Rousseau, these were the main driving force of the human being, the origin of all knowledge: society, knowledge, and languages are born from pleasure, desire, and their opposites.[8] Since then, feelings have been treated as natural phenomena that, properly guided through a suitable moral education, are valuable for social life.[9]

In addition to this, we have the "atrocious influence and powerful effect" that women supposedly exercised over men. In a more constructive sense, the literature of the period underlines "their beneficial influence on man, guiding his passionate excesses and turning him into a responsible subject in his public and private obligations."[10] Opinions such as that of Pablo de Olavide, included in the Basque enlightened project to educate women, emphasize this idea "of educating masculine feelings to build a civilized society" through the influence exerted by women.[11] The *Gaceta de Buenos Aires* of 1811 published a similar message: "If mothers and wives were to study how to inspire their children, husbands, and domestics with these noble feelings, and if those ... were to employ the empire of their beauty and natural artifice to conquer the unnatural, and electrify those who are not, what progress would our system not make?"[12]

Using a female figure to symbolize national feeling therefore made perfect sense. First, because of the image of femininity as a bridge or link between the people and political power, inviting the nation to join the new political project—taking into account, in addition, the mediating role they had. Second, femininity was always linked to the capacity for feeling, an unbeatable image if discussing representing national sentiment. The patriots who faced Napoleon could be expected to have a similar passion. To paraphrase Thomas, "this love is responsible for the complete selflessness and their consequent dedication to the Nation."[13] Last, the hypothetical influence that women had over men could also have served as an argument to build the image of the heroine. In fact, we cannot rule out that, in such a war context, this symbol indirectly appealed to manliness, pride, or "masculine ardor." Or to paternalism.

The *Manifiesto de Cartagena* of 1812 is the first important public document written by Simón Bolívar. In this manifesto he sees himself as the son of a punished, feminized city, which he must liberate. The duty of a good patriot would be to liberate the Nation-Homeland-Mother. In his *Carta de Jamaica* (Letter from Jamaica), on the contrary, the mainland is represented as an evil stepmother. We see, therefore, the space that gender representations have in allegorical and pro-independence speeches.[14]

A century later, the politician and military man of Basque descent José Gómez de Arteche y Moro de Elexabeitia wrote *La mujer en la Guerra de la Independencia* (Women in the War of Independence). In this work he gives an absolutely laudatory discourse on the Spanish women who fought Napoleon, a dissertation inspired by the speeches that arose during the war. His main objective was to exalt their role as mothers of the homeland thanks to the feelings inspired by their nature and religious faith:

> Spiritualism, however, elevates in women their feelings of piety, religious faith and love for the family, to the point of uniting them with that of the home, which ends up being confused with that of the Fatherland. *Matria*, the Greeks called it; and it is not surprising, according to the nature, character and duties of motherhood that make women intimate participants in the destiny of the nation . . . slave of these noblest feelings, women become the vehicle for affirming them in men and transmitting them to their children.[15]

In the opinion of this member of the Royal Academy of History, the Catholic religion, motherhood, and love of country were the driving forces of the Spanish fight against the French. "Throughout the 19th century, Spanish nationalism managed to domesticate and naturalize the memory of 1808 to adapt it to the prevailing gender discourses"[16]:

> And you, Ladies . . . not satisfied with inspiring in your children and relatives the patriotic spirit that would exalt them . . . do not deny such noble sentiments and also inspire in your people, in your children above all, that religious faith, that love for the native country, that generous dispossession of fortune and rank, even of life, which constitute and will always constitute the greatest glory of man, of the family and of the Homeland.[17]

In postwar Spain, a singular phenomenon happened, as the female authors who stood out before and during the conflict stopped publishing. Thus, in the early years of the nineteenth century, a kind of gap emerged between the Enlightenment and Romanticism.[18]

The need to generate national political images and discourses coincides with female participation. That is to say, at least during the Spanish War of Independence and the American revolutionary processes, the rhetoric was congruent with actions in the everyday sphere, since they also suffered the consequences of the war, fighting against the enemy and being called on to do so. However, from an allegorical point of view, the images changed significantly. And the same happened in the sphere of actions.

Although many participated in the fight, only a small number are part of our collective memory. Due to endogenous issues corresponding to the national construction of each of the American nations, some women were glorified to the detriment of others, as happened in Spain. Each woman's dedication to independence or the Hispanic monarchy differs, like the subsequent recognition of their actions or their ideological use. And in this case, as happens with the heroes of the American independence, women of Basque origin overcome. To Iturbide or Bolívar, we add Azurduy, Salavarrieta, or Sáenz.

The reasons for this Basque prominence have already been explained, with the outlining of their influence within political, economic, and social structures. American elites led parts of the independence movements; although these were not exclusively Creole revolutions, that actors of Creole origin played an oversized role is part of a national historiography that emphasizes their prominence for ideological reasons:

> Often, the narrative of what happened tends to suggest that independence was Creole, white male. The traces of subaltern men and women are lost in the meanders of history. The usual reading tends to consider the emancipatory process of the early 19th century as a revolution from above, promoted and instigated by an enlightened minority that wanted to privately ben-

efit from the breaking of the classic colonial bond. This vision tends to suppress the tensions and inflections of the process and the diversity of subjects and experiences in favor of a view that sees exclusively the result: the imposition of a new order with Creole hegemony.[19]

In this situation, "records of the women who participated in the Wars of Independence favor the upper classes, particularly white, urban women. This reflects the contribution of the Creole elite to the movement."[20] For this reason, American women with Basque surnames occupy a large part of the chronicles.

The construction of the heroine is, moreover, a complex subject of analysis, full of varied approaches. As a previous step to this accumulation of images and discourses, political circumstances demanded its action. It happens in revolutionary France, in the future United States of America, Haiti, and the Old World. And as the speeches cross the continent, the representations emerged united.

The fight of American women took place in a context of exceptional need. As Ciriza Jofré reflects, "the independence revolutions opened spaces in which, for a brief time, other practices and relationships were possible that denaturalized the idea that there were inferior human beings by bodily destiny. . . . A generation of men and women put their desires for emancipation on the agenda."[21] Beatrice Bruce and Gabriela Gresores discuss the alteration of the gender system during the war, where American women found new spaces thanks to the temporary break in the ordinary social order.[22]

Because of this, women went from rejection to participation in a matter of years. The American press was established as one of the supports or vehicles for this transformation. If in 1794 the *Gaceta de Lima* (Lima Gazette) referred to women as "born to soften the habits of man, they should not take an active part in discussions, whose ardor is incompatible with the balance and sweetness that form the enchantment of their sex,"²³ the *Gaceta de Caracas* (Caracas Gazette) of 1811 published the "Representation that the fair sex makes to the Government of Barinas," which represents a substantial change:

> The female sex, Sir, does not fear the horrors of war: the explosion of the cannon will only encourage it: its fire will kindle the desire for freedom, which it will maintain at all costs in service to the Fatherland. In virtue of this and wishing to enlist in service to make up for the defect of the military who have left for San Fernando, they beg Your Excellency to please keep them in mind and assign them where you deem appropriate under the assumption that they will not omit sacrifices that concern security and defense.²⁴

The Basque Creole José Joaquín Fernández de Lizardi, married to the Basque Creole Dolores Orendáin and founder of *Pensador Mexicano* (a Mexican newspaper founded in 1812), praises in his work the Mexican women who fought for independence by serving as symbols. However, he is remarkable for his defense of female education as a political issue, since the construction of a new, free state depended, according to him, on the education that women could receive. As we can see, he shares many of the discourses on femininity spread throughout the Atlantic world, including that of Olavide. Women would be destined to "support family education and dignity;" that is, their necessary support for the independence process would have to be given from their domestic role. As a consequence, female education was truly important "in the configuration of the new American identity": "Be faithful to your husband, love him very much, take care of and educate your offspring in the holy fear of God; Inspire her with good morals and a great love for her country and its freedom, and you will be a woman useful to the State, you will make your husband and your children happy and, adorned with solid virtues, you will await death in peace and you will go to heaven with a tunic, a cloak and satin shoes."[25] Certainly, these are statements that are not far from the words written a century before by General Montiano.

Another general with similar ideas is Manuel Belgrano. In an article written for *Correo de Comercio* (Argentine newspaper created in 1810), he acknowledges the lack of female education, arguing that "the success or failure of independence depended on it" because mothers were responsible for educating future citizens. Following this line, "the Peruvian newspaper *El Investigador del Perú* (1813) considers that women should have access to a quality education, since, as Belgrano believed, the future of the new citizens was in their hands."[26]

After the war, the hegemonic discourses on femininity continued in a specific direction. During the revolutionary period, women were called on to collaborate following the canons or archetypes of domesticated femininity, an aspect that was reinforced at the end of the conflict thanks to models such as the "angel of the home" or the American republican mother.[27] In this sense, the reflections developed by Mary Nash and collected by Tocino Espigado stand out. Hispanic feminism would be, from a historical point of view, more social than political, focused on education and work, and emphasizing arguments "of a maternalistic and domestic-functional type" rather than political.[28] That is, close to the discourse on social motherhood.

The different Latin American nationalist historiographies of the nineteenth century choose "two ways of erasing" the intellectual and political contributions of women. On the one hand, they recognize women's contributions as mothers or wives exclusively, as we see in the Spanish case. On the other hand, they "[exalt] the participation of women in romantic tones, turning them into manageable heroines from a private perspective of love for the homeland or freedom: self-sacrificing wives, heroic mothers, protectors of prisoners, sisters of men who sacrificed their lives."[29] In this case, a woman's only reference point is men; her setting of action, the home.

Leona Vicario was accused of having participated in the Mexican insurgent movement out of love, motivated exclusively by her feelings for another hero of the country, Andrés Quintana Roo.[30] Historians such as Lucas Alamán feed these discourses by reinforcing the image of the heroine as domestic, without highlighting the importance of the actions of Leona Vicario "as an intelligence agent, campaign financier and collector of food and supplies for the troops, spending her entire fortune on it." They turn them, of course, into nationalist symbols, rejecting their historical agency.[31] In this regard, García López concludes the following:

> Once peace was achieved, their valuable intervention was presented from a manipulative discourse that silenced their prominent role in the process, relegating them to a secondary level, which minimized their patriotism by attributing the reasons for their involvement to sentimental reasons, denying their capacity for independent thought and decision, which only praised the work typical of their sex, but which denigrated the attitudes and actions of those women who developed in a masculine environment, who expressed their own thoughts and claimed a leading role in the public sphere, reserved for men.[32]

Another of the most prominent cases is that of Manuela Sáenz, reduced by most traditional historiography to the role of the official lover of Simón Bolívar.[33] In this historical reading, she was portrayed "between darkness, heroism, madness and sexual and sensual excess."[34] However, when history came to be examined through feminist critical theory, this perception was revised. Even so, at first, Manuela Sáenz was a victim of early feminist historiography that was almost exclusively interested in great female figures, which Asunción Lavrin calls "great women syndrome,"[35] and depicted as an exceptional case.

The figure of Policarpa Salavarrieta, "La Pola," is also the target of those who built the collective national mythology. As early as 1820, the writer Domínguez Roche "created a heroine and a social drama that attempted to found a nation of citizens. At that time, the figure of Policarpa could have been like Marianne, the symbol of French freedom. Despite this, this myth did not work in 1820; it was not widely accepted."[36] Nevertheless, "with the tragedy of La Pola, a founding mythology was being created on the way, which, somehow, comes close to the secularized forms of the modern State."[37]

The way in which the emerging nations of the nineteenth century received, managed, and explained the military actions of women is complex. Patriotism is not only a matter for men,[38] although its representation is. The construction of the heroine was in the hands of the cultural and masculine elites of the nineteenth century, and they preserved, fed, and reconfigured the androcentric and patriarchal schemes of the period. And at this point, a difficulty emerges: nineteenth-century historiography, but also that which followed, tended toward the analysis and representation of the most heroic acts, never the most "normal" ones. The construction of a national epic requires this focus. In turn, two problems arise: female action, related to more "ordinary" acts, is obscured, and a "heroic and homogenizing historiographic conception" forms where women have no place:

> It is not the female voice that is heard, but rather idealized images that are frozen.... Furthermore, following an established masculine model, heroic action is prioritized, leaving the daily experience of war and its impact on concrete practices and on the bodies themselves stifled. This action can be understood as the "officialization" of a knowledge that takes up aspects of female participation in the war to build with them a compact and coherent tradition with the already established one and to continue perpetuating the same cognitive and existential order. But, it is not about making the subalternized half of the sky enter into an established ontology, but rather about breaking with that unified and unifying memory, and giving room to readings from other perspectives.[39]

"It seemed that 'feminine patriotism' had a sense and function different from that of men, and this difference reflected the perceptions and expectations surrounding the figure of woman."[40] As Merry E. Wiesner-Hanks said, "national symbols, rituals, and myths are gendered and trace both women's contribution to nation-building and their exclusion from it by the state and its institutions."[41]

How is this figure of the heroine, excluded from her own lived reality, constructed and justified? On the one hand, we know the importance that gender discourses had in the construction of the national myth. On the other, women in the Hispanic sphere, both in the Iberian Peninsula and America, were invited to participate in the fights following the canons of social motherhood. The problem arises with the so-called deviants: those who break with the established patterns. The most famous figures, future heroines of the nation, are manipulated objects, constructions consistent with the hegemonic stereotypes of the period that come to blur the real historical agent. And one of the discourses of exclusion that will unite some of them, whether in Europe or America, is that of the virile woman.

NOTES

1. Romeo Mateo, "Españolas en la guerra," 68.
2. Espigado Tocino, "Las mujeres," 68.
3. Gloria Espigado Tocino, "Pasiones políticas: La representación de la mujer política en el siglo XIX," *Historia social* 81 (2015): 153.
4. Espigado Tocino, "Pasiones políticas," 155.
5. Oliván Santaliestra, "Por una historia," 61–77.
6. Crawford, "Revisiting Monarchy," 166.
7. Antonio Zirón Pérez, "Antropología filosófica y afectividad," in *Cultura y afectividad. Aproximaciones antropológicas y filosóficas al estudio de las emociones*, ed. Edith Calderón Rivera and Antonio Zirón Pérez (Mexico City: Universidad Autónoma Metropolitana, 2018), 14. See also Mónica Bolufer Peruga, "Sociabilidad mixta y civilización:

Miradas desde España," in *Educar los sentimientos y las costumbres: Una mirada desde la historia*, ed. Mónica Bolufer, Carolina Blutrach, and Juan Gomis (Zaragoza: Institución Fernando el Católico (CSIC), 2014), 150–53; María Luisa Candau Chacón, "Las mujeres y las emociones en la Edad Moderna," in *El siglo XVIII en femenino: Las mujeres en el Siglo de las Luces*, ed. Manuel-Reyes García Hurtado (Madrid: Síntesis, 2016), 113–20; David Hume, *Tratado de la naturaleza humana*, ed. Félix Duque (Madrid: Editorial Nacional, 1981), 87; María José de la Pascua Sánchez, "La escritura privada y la representación de las emociones," in *Educar los sentimientos y las costumbres: Una mirada desde la historia*, ed. Mónica Bolufer, Carolina Blutrach, and Juan Gomis (Zaragoza, Spain: Institución Fernando el Católico [CSIC], 2014), 93–94.

8. Iglesias, *Razón, sentimiento*, 354–55.
9. Bolufer Peruga, "Afectos razonables," 42; Bolufer Peruga, "En torno," 35; María Luisa Candau Chacón, "Emociones diversas," in *Las mujeres y las emociones en Europa y América. Siglos XVII–XIX*, ed. María Luisa Candau Chacón (Santander, Spain: Universidad de Cantabria, 2016), 11–12; Luisa Elena Delgado, Pura Fernández, and Jo Labanyi, "Cartografía de las emociones en la cultura española contemporánea: Teorías, prácticas y contextos culturales," in *La cultura de las emociones y las emociones en la cultura española contemporánea (siglos XVIII–XXI)*, ed. Luisa Elena Delgado, Pura Fernández, and Jo Labanyi (Madrid: Cátedra, 2018), 16; Morant Deusa, "¿Qué es una mujer?," 147–52; María Sierra, "Entre emociones y política: La historia cruzada de la virilidad romántica," *Rúbrica Contemporánea* 4, no. 7 (2015): 17.
10. Bolufer Peruga, "Afectos razonables," 47.
11. AMB, 03-C/123-006; APV, Fondo Álava, legajo 3; Bolufer Peruga, "Afectos razonables," 47.
12. Daniel Morán, "Las 'jacobinas de la revolución': Imágenes y representaciones de la mujer en la prensa de Buenos Aires (1810–1816)," *Tiempos Modernos* 37 (2018): 156.
13. Morant Deusa, "¿Qué es una mujer?," 147–52.
14. Catherine Davies, Claire Brewster, and Hilary Owen, *South American Independence: Gender, Politics, Text* (Liverpool, UK: Liverpool University Press, 2011), 37–41.

15. José de Arteche and Moro de Elexabeitia, *La mujer en la Guerra de la Independencia* (Madrid: Hijos de J. A. García, 1903), 5–6.
16. Romeo Mateo, "Españolas en la guerra," 71.
17. Gómez Arteche and Moro de Elexabeitia, *La mujer*, 25.
18. Espigado Tocino, "Europeas y españolas," 59; Espigado Tocino, "Las mujeres," 70–71.
19. Ciriza Jofré, "Genealogías feministas," 619.
20. Brewster, "Women," 26.
21. Ciriza Jofré, "Genealogías feministas," 615.
22. Beatrice Bruce and Gabriela Gresores, "Cómo vivir en un mundo en llamas: Impacto de la Guerra de la Independencia en la cotidianeidad de las mujeres," *Cuadernos FHyCS-UNJu* 48 (2015): 24.
23. García López, "La participación," 35.
24. García López, "La participación," 36–37.
25. María José García Rodríguez, "La figura de la mujer en Lizardi: *Noches Tristes y Día Alegre y Don Catrín de la Fachenda*," *Cartaphilus. Revista de investigación y crítica estética* 13 (2014): 158–66.
26. Morán and Rivera, "Libertadoras," 16–17; Morán, "Las 'jacobinas,'" 153.
27. McClelland, *The Education*, 56.
28. Espigado Tocino, "Mujeres y ciudadanía," 172.
29. Francesca Gargallo, "Las mujeres, sus ideas, sus escritos y sus actos en la Independencia nuestroamericana," *Coloquio Políticas de la Alteridad* (Mexico City: Universidad Autónoma de la Ciudad–Plantel del Valle de México, 2010), 3.
30. Erika Pani, "'Ciudadana y muy ciudadana'? Women and the State in Independent Mexico, 1810–30," *Gender and History* 18-1 (2006): 9.
31. Pani, "'Ciudadana y muy ciudadana'?," 3–4.
32. García López, "La participación," 46.
33. Taxin, "La participación," 85.
34. Patrícia-Victòria Martínez I. Àlvarez, "Memoria feminista para pensar a Manuela Sáenz: Un recorrido por su política y sus territorios," *Debate Feminista* 65 (2023): 3.
35. Asunción Lavrin, ed., *Latin American Women: Historical Perspectives* (Westport, CT: Greenwood Press, 1978), 4.
36. Mojica, "La leyenda," 154.
37. Mojica, "La leyenda," 149–50.

38. Brewster, "Women," 22.
39. Bruce and Gresores, "Cómo vivir," 16.
40. Pani, "'Ciudadana,'" 8.
41. Wiesner-Hanks, "Crossing Borders," 374.

CHAPTER NINE

The Problem of the Virile Woman in War Times

References to virile women and manly women tend to be mixed together. The term *virile* is understood in a positive way—"that which belongs to men." *Manly*, on the other hand, is used in a mocking way. In contrast to the "learned manly" attitude criticized by some members of the RSBAP, there were many testimonies praising Basque women with virile attitudes. In the American wars of independence, these arguments surfaced again—frames of reference that had been in place since long before. For instance, when Isabella of Bourbon, wife of Philip IV, died, some underlined that "she would have exercised the regency with great dignity and prudence but also with firm poise and a 'manly' heart."[1]

In Mexico in 1795, just a few years before the events narrated took place, the former regent of the Mexican audience sent a complaint to the Inquisition tribunal about a pamphlet. This satire of misogynistic literature was titled *Sermón* and asserted, among other things, that women were worse than demons, responsible for condemning the entire universe for original sin and that "man and the world were lost because of them." The pamphlet inherited a tradition that had defended for centuries a model of femininity based on two sole examples, that of the Catholic virgin or that of the manly woman—"like those martyrs or saints who managed to dissolve their femininity by sacrificing parts of their body or overcoming their natural instincts such as that of motherhood."[2] At the end of the eighteenth century, satirical speeches such as the

Sermón spread this positive image of the virile woman, removing her femininity through a strategy of "degradation or devaluation."[3] The best of women, these texts emphasize, is their virile qualities, since femininity and its features condemn the entire world.

Some praise eighteenth-century femininity, like some of the cultural elites of the period. There are also those who detest such traits, rejecting femininity and praising women with virile attributes. And there are those who see in such virility an aberration against the nature of the "fair sex." Such is the case, late in the nineteenth century, of Ricardo Palma and his version of Manuela Sáenz, whom he met in person: "Doña Manuela was a mistake of nature, who in sculpturally feminine forms embodied spirit and manly aspirations. She did not know how to cry, but rather how to become angry like men of a tough personality."[4] The political woman, with political aspirations, is denaturalized by one of the most influential writers and politicians of nineteenth-century Peru.

According to some testimonies, Manuela "disregarded" her feminine features by smoking and sometimes dressing in masculine clothes.[5] She certainly came to be seen as a virile, exceptional, or unnatural woman. The important thing about the portrait, however, is that it is drawn from a critical point of view. Her main chroniclers, such as the aforementioned Palma, placed the Libertadora within masculine politics, the politics "of others" that is not her own, the feminine one.[6]

The Frenchman Jean-Baptiste Boussingault relates that, at the time of their meeting, Manuela Sáenz presented herself "in military uniform, wearing a moustache and riding her horse." She had been named colonel of the liberation army. The interesting thing about her portrait lies, however, in the praise of her masculine features: "he could be a 'great friend,' speaking of this in the masculine, ascribing the positive in her to a masculine quality. Whereas, to describe her as a woman, in her condition as a lover, he refers to something negative: infidelity."[7] In one of his letters, Simón Bolívar describes her as "my dearest officer of the Colombian army," a companion whom he acknowledged had "more pants than any of his officers."[8]

Another American heroine with Basque ancestors, Policarpa Salavarrieta, was objectified in a similar way. In the cited work by Domínguez Roche, we see how the author praises her patriotism, emphasizing her virility. "The individual decision to sacrifice her life for the homeland from her particular condition of 'virile woman' turns La Pola into a woman who makes her decisions with a clear conscience of destiny, which makes her worthy of Roman virtue, the main attribute of the hero."[9] This is not a critical discourse toward femininity, although the value that the author gives to her political action is due to her virile attitude. Indirectly or implicitly, he joins that misogynistic vision that undervalues women.

Francisca de Zubiaga was a Creole lady of Basque origin married to the also Basque-American Agustín de Gamarra. She was another of the great heroines of the independence. Known as La Mariscala (The Field Marshal), she accompanied and fought alongside her husband until, between 1829 and 1833, he occupied the presidency of the newly created Peruvian Republic. Does she share, apart from origins, any other attribute with the aforementioned? Zubiaga was harshly rebuked for having made a place for herself in the Peruvian political scene. To criticize her, some authors used her lack of feminine delicacy, a manly attitude contrary to hegemonic gender archetypes. A century after her death, in fact, Abraham Valdelomar continued to promote this image: "She begins to handle the gun, the sword, horse riding. She attends the manliest shows; she is passionate about cockfights, she bets; she likes the company of men; she is not very interested in that of women, and she begins to be the guiding arm in her husband's destiny."[10]

Simón Bolívar, one of the great protagonists of the revolutionary period, wrote about the Socorro women of 1780. In his *Alocución a las matronas del Socorro,* read in public in February 1820, the Liberator builds a myth that praises the warlike attitude of these virile women, a patriotic speech designed to bring women to the independence cause. "Through the *Alocución* to virile women, masculinity is still predicated on heroism and enlightenment, and femininity on beauty, innocence, the sacred, the tender and the family. Women will be excluded from the polis unless they act, unnaturally, like men in these 'unnatural' circumstances":

> To the illustrious matrons of Socorro: A people that has produced manly women, no human power is capable of subduing. You, daughters of El Socorro, will be the downfall of your oppressors. They, in their frenzied fury, profaned the most sacred, the most innocent, the most beautiful of our species; they trampled you underfoot. You have raised your dignity by hardening your tender heart under the blows of the cruel. Heroic El Socorro women: the mothers of Sparta did not ask for the life of their sons, but for the victory of their country; those of Rome contemplated with pleasure the glorious wounds of their relatives; they encouraged them to achieve the honor of dying in combat. More sublime you in your generous patriotism, you have taken up the lance; you have placed yourselves in the ranks and ask to die for the country. Mothers, wives, sisters, who can follow in your footsteps in the race of heroism? Are there men worthy of you? No, no, no! But you are worthy of the admiration of the Universe and the adoration of the liberators of Colombia.[11]

"Referring with surprise to the quality of heroism in women, he [Bolívar] emphasizes that this is an eminently masculine characteristic, which is why he considers them 'manly women.'"[12] José Joaquín Fernández de Lizardi's essay *Heroínas Mexicanas* describes four of them: they "appear as strong protagonists, motivated by their opinions and by reason rather than by feeling. Sometimes he compares these women to men, without making them appear as the weaker sex."[13]

We can see, therefore, how some male protagonists of the period, although also later, helped build this image of the virile woman, a portrait mixed with that of the heroine. Several of them do so from a positive perspective. Their objective is to praise the role of those women who, with "patriotic ardor," fought against the enemy, overriding the stereotypes of femininity. Although the graces of the "fair sex" are found in other elements or behaviors, such as sensitivity or modesty, they gladly assume their virility when fighting. That is to say, "due to the vision that was held of women at the time and the expectations of the role that they should fulfil in society (staying in private space, the domestic sphere and being a good mother and wife), their bravery and contribution to the independence of the continent are repeatedly linked to masculinity."[14]

The construction of the heroine is cultivated by frames of reference such as gender, because "praising masculine heroines, as some of her contemporaries did, meant simultaneously highlighting gender difference and the possibility of overcoming it."[15] This is one of its bases, although the critical interpretation that we can make from a historical point of view is complex.

The speech of the virile woman is mutable and adapts to different times and latitudes, according to the needs expressed by a specific androcentric and patriarchal society. The essential point is that the inequalities between men and women support the framework. In the case in question, it is a positive construct that praises the work of certain women, although it implicitly rejects feminine weakness. For this reason, they also defend the role of domesticated femininity.

One of the most interesting characteristics of this representation is its ability to adapt and permeate the length and breadth of the Atlantic Ocean. These virile women are accepted because the situation demands it, demonstrating an incredible capacity for adaptation that responds to a notable historical fact: when we talk about Atlantic or transnational history, androcentrism, patriarchy, and misogyny are elements that unite different countries. It is a common element, among many others, of an Atlantic world full of changing casuistry.

Throughout the seventeenth and eighteenth centuries, some Basque women, particularly on the coast, were represented as virile. The circumstances of these spaces required their involvement in economic and social spheres. Father Larramendi, one of the great defenders of the virility of Guipuzcoan women, developed this rhetoric out of personal interest, in this case, to reinforce his discourse on the Basque Country. Simón Bolívar did so in defense of his American political project. The enlightened Basques, on the contrary, sponsored the figure of domesticated femininity, rejecting the masculine one, also out of personal interest. In their case, to preserve their social microcosm. As a whole, some challenged the weakness and futility of domesticated femininity, such as the Jesuit Larramendi. Others, such as the Basque and American elites—Bolívar, Belgrano, and others—admired it.

There are several voices that demanded women participate in different conflicts. The cultural elites of the period appealed to social motherhood, although they also accepted women who interfered in the public arena and whose contributions were not ignored. It is then that they recognized their collaboration, arguing that their successes come from their virility, since femininity would be far from the historical figure who gets involved, successfully, in politics and war. The reasons for this recognition could be multiple, although the need for the context, due to its extraordinary exceptionality, explains part of its development. They accept their contributions by reformulating their discourses.

It is important to understand how the patriarchal system of the time worked. The regime of male domination developed in Europe and assimilated by the American elites is based, in part, on a system that Arlette Farge describes as "compensatory." Through this mechanism, women were dominated and gratified, so they assimilated and sustained this system. Patriarchal power, consisting of a "pyramid of subsequent or adjacent powers," had the capacity to generate and offer compensation of all kinds to dominated women, spaces of autonomy, and power that compensated for their social situation. Motherhood or widowhood were part of this "turn over," a mechanism that broke with female solidarity and helped sustain the framework.[16]

Patriarchy, as a social construction, is not perfect or absolute,[17] but it is close to being so. For this reason, it creates demands or needs that are contradictory,[18] demonstrating an astonishing capacity to adapt to circumstances. Thus, when Basque, Spanish, and American women participate in the war, they do so because the situation requires it. They are allowed to interfere exceptionally. And although this participation conflicts with the hegemonic category of femininity and the patriarchal framework as a whole, the system has the capacity to make its discourses more flexible in order to use them. The constructs of the heroine or the virile woman demonstrate this capacity for adaptation—the "confidence" of the patriarchy that we also observe, for example, in feminine power, limited as it may be portrayed.[19] The interplay between circumstantial needs, such as the wars of independence, and the compensation, recognizing the female warriors, is essential.

In the feminized communities of the Basque coast, the wife was granted a certain capacity to command. In the popular revolts, we also observe how the communities offered women an important role, although both situations were contrary to the main idea about femininity, challenging the prevailing misogyny and the socioeconomic framework. It was tolerated out of necessity, offering certain compensations in exchange: "women obtain compensations of all kinds from the system, among them a certain number of powers that allow us to understand the degree of consent that they grant it and without which it will not be able to work."[20]

A clear example, again, is the virile woman. Although in the years before the wars of independence this figure, the one who fought under the French flag, was criticized by the press in New Spain, during and after the conflict, her image was shaped. These women broke with sexual and gender norms, for which they were judged. Some authors, however, praise these figures when they fought on the side they supported, despite the fact that these women did not represent their ideal of femininity.

Another example is motherhood. At a time when new nations are beginning to be formed, the role of the mother-educator is a fundamental key in the transmission of new national feeling. That is why motherhood is put on a pedestal, as an additional compensation: "her deficit as a public being would be compensated by the surplus of her domestic being, according to the already well-studied discourse that portrayed her as the angel of the home."[21]

It is clear that heroines are constructs belonging to nationalist mythology, not real historical agents. It is striking that most of the women who contributed to the war while respecting gender norms remained anonymous, although there are notable exceptions, such as the Mexican Mariana Patriots. Those who stood out in combat, however, were recognized as heroines, public figures belonging to the use of national discourse. The reality, however, is the opposite, because beyond the national myth, most of the women who fought with their own weapons ended up being trampled.

NOTES

1. Laura Oliván Santaliestra, "Gobierno, género y legitimidad en las regencias de Isabel de Borbón y Mariana de Austria," *Historia y política* 31 (2014): 40.
2. María Isabel Terán Elizondo and Sonia Ibarra Valdez, "Crítica y ¿defensa? de las mujeres en un "sermón" satírico novohispano prohibido por la Inquisición (1795)," *Edad de Oro* 38 (2019): 308.
3. Terán Elizondo and Ibarra Valdez, "Crítica y ¿defensa?," 306.
4. Ciriza Jofré, "Genealogías feministas," 627.
5. Vilalta, "Historia," 68.
6. Martínez I. Àlvarez, "Memoria feminista," 12–13.
7. Morán and Rivera, "Libertadoras," 5.
8. Morán and Rivera, "Libertadoras," 15.
9. Mojica, "La leyenda," 148.
10. Morán and Rivera, "Libertadoras," 17.

11. Davies, Brewster, and Owen, *South American*, 46–47.
12. Morán and Rivera, "Libertadoras," 15.
13. Chambers, "¿Actoras políticas," 303.
14. Morán and Rivera, "Libertadoras," 14.
15. Chambers, "¿Actoras políticas," 307.
16. Arlette Farge, "La historia de las mujeres: Cultura y poder de las mujeres; Ensayo de historiografía." *Historia Social* 5 (1989): 88–95.
17. Susan D. Amussen, "The Contradictions of Patriarchy in Early Modern England," *Gender and History* 30, no. 2 (2018): 343–44.
18. Amussen, "Contradictions," 344–345.
19. Allyson M. Poska, "The Case for Agentic Gender Norms for Women in Early Modern Europe," *Gender and History* 30, no. 2 (2018): 356.
20. Farge, "La historia," 89–92.
21. María Sierra, "Entre emociones y política: La historia cruzada de la virilidad romántica," *Rúbrica Contemporánea* 4, no. 7 (2015): 17.

CHAPTER TEN

The Punishment Suffered by Women

Manuela Sáenz de Vergara y Aizpuru, "La Libertadora," was "the prototype of a woman who did not fit into the patriotic morality of the society that emerged after independence in the newly born American countries and for this reason she was insulted and rejected, even named as a defect of Bolívar."[1] After the fight, the Libertadora was seen as a political threat and was driven into exile. In the words of the second president of Ecuador, Vicente Rocafuerte, addressed to the first, Juan José Flores y Aramburu, "Madame de Staël was not as harmful in Paris as Sáenz is in Quito. . . . Women (of loose morals) prized for good looks and used to cabinet intrigues are more harmful than an army of conspirators." Just two weeks earlier he warned, "She is the one called to rekindle the revolutionary flame."[2]

Sáenz's contributions to the independence processes of Ecuador, Peru, and Colombia were never enough. Nor was the defense that some "liberal women" of the city of Bogotá made of her when she was banished five years before.[3] The Peruvian government, for its part, denied her a pension after having awarded her with the Order of the Sun.[4] Exiled in the town of Paita, Peru, "for the next 25 years she survived by selling tobacco, translating and writing letters to the United States on behalf of the whalers who passed through the area, and making embroidery and sweets on request. . . . Her body was buried in a common grave and cremated."[5]

Policarpa Salavarrieta was arrested, imprisoned, and executed in 1817.[6] She was twenty-two years old.[7] The words of courage attributed to her at the end of her days,[8] as well as her youth, helped spread her legend. From then on, her sacrifice was used as a model.[9]

Francisca de Zubiaga, wife of the Peruvian president Francisco Gamarra, also did not enjoy a long life. "Her prominence in the upper levels of power between 1829 and 1833, reserved for men and therefore forbidden to her gender, earned her the repudiation of the conservative Peruvian society that emerged from independence and the banishment and exile in Valparaíso where she died on May 8, 1835, a victim of tuberculosis, poor and anonymous." When she fell into disgrace, many offensive comments were published about her: "Here lies the most insolent woman // that the world has ever had // another more criminal has never been seen."[10]

In war times, Juana de Azurduy was respected, like the day she was received with honors by Colonel Manuel Pérez de Uriondo—both of Basque origin. After the war, Simón Bolívar visited her and, seeing her difficulties, granted her a life pension. After years of fighting, years in which General Manuel Belgrano recognized that "her heroic actions and the courage shown by her were 'uncommon to people of her sex,'" Juana ended up surviving, together with her daughter, living in a modest roadhouse.[11] Her assets were seized, as well as the pension that General Antonio José Sucre had granted her years before.[12] After her death, she was buried in a common grave.

Like the previous anonymous American women, also of Basque descent, they suffered the most horrible punishments. Several of them were arrested because of their relatives' political affiliation, as though they had no ideas of their own, or as instruments used to punish their male relatives. Just as happened to the noblewoman from Vitoria, María Águeda de Valencegui, the Mexican María Josefa Marmolejo de Aldama was arrested to punish her relatives. Like the former, María Josefa was part of the elite. In the Mexican independence conflict, in fact, soldiers like Félix Calleja or Agustín de Iturbide "used the strategy of arresting and shooting the entire families of the insurgents: firstly, to force them to surrender; secondly, when they wanted revenge."[13]

There were also cases, barely investigated, of women executed for their actions, for their direct participation in the conflict. In

Ecuador, Bárbara Espalza, María Josefa Riofrío, and Dolores Zabala "were executed on October 18, 1809 for trying to rescue the independence hero Manuel Zambrano."[14] Years later, in the *Plaza Grande* of Quito, the heads of Rosa Zárate and her husband were displayed. They had been militants on the rebel side for years, and their executions served as a warning.[15] On the other hand, acts of such magnitude implicitly suggested "that women were considered active political participants."[16] Treating women in this way produced, in fact, great social commotion, given the paternalistic culture of the period. The paradox is that they were punished like men although many of the speeches of the period portray them as having no political ideas or motivations of their own.[17]

In the Basque Country, women from both sides also suffered repression, punishment, and death. One of the most terrible cases happened near Mondragón, in the province of Gipuzkoa. As Commissioner Lagarde informed Emperor Bonaparte, "some women were massacred by the guerrillas using the expedient method of tying cartridges of gunpowder to their chests and causing them to explode."[18]

On the American continent, women from all classes and conditions were executed as well. Following the trail of Basque surnames, we find figures such as Carmen Olano, who in 1816 was shot for trying to persuade Spanish soldiers to desert, or María Josefa Lizarralde, executed in the square of Zipaquirá, Colombia, for trying to corrupt a guard.[19]

Seditious words were also considered serious crimes by the Spanish regime. For this reason, Antonia de Ochoa from Veracruz and Francisca Michelena, among others, were arrested and locked up in a convent.[20] Leona Vicario suffered the same fate, in this case, in one of the institutions associated with the Basques in Mexico City, the College of Belém.[21] The reaction of the viceregal authorities was, generally, to confine them in houses of refuge, institutions built in the sixteenth and seventeenth centuries and dedicated to the reform of immoral women such as vagrants, divorcées, or prostitutes. Although at the beginning of the conflict there were few women imprisoned, as the conflict progressed their number increased. Iturbide sent a total of one hundred women to the refuge in Guanajuato as a reprisal against the rebels of the Bajío. The order was clear: arrest all the wives of the insurgent group.[22] In fact, it is estimated that in Mexico, 55 percent of women were imprisoned because of their family connection to or romantic relationship with a rebel.[23]

Economic repression was another of the most commonly used practices, a punishment used against women of the Basque elite during the Napoleonic Wars. A paradigmatic example of what happened in America can be found in the Junta de Secuestros (Seizure Board) organized by the royalist side in territories such as Colombia. The seizure of property was "used as an instrument of repression to undermine the enemy's potential," leaving "the families of the 'conspirators' orphaned and in misery."[24] María de los Ángeles Zandaeta, from Venezuela, was one of those expropriated.[25] Meanwhile, in the Colombian town of Riohacha, the authorities started a lawsuit against the widows who, after the execution of their husbands, yelled subversive calls against the social order from their windows. It was the year 1819.[26]

Finally, one of the most brutal methods of repression was rape. In the context of the wars of independence, "the ethical standards that governed their societies were suspended and a particular treatment of female sexuality was included as part of warrior behavior: rape. The female body was taken as territory and the act of forcibly taking possession of it was a metaphor for triumph."[27] Though there is a lack of documentation—rape against women was barely mentioned because these documents focused on male honor[28]—the truth is it was a common practice.

NOTES

1. García López, "La participación," 43.
2. Taxin, "La participación," 107.
3. Taxin, "La participación," 105.

4. Martínez I. Àlvarez, "Memoria feminista," 5.
5. García López, "La participación," 45.
6. Mojica, "La leyenda," 146.
7. García López, "La participación," 40.
8. Morán and Rivera, "Libertadoras," 13–14.
9. Cherpak, "The Participation," 8.
10. García López, "La participación," 42.
11. Mora Valcárcel, "Una mujer," 506.
12. Morán and Rivera, "Libertadoras," 13.
13. Palacio Montiel, "La participación," 85.
14. Taxin, "La participación," 92.
15. Cherpak, "The Participation," 7.
16. Taxin, "La participación," 93.
17. Chambers, "¿Actoras políticas," 302–6.
18. Martín-Valdepeñas Yagüe, "Mis señoras traidoras," 101.
19. Cherpak, "The Participation," 6.
20. Palacio Montiel, "La participación," 86.
21. García López, "La participación," 39.
22. Pani, "'Ciudadana,'" 5.
23. Robinson, "La reclusión," 227–34.
24. Pita Pico, "Resistencia," 622.
25. Cherpak, "The Participation," 9.
26. Brown, "Adventures," 41.
27. Bruce and Gresores, "Cómo vivir," 18.
28. Brown, "Adventures," 41.

CHAPTER ELEVEN

The Noncitizen

The critical needs of the moment made it possible for many to transcend social walls,[1] being, in a way, tolerated by the general public, although also criticized. At the end of the wars, however, the speeches were settling in the way laid out by the androcentric and patriarchal culture of the period.

Women were immediately excluded from citizenship, a crucial legal figure in the states born out of the Atlantic revolutionary cycle. Europe and America broke with the Ancien Régime, although only partially; a large part of the population was excluded. The social, economic, and cultural forms that shaped gender relations continued to be in force, a common aspect for the entire Atlantic world.

From a political view, the public and private spheres became more separated with the birth of new nations, the political citizen, and the figure of the mother-wife.[2] This new domestic woman responded to "the need of the middle classes to establish new social and ideological conditions for their own identification in an emerging society" that demands "the redefinition of social subjects, as well as the invention of new generic identities." As a result, "men would be catalogued as political creatures and women as domestic creatures."[3]

Women's circumstances changed with the reconfiguration of postrevolutionary society: "at the moment of formulating social space in two clearly differentiated spheres, the public, domain of the political, and the private, domain of the domestic, the decision is made to exclusively attribute the former to men."[4] This subtraction of the public consolidated sexual hierarchies and postponed the emancipation of women in a context where, not by chance, powerful voices, such as those of Olympe de Gouges and Mary Wollstonecraft, emerged.[5]

The citizen as a subject of political rights who participates in the government of his political community is a historical product[6] that comes to embody "the legal-formal conception of subjectivities."[7] This is a matter of great interest. Subjectivity is not something "natural"; it is a historical construct so important that in its Hegelian reading it is considered the philosophical principle of modernity, from René Descartes to Immanuel Kant.[8] The importance of the self, of the rational being, forever transforms European and American societies, producing the "redefinition of social subjects" and creating new gender identities.[9]

For Michel Foucault, subjectivity is built through discourses about the body, scientific claims about sexual difference that connect with a sexuality understood as a historical product related to intimacy and subjectivity. According to his "repressive hypothesis," since the seventeenth century there has been a cultural tendency that forbids mentioning sex, something that, on the contrary, helped develop another series of discourses that saturated the female body with sexuality. The new body politics developed in the nineteenth century follows the model of Jeremy Bentham's Panopticon, based on subjectivity and self-surveillance or self-coercion, which reminds us of Norbert Elias. Therefore, subjectivity "is nothing more than the product of an education of the body by which each individual becomes his own jailer," a disciplined and disciplinary power.[10]

Cartesianism has been shown to result in the individualism-egalitarianism complex, which offers an exclusive and excluding category of citizen.[11] This subtraction, another milestone in the history of women,[12] is based on the efforts made by authors of the period concerned with disguising the already classic principle of sexual difference as complementarity,[13] a critical assault that happens from the very moment in which Cartesian rationalism universalizes the "autonomous capacity to judge," also extensible to women.[14] In this context, the power of men and the inequality between the sexes were problematized,[15] a "reopening of the question of the sexes" to which should be added the questioning and reorientation of "the patterns of behavior in relations between the sexes in light of modern philosophical postulates that, in the case of women, would lead to the model of the domestic woman."[16] The famous disciple of Descartes, Poullain de la Barre, formulated the most "radical" proposal following the postulates of his master: an absolute equality between women and men, also political, which early thinkers of the eighteenth century challenged.[17]

This is how the dissertations on the complementarity between the sexes,[18] those related to intellectual, physical, and moral differences, and those based on scientific or "biological" arguments, emerged in the Enlightenment. This would serve to justify their subordination.[19] They would never be citizens because they were mothers and wives,[20] a denial of rights based on their "different moral and physical nature" and denounced by thinkers such as Wollstonecraft.[21] However, some of these speeches had a constructive and revolutionizing tone, filling women's new civic role with public utility and political virtuosity. In their role as mothers committed to the education of future citizens, women found a new existential dimension.[22]

Going deeper into this matter, "Celia Amorós proposes defining the feminine sphere as the space of the identical" based on the fact that no attribute would impact more on them than the fact of being a woman: "the feminine identity, being identical, implies not having a principle of individuation, not being, therefore, subjects."[23] There is an extended confusion about the concepts of equality and identity, as equality is "understood as a kind of generalized identity where every subject is identical to any other,"[24] a common mistake that fails to hide the fact that "the concept of equality refers to a certain type of relationship between individuals."[25]

"In the private space, what we call in Philosophy the principle of individuation does not happen," which turns the public sphere into an egalitarian territory where individuals share power. This turns the private sphere into the space of the identical, where individuation does not exist because it is unnecessary.[26] The public sphere, the polis, is thereby proposed to be a place of competence between equals and where the individual is distinguished from others in contrast to the private and family sphere, that mysterious place made up of the identical, but not equal.[27] The historian Capel Martínez identifies it with these words: "the notion of citizen that ends up imposing itself is the one established by reference to the private sphere: the wife of the citizen," a euphemistic or empty concept of citizen that is explained from the above.[28]

Separate spheres have been, therefore, a central element of patriarchal liberalism from its origins. Liberalism and democracy cannot be understood without the exclusion of women from the public sphere of "true intersubjectivity,"[29] and is used as its sustenance—morally with the development of these discourses and materially by carrying all the reproductive work on their shoulders.[30] This integral relationship between spheres and the resulting status of nonindividual feminine—thanks to the fact that the contractualists of the seventeenth century decided to exclude women from the space of *frater*, or equals[31]—would result in that patriarchal liberalism mentioned and the doubt of whether women should be integrated into that scenario or renounced from the category of citizens. This is what has come to be called the "Wollstonecraft dilemma"[32] or the "Pateman dilemma."[33]

As long as she was not considered the subject of the social contract or as the interpreter of her own will, which falls on the male head of the family,[34] a woman would not be illuminated by the Age of Enlightenment but remain "under indirect light," in the words of Wollstonecraft.[35] For this reason, contemporary feminism has its roots in the eighteenth century, when it dealt with women's political and civic rights "as a result of the redefinition of the concept of citizenship produced in its final decades."[36] This movement became the last and most radical proposal carried out by the Enlightenment.[37]

On the American continent, Ciriza Jofré points out that "the appeal to equality was, for them, a source of tension, since the 'new American regime' did not suppress the forms of patriarchal domination, the relations of servitude and exploitation, racism and the conviction of the inferiority of Indians, blacks, castes and women. However, unequal treatment was no longer considered legitimate."[38] Along these lines, Erika Pani highlights that "after the revolution, the citizen, as a member of the sovereign entity—the people, the nation—represents one of the key participants in the new political order. The exclusion of women, therefore, responds—perhaps above all—to particular ways of imagining this political actor."[39] Despite this, authors such as Matthew Brown point out that

> the involvement of women in the conflict meant that women occupied "a contested seat at the revolutionary banquet" in the immediate post-war period. Female involvement in the Wars of Independence presented the possibility that women could take a greater part in society in peacetime, and male elites therefore took care to ensure that "women were to relate to the republic via their subordinate position within the family."[40]

As an anecdote, the *Gaceta de México* reported on May 6, 1794, about the streets of Paris during the War of the Pyrenees. Talking about a singular episode involving several women, the editor of the newspaper spread this idea of femininity that had been repeated for years, also criticizing the political aspirations of the most aggressive Parisian women. Their goals were far from their natural role, focused, as Olavide rightly indicated, on "softening men's habits":

> Three days earlier, there had been reports of disorders in Paris by women. Many of them, adopting the name of Jacobins, appeared in the markets and other places wearing red caps and

trousers or breeches, and wanted other citizens to wear the same dress. Sixty of these legislators gathered together, running through the streets and squares insulting those who were not dressed like them, and many were whipped by the Jacobins. It became necessary for the Committee of Public Safety to take a hand in this serious matter. There, two questions were discussed: Can women exercise political rights and take an active part in the Government? Can they deliberate among themselves, gathered in a popular society? The Committee decided against it on the grounds that: "Women are not susceptible to the care and qualities that the Government demands, such as a severe impassivity and self-abnegation: they do not have the moral or physical strength that the exercise of the political rights of the citizen demands. If they were to devote themselves to these painful and useful functions, they would have to sacrifice for them the most important cares to which nature calls them. Born to soften the morals of man, they should not take an active part in discussions, the ardor of which is incompatible with the moderation and gentleness that form the enchantment of their sex. Moreover, women by their organization are prone to an exaltation that would be fatal in the examination of public affairs."[41]

After the war, the model of the republican mother triumphed in the United States.[42] The private role of the former colonial woman was then endowed with a fundamental public responsibility: raising the citizens of the new republic.[43] This domestic role justified her exclusion from the public sphere, although she had a social, civic, and community responsibility. In fact, motherhood emerged as another compensatory sphere.[44] This model also prevailed in postcolonial Mexico, as José Joaquín Fernández de Lizardi rightly stated—"if the woman fails, the bases of society will shake."[45] Meanwhile, the pamphlet *La mexicana independiente* vindicated the women of the new nation:

If we are already in enlightened times when everyone can express their ideas: If everyone writes what they think, what they want, what they know or what they can: If the lavish day of the oath of our happy independence gives merit to be celebrated by the wise, the ignorant, the rich, the poor, the child, the old, the noble and the commoner, because everyone is born with their natural philosophy, I do not know why only men should have permission to write, discuss and philosophize, and not women, to whom heaven granted, like every living being, two fingers on their foreheads [a Spanish expression meaning ability to reason].[46]

The public utility of women is established by their capacity as educators following the postulates of Rousseau, their role as mothers at the service of the nation.[47] The female gender is rebuilt from this new civic function, offering a "new image of women as citizens useful to the country," although they are still far from the legal category of citizen, being considered, ultimately, as "citizens providers."[48] In this way, the emerging American nations "created patterns of inclusion and exclusion of women in the various state institutions related to the spaces of political sociability and the configuration of the political arena."[49] As Pani says, "gender also structured the public space that emerged with independence and which occupied a central place within the new political imagined space."[50] They were, ultimately, "excluded from freedom."[51]

In the newly created Colombia, women "did not have the appropriate spaces for organization to demand improvements in their social conditions or to claim their rights in accordance with the legal and political changes promised by the leaders of the revolution. . . . Once the political and military effervescence was over, they would return to their traditional roles."[52]

Something similar occurred in Spain, including in the Basque Country. "The legal situation of women, at the beginning of contemporaneity, was lacking the recognition of those political rights that men achieved when the change from subjects to citizens took place."[53] However, throughout the nineteenth century, "the demands of Spanish women . . . focused on educational and labor requests and appeals for reform of the codes that regulated family life and the marriage contract, prioritizing them over voting rights."[54]

From a broad concept of citizenship, where we add the civic and social dimension to its electoral dimension, we better understand that Spanish women focused their fights on these types of claims, prioritizing them over those of a political nature.

Consequently, at the beginning of the new era, the individual freedom of man was based on female isolation.[55] Even so, in the old Hispanic sphere, there were voices that demanded political equality between men and women, because as the Basque-Mexican Lizardi stated in his *Pensador Mexicano*, "women should not only participate in parliamentary debates, but ... as citizens they should be able to elect and be elected."[56]

NOTES

1. Morán and Rivera, "Libertadoras," 3.
2. Elena Barbieri and Rosa de Castro, "Ciudadanía y feminismo: Categorías a debatir," *Actas de las XIII Jornadas Rosarinas de Antropología Socio-cultural* (Rosario, Argentina: Universidad de Rosario, 2016), 7.
3. Gloria Franco Rubio, "La contribución literaria de Moratín y otros hombres de letras al modelo de mujer doméstica," *Cuadernos de Historia Moderna* 6 (2007): 224.
4. Franco Rubio, "La contribución," 225.
5. Isabel Alonso and Mila Belinchón, *1789–1793: La voz de las mujeres en la Revolución francesa; Cuadernos de quejas y otros textos* (Barcelona: La Sal, 1989); Barbara Caine and Glenda Sluga, *Género e Historia: Mujeres en el cambio sociocultural europeo, de 1780 a 1920* (Madrid: Narcea, 2000), 21–48; Paule-Marie Duhet, *Las mujeres y la Revolución (1789–1794)* (Barcelona: Península, 1974); Cristina Molina Petit, *Dialéctica feminista de la Ilustración* (Barcelona: Anthropos, 1994); Alicia H. Puleo, *La Ilustración olvidada: La polémica de los sexos en el siglo XVIII* (Barcelona: Anthropos, 1993); Mary Wollstonecraft, *Vindicación de los derechos de la mujer* (Madrid: Istmo, 2005).
6. Barbieri and Castro, "Ciudadanía y feminismo," 1–3; Capel Martínez, "Preludio," 157.

7. Celia Amorós Puente, *Mujer: Participación, cultura política y Estado* (Buenos Aires: Ediciones de la Flor, 1990), 23.
8. Gabriela Castellanos, "Género, poder y postmodernidad: Hacia un feminismo de la solidaridad," in *Desde las orillas de la política. Género y poder en América Latina*, ed. Lola G. Luna and Mercedes Vilanova (Barcelona: Universidad de Barcelona, 1996), 27–30.
9. Franco Rubio, "La contribución," 224.
10. Castellanos, "Género, poder," 32–37.
11. Iris Marion Young, "Vida política y diferencia de grupo: Una crítica del ideal de ciudadanía universal," in *Perspectivas feministas en teoría política*, ed. Carme Castells (Barcelona: Paidós, 1996), 99; Amelia Valcárcel, "Moralización de la política," *Revista del Centro de Estudios Constitucionales* 8 (1991): 159.
12. Franco Rubio, "La contribución," 228–29.
13. Capel Martínez, "Preludio," 163.
14. Celia Amorós Puente, "Dimensiones del poder en la teoría feminista," *Revista Internacional de Filosofía Política* 25 (2005): 13.
15. Amorós Puente, "Dimensiones," 13.
16. Franco Rubio, "La contribución," 225; Mónica Bolufer and Montserrat Cabré, "La Querella de las Mujeres: Nuevas perspectivas historiográficas," *Arenal* 20, no. 2 (2013): 235–341.
17. Amorós Puente, *Mujer: Participación*, 24–25.
18. Franco Rubio, "La contribución," 252.
19. Celia Amorós Puente, "Simone de Beauvoir: Entre la vindicación y la crítica al Androcentrismo," *Investigaciones Feministas* 0 (2009): 12; Barbieri and Castro, "Ciudadanía y feminismo," 4–7; Capel Martínez, "Preludio," 161–62.
20. Barbieri and Castro, "Ciudadanía y feminismo," 7.
21. Encarna Bodelón, "Feminismo y Derecho: Mujeres que van más allá de lo jurídico," in *Género y dominación: Críticas feministas del derecho y el poder*, ed. Gemma Nicolás and Encarna Bodelón (Barcelona: Anthropos, 2009), 98.
22. Capel Martínez, "Preludio," 172–79.
23. Clara Serra Sánchez, "El feminismo a principios del siglo XXI: Sobre hechos y derechos en clave ilustrada," *XLVII Congreso de Filosofía Joven* (Murcia, Spain: Universidad de Murcia, 2010), 7.
24. Serra Sánchez, "El feminismo," 5.

25. Celia Amorós Puente, *La gran diferencia y sus pequeñas consecuencias ... para las luchas de las mujeres* (Madrid: Cátedra, 2007), 88.
26. Amorós Puente, *Mujer: Participación*, 9–10.
27. Tomeu Sales Gelabert, "Crítica y teoría feminist: Por una nueva agenda feminista," *Astrolabio: Revista Internacional de Filosofía* 20 (2017): 182; Serra Sánchez, "El feminismo," 5.
28. Capel Martínez, "Preludio," 179.
29. Amorós Puente, *Mujer: Participación*, 30.
30. Young, "Vida política," 103; Carole Pateman, "Críticas feministas a la dicotomía público/privado," in *Perspectivas feministas en teoría política*, ed. Carme Castells (Barcelona: Paidós, 1996), 42–51.
31. Sales Gelabert, "Crítica y teoría," 186.
32. Barbieri and Castro, "Ciudadanía y feminismo," 7.
33. Sales Gelabert, "Crítica y teoría," 183.
34. Amorós Puente, *Mujer: Participación*, 28.
35. Amorós Puente, "Simone de Beauvoir," 10.
36. Capel Martínez, "Preludio," 156.
37. Amorós Puente, *Mujer: Participación*, 7.
38. Ciriza Jofré, "Genealogías feministas," 624.
39. Pani, "Ciudadana," 6.
40. Brown, "Adventures," 45.
41. *Gaceta de México*, May 6, 1794.
42. Cogliano and Phimister, *Revolutionary America*, 190.
43. McClelland, *The education*, 57.
44. Farge, "La historia," 94–95.
45. García Rodríguez, "La figura," 159–66.
46. Ciriza, "Pensar el bicentenario," 123.
47. Lorenzo Rustighi, "The Good Prince or the Good Mother: Reassessing the question of Gender in Rousseau's political theory," *Gender and History* 30, no. 1 (2018): 30–51.
48. Gálvez Ruiz, "La construcción," 126.
49. Pilar García Jordán and Gabriela Dalla-Corte Caballero, "Mujeres y sociabilidad política en la construcción de los Estados nacionales," in *Historia de las mujeres en España y América Latina*, vol. 3, ed. Isabel Morant Deusa (Madrid: Cátedra, 2006), 560.
50. Pani, "'Ciudadana,'" 16.

51. Morán and Rivera, "Libertadoras," 3; Chambers, "¿Actoras políticas," 308–9.
52. Pita Pico, "Resistencia," 628–29.
53. Amelia Sanchís Vidal and María José Ramos Rovi, "Afrancesadas y majas: Presentes en la guerra e invisibles en las Cortes; Análisis feminista," *Raudem: Revista de Estudios de las Mujeres* 2 (2014): 173.
54. Espigado Tocino, "Mujeres y ciudadanía," 172.
55. Espigado Tocino, "Mujeres y ciudadanía," 174–75; Anna Becker, "Gender in the History of Early Modern Political Thought," *Historical Journal* 60, no. 4 (2017): 861.
56. Pani, "'Ciudadana,'" 11.

Conclusion

"The achievement of *feminist memory* is the course from the abstract of the nation, politics, homeland, freedom and also love, to the real sense with which girls and women can measure themselves today when listening to the experience of women like Manuela Sáenz."[1] These words from Martínez I. Àlvarez help explain part of my purpose.

There are many female experiences that I have tried to portray throughout these pages. Basque women have been the subjects of much of the analysis in this study, but I also wanted to highlight the different American figures with Basque origins who were protagonists in those years. And I would like to make an important clarification to avoid cultural or historiographical appropriation of their figures: they are American women with Basque ancestors. Nothing more.

Thanks to these women, we have approached a variety of topics, objects of analysis that have an evolving journey and a strong future. On these elements I would like to explain some final considerations.

First, I underline the importance of the framework used. On both shores, the experiences of Basque and American women in the context of the Atlantic Revolutions reveal a multitude of differences and similarities. The analogy between the hegemonic discourses on femininity is a clear example. Experiences vary, even more so when factors such as race, ethnicity, and socioeconomic status are taken into account. And despite this, the speeches on femininity developed at the end of the eighteenth century in the Basque Country and in America seem identical. The American

Republican mother, the angel of the home, and the women of the Hispanic American sphere share identical values.

As Ian Tyrrell said, "transnational history refers to a broad range of phenomena cutting across national boundaries."[2] The construction of femininity and gender relations are, without a doubt, one of these phenomena. However, I would like to emphasize that these constructions seem to be oriented toward high-society ladies, on both sides. Although these discourses appeal to a large majority, the incredible variety of experiences reveals an astonishing plurality. The importance of social origin and other categories, such as race or gender, seem critical when it comes to establishing social models and relationships but also power. And as part of these archetypes, we find elements such as that of the virile woman, which complete the previous ones.

I also point out the manifestations made by Espigado Tocino inviting us to go beyond national models and focus our attention on broad geographic and chronological spaces such as the Atlantic world and its revolutions so that we can better understand "a scenario with adequate entity to frame the female responses observed in similar transition processes."[3] This has been part of my work, to bring together different female experiences in order to compare, connect, share, and understand. One of the most accurate conclusions I can make is that of similarities, since many Basque and American women shared a destiny or were exposed to similar discourses, archetypes, and gender relations. Differences, of course, can always be found.

The role of women, gender relations, and the meaning of femininity itself changed between the sixteenth and nineteenth centuries. The participation of Basque women in the most turbulent events during these centuries suggests a role accepted and demanded by society as a whole that placed them as contributors, although on different levels. Sometimes they rise up as the voice of the rebellious people, take part in specific actions, instigate the rebels, and even arbitrate with the authorities. A clear change that can be seen between the rebellions that took place in the modern age and the Atlantic Revolutions is related, precisely, to their actions. In some way, women became involved in a different way, moving from a kind of verbal and symbolic action to one of a more practical nature by participating directly.

However, it seems clear that before the revolutionary cycle, contributions in these events were limited by social categories. Women from the elite and those from low socioeconomic backgrounds do not seem to share the same fate, whatever their position within these events. In the Atlantic Revolutions, on the contrary, this seems to change.

In this context, the facts challenge all the people involved, whatever their social origin. This is a substratum, by the way, that is about to change. One of the big questions I ask myself is whether there was a significant transformation in the role played by women during the conflicts that announced the change of the era. It seems that such a change happened. The action of women, or the testimonies about it, refer to a participation in a multitude of areas, although respecting, for the most part, the feminine canons of the period, such as those referring to social motherhood. The majority of them were invited to collaborate following these schemes. And so they did. On the contrary, there were also many women who exceeded and transgressed these parameters.

In this regard, we must ask ourselves whether social differences played an important role, whether women from one social level or another contributed in a similar manner. And respecting the individual experience, since we will always find exceptions, it seems that there were some differences. The hegemonic discourses on domesticated femininity infiltrated more deeply within the most privileged groups, affecting their participation in the various events. This is what the Basque, Hispanic, and American examples seem to indicate.

Elite women were involved in respecting these canons, which led them to participate in social gatherings, patriotic festivities, donations, espionage work, and much more. These were actions between their existential and normative universes that were allowed, and even required, due to circumstances. In reality, it was something that involved all women, both in the Basque Country and in America. However, women belonging to the wealthy classes were much more receptive to the enlightened discourses of the time. In fact, the Spanish monarchy publicly recognized only those women who obeyed gender rules.[4]

Although all of these women, regardless of their social origin, participated in a multitude of tasks and responded to the aforementioned canons, the social origin of those who took up arms seems, at the very least, unclear. The cases analyzed indicate a majority coming from the lower classes, anonymous women who fought, in many cases, dressed as men. This does not mean that there were no opposite cases, such as Manuela Sáenz herself, of wealthy women who fought directly in battles. However, it seems that more often the transgressive women came from the humblest social levels, those who were less exposed to elitist standards.

Speaking about their credit at the time, there also seems to be a certain difference from the social point of view. The Mexican women who went down in history as Beneméritas de la Patria (Distinguished of the Nation) belonged to the upper class. Such are the examples of Josefa Ortiz, Leona Vicario, and Güera Rodríguez.[5] Gertrudis Bocanegra, executed in 1817 for supporting Xavier Mina's expedition, never enjoyed such recognition.[6] She belonged to a lower socioeconomic class. At that time, belonging to one class or another was decisive. Gender differences were built by elements that go beyond sexuality, such as values of all kinds or identity components such as the social hierarchy itself.[7]

Another complex element is the development of discourses on virility. In the Basque Country, there were already opinions of this kind in the seventeenth and eighteenth centuries, and they were used in different ways. On the one hand, there were those that portrayed women as strong, noble, and hardworking. For the enlightened Basques, the manly woman was the ridiculous woman who emulated the man. It is really interesting how these discourses were incredibly flexible, being used by American cultural elites to praise or criticize women who participated in the conflicts. The reasons changed and were used according to the situation and the author's intention, on a transnational scale.

In her analysis of Domínguez Roche praising La Pola, Sarah de Mojica develops an interesting idea: "Because of her unconditional aspiration for freedom, a virtue that gives her heroic stature, Policarpa decides to subject her body as a woman condemned to torment by the despotic social regime, in order to rebuke, with a reckless and virile attitude, her break with the monarchical State."[8] In this case, acting using masculine qualities seems decisive when it comes to making a difference in the political arena, which leads me to the following question: Was it essential to embrace masculinity in order to make a difference in the political arena? Can women be seen as historical agents of transgression and change in a feminist sense? Ladies of high society, at least, did not reject femininity to exercise their political power. In any case, we do not know precisely the reasons that led these transgressors to choose one life or another, to develop more fluid identities from a gender perspective, or to make certain life decisions.

The testimonies used show the capacity of the patriarchal culture of the time to manipulate its discourses, adapting them to contemporaneous needs. Although some of these explanations could justify the normative transgression, the truth is that the system was showing great flexibility, feeding the aforementioned compensatory mechanism. One of the keystones of this androcentric and patriarchal system is its capacity to compensate or reward women, creating a solid social balance despite its own contradictions.

Ultimately, we must understand this set of discourses about the virile woman as mobile or fluid, adaptable to circumstances and performed by a multitude of historical agents. Countless women joined the fights adopting physical, symbolic, and psychological qualities attributed to masculinity of the time, from the women in the Basque Country and old Europe who fought dressed as men to the Mexican and American women.[9] Some were arrested "for wearing pants,"[10] others were tolerated, several were praised, and many were criticized. And what about the motives? As Claire Brewster said, "their motives for taking part are likely to be as individual as the women themselves. Some were doubtlessly politicized as a result of the death, injury, exile or imprisonment of their fathers, brothers, spouses and lovers; others followed the examples of their families and friends in distributing messages; and it is fair to assume that the spirit of adventure offered by the unrest may have lured some of them into action."[11]

The context is also important. According to part of the historiography, the notion of sexuality was born between the seventeenth and nineteenth centuries—that is, it was then that people in Western society discovered they had individual sexualities, "a quality defined by sexual object choice. . . . Before this point there were sexual acts, but after this point people came to understand that they had a sexual identity or sexual orientation... 'acts versus identities,' 'modern versus premodern.'"[12] Continuing with this consideration, was the virile woman an identity product defined from the outside or an act of a sexual nature? Remember that each of the pieces that constitute gender relations are historical, cultural, and social products. And the discourses on virile women have no other purpose other than to catalog them, always with the intention of subjecting them to a purpose, in a pejorative or more positive way. According to those who portrayed them, women showed qualities or abilities typical of men, escaping from or beating their nature.

As for the consequences, we also see differences. Those who were combative were praised or, at least, tolerated. That this "window"—of permissibility—opened during the period is indisputable. Once the conflicts were over, however, divergences arose. Women with political influence were attacked, punished, and rejected. They were also excluded using discursive elements related to female virility, such as being classified as subjects against nature. However, some of the prominent ladies were never punished; in fact, women like Ana María de Iraeta were rewarded.[13]

Many women had their political ideas rejected. In the case of Mexico, for example, we find an interesting analysis of the speeches made by lower-class women who were on trial; these women had been accused of political and moral crimes and generally sentenced for moral crimes, given their "natural fragility" and inability to have their own ideas.[14] In their trials, they made strategic use of gender. Many were persecuted and punished for family connections. This contrasts with reality because in Mexico there have been documented cases of rebel women with strong political ideas who overcame personal and family casuistry.[15] The same happened in the Basque Country. The fact that many women were punished like men were contradicts the messages that deny their ideals and the paternalistic culture of the period, emphasizing its ambiguity.[16]

For this reason, it is necessary to change our view. As Martínez I. Àlvarez points out, the question does not lie in whether or not women participated in political events, since there are not two histories of men and women. Perhaps the significant thing is to discover the stories used to remove them from power or those that placed them only in relation to others' politics—that is, in a masculine politics that is not their own.[17]

This image of women lacking political opinions is in line with the ideal of domesticated femininity. The enlightened Basque men granted women in their social and family environment a certain capacity to arbitrate in political affairs, based on their basic frame of reference: the home (though it, too, can be political). However, they were excluded from citizenship and without political rights.

The American nations are clear about the role of their women. In France, the Basque Country, and the United States, the role of the mother who raises the future citizens of the nation triumphs.

This task was already an obligation in the minds of enlightened people like Pablo de Olavide in 1768, years before the Atlantic Revolutions. Their natural fragility and their special capacity as sensitive and nonrational beings made them ideal for domestic work. In reality, patriarchy reformulated itself, continuing with a historical pattern and leaving reproductive work in the hands of women once again. However, this phenomenon formed the basis for a future transformation. On the one hand, we clearly observe how these discourses placed mothers at the epicenter of national construction, not so much from a political point of view but from symbolic, social, and cultural levels. Without being full subjects, they participated with great symbolic, and also practical, significance in the nation's construction. On the other hand, the idea of political equality marked a turning point: consider how close this generation is, in chronological terms, to the feminist emerging.

What is clear is that these women were not passive historical agents but active protagonists of historical events, such as the Atlantic Revolutions. They were not rebels against patriarchy, even though they managed to outline a fundamental period for understanding subsequent changes. They fought for their ideals, whatever they were.[18]

I would also like to reflect on what Beatrice Bruce and Gabriela Gresores have observed: we could be observing a kind of "female empowerment in dire times." "Repression as the putting into action of a perpetual relationship of force is cracked by the temporary absence (displacement to the battle front) or permanent absence (death) of the dominant male subject."[19] The number of transformations and the war "make it possible for some women to assume an active social role in this situation, challenging sex-gender norms."[20] This empowerment in situations of male absence, in this case due to war, could be happening simultaneously in spaces such as the maritime Basque Country. "Likewise, active adaptation to the new situation generates original practices that allow the dismantling of the prevailing stereotypes of femininity and give way to self-esteem."[21]

Should we include the important role played by Basque women within these parameters? During the Napoleonic Wars, 20 percent of women judged throughout Spain were of Biscayan origin, a notable statistic.[22] Their role in economic structures was also important. And finally, we have the emergence of discourses on virile women, which we could understand as discursive practices that break or dismantle hegemonic stereotypes about femininity. In other words, in times and spaces where women took on tasks reserved for men due to their absence, these arguments arose to identify, explain, reinforce, or even denigrate their exceptional performance. They were, after all, far removed from their normative framework. And the Basque case could, for this very reason, be connected to part of the female experiences observed in the Atlantic world during the war. In fact, their experience can also be assumed as part of a transnational history: "in all its forms is a study of relationships, interactions, and intertwining. These interconnections also shaped the experiences of people who did not move a meter, for any fixed location can also be saturated with transnational relationships."[23]

The observed female realities, although distant, share common points. Countless Basque and American women, from all over the Atlantic world, are connected. Within the diversity, there will be symbolic practices, as well as experiential ones, that unite them all. And patriarchal domination, with its mechanisms of imposition and compensation, is one of them.

Finally, I end with a warning: the recognition of women's participation in the Atlantic Revolutions is based on a masculine perspective, an androcentrism that leaves an indelible mark. If the society of that time adulterated the stories, how can current historiography counter this bias? There is still a long way to go, because let us not forget that "the silence about the female presence has more to do with those who write history than with its protagonists."[24]

Conclusion | 151

As always, I owe a debt of gratitude to the voices excluded from the story.

NOTES

1. Martínez I. Àlvarez, "Memoria feminista," 4.
2. Ian Tyrrell, "Reflections on the Transnational Turn in United States History: Theory and Practice," *Journal of Global History* 4, no. 3 (2009): 454.
3. Espigado Tocino, "Europeas y españolas," 49–50.
4. Espigado Tocino, "Mujeres y ciudadanía," 182–184.
5. Palacio Montiel, "La participación," 77–78.
6. Moisés Guzmán Pérez, "Gertrudis Bocanegra y el Proceso de Construcción de la Heroína en México," in *Las mujeres en la Independencia de América Latina*, ed. Sara Beatriz Guardia (Lima: CEMHAL, 2010), 59–62.
7. Nerea Aresti Esteban, "Género e identidad en la sociedad del siglo XVII," *Vasconia* 35 (2006): 49–62.
8. Mojica, "La leyenda," 149.
9. Brewster, "Women," 22.
10. Palacio Montiel, "La participación," 71.
11. Brewster, "Women," 26.
12. Wiesner-Hanks, "Crossing Borders," 360.
13. Torales Pacheco, "Tres viudas," 205–27.
14. Alejandra Guadalupe Hidalgo Rodríguez, "Los discursos sobre la participación de las mujeres en la Guerra de la Independencia: Casos del occidente mexicano," in *Mujeres y emancipación de la América Latina y el Caribe en los siglos XIX y XX*, dirs. Irina Bajini, Luisa Campuzano, and Emilia Perassi (Milán: Ledizioni Milano, 2013), 57–64.
15. María José Garrido Asperó, "Entre hombres te veas: Las mujeres de Pénjamo y la revolución de independencia," in *Disidencia y disidentes en la historia de México*, ed. Felipe Castro and Marcela Terrazas (Mexico City: UNAM, 2003), 169–90; Palacio Montiel, "La participación," 88.
16. Chambers, "¿Actoras políticas," 302.

17. Martínez I. Àlvarez, "Memoria feminista," 3–13.
18. Brewster, "Women," 33.
19. Bruce and Gresores, "Cómo vivir," 18.
20. Arcos and Salomone, "Mujeres," 206.
21. Bruce and Gresores, "Cómo vivir," 18.
22. Fernández García, "Transgresión total," 143–44; Sánchez Arreseigor, *Vascos contra Napoleón*, 175–87.
23. Wiesner-Hanks, "Crossing Borders," 377.
24. Vilalta, "Historia," 63.

BIBLIOGRAPHY

Abreu Ferreira, D. "Fishmongers and Shipowners: Women in Maritime Communities of Early Modern Portugal." *Sixteenth Century Journal* 31, no. 1 (2000): 7–23.

Aguado, A. M., Capel, R. M., González Calbet, T., Martínez López, C., Nash, M., Nielfa, G., Ortega, M. [et al.]. *Textos para la historia de las mujeres en España*. Barcelona: Cátedra, 1994.

Aguirrezabala, Marcel, and Marcela V. Tejerina. "Entre quejas confiadas y súplicas de amparo: Una aproximación a la condición de las mujeres en el Río de la Plata a fines del siglo XVIII." *Palobra* 13 (2013): 18–29.

Agustín de Montiano y Luyando, primer Director de la Real Academia de la Historia. Madrid: Real Academia de la Historia, 1926.

Alamán, Lucas. *Historia de Méjico*. Vol. 1. Mexico City: Editorial Jus, 1968.

Alberdi Lonbide, Xabier. *Conflictos de intereses en la economía marítima guipuzcoana: Siglos XVI–XVIII*. PhD diss., UPV/EHU, Vitoria-Gasteiz, 2012.

Alberdi Lonbide, Xabier. "Reforma de la administración de los recursos navales de Gipuzkoa a principios del siglo XVIII: La búsqueda de un nuevo equilibrio entre la política naval y económica de la Monarquía y las actividades de los principales hombres de negocios de la provincia." In *Una década prodigiosa. Beligerancia y negociación entre la Corona y las provincias vascas (1717–1728)*, edited by Álvaro Aragón Ruano and Alberto Angulo Morales, 69–93. Bilbao: UPV/EHU, 2019.

Alonso, Isabel, and Mila Belinchón. *1789–1793: La voz de las mujeres en la Revolución francesa; Cuadernos de quejas y otros textos*. Barcelona: La Sal, 1989.

Alonso Seoane, María José. "El último sueño de Pablo de Olavide." *Cuadernos Dieciochistas* 4 (2003): 47–65.

Altonaga Begoña, Bakarne. "Generoa Antzinako Erregimenean: Manuel Larramendiren ikuspuntua eta bere itzala." *Sancho el Sabio* 2, número extraordinario (2018): 107–27.

Altonaga Begoña, Bakarne. "Mujeres viriles en el siglo XVIII. La construcción de la feminidad por el discurso foralista de Manuel de Larramendi." *Historia Contemporánea* 52 (2016): 9–42.

Álvarez Barrientos, Joaquín. "Reunirse y conversar: Las tertulias del siglo XVIII." *Ínsula* 738 (2008): 1–9.

Álvarez Gila, Óscar, and Alberto Angulo Morales. *Las migraciones vascas en perspectiva histórica (Siglos XVI–XX)*. Bilbao: UPV/EHU, 2002.

Amelang, James S., and Mary Nash. *Historia y género: Las mujeres en la Europa Moderna y Contemporánea*. Valencia, Spain: Edicions Alfons el Magnànim, 1990.

Amorós Puente, Celia. "Dimensiones del poder en la teoría feminista." *Revista Internacional de Filosofía Política* 25 (2005): 11–34.

Amorós Puente, Celia. *La gran diferencia y sus pequeñas consecuencias... para las luchas de las mujeres*. Madrid: Cátedra, 2007.

Amorós Puente, Celia. *Mujer: Participación, cultura política y Estado*. Buenos Aires: Ediciones de la Flor, 1990.

Amorós Puente, Celia. "Simone de Beauvoir: Entre la vindicación y la crítica al Androcentrismo." *Investigaciones Feministas* 0 (2009): 9–27.

Ampudia de Haro, Fernando. "Cortesía y prudencia: Una gestión civilizada del comportamiento y de las emociones." In *Accidentes del alma: Las emociones en la Edad Moderna*, edited by María Tausiet and James S. Amelang, 123–43. Madrid: Abada Editores, 2009.

Amussen, Susan D. "The Contradictions of Patriarchy in Early Modern England." *Gender and History* 30, no. 2 (2018): 343–53.

Andújar Castillo, Francisco. "Interpretar la corrupción: El marqués de Villarrocha, Capitán General de Panamá (1698–1717)." *Revista Complutense de Historia de América* 43 (2017): 75–100.

Andújar Castillo, Francisco. *El sonido del dinero: Monarquía, ejército y venalidad en la España del siglo XVIII*. Madrid: Marcial Pons Historia, 2004.

Andújar Castillo, Francisco. "Venalidad y gasto militar: Sobre la financiación de la Guerra de los Nueve Años." In *Un Estado military:*

España, 1650–1820, edited by Agustín González Enciso, 395–422. Madrid: Actas, 2012.

Angulo Morales, Alberto. "El clero y los productos coloniales en la España septentrional: Consumo, contrabando e inmunidad eclesiástica (siglos XVII–XVIII)." In *Entre el fervor y la violencia: Estudios sobre los vascos y la Iglesia (siglos XVI–XVIII)*, edited by Mª Rosario Porres, 187–216. Bilbao: UPV/EHU, 2015.

Angulo Morales, Alberto. *De Cameros a Bilbao: Negocios, familia y nobleza en tiempos de crisis (1770–1834)*. Bilbao: UPV/EHU, 2007.

Angulo Morales, Alberto. "De la congregación de Cantabria o San Ignacio al proyecto de la Bascongada: El grupo de presión vasco en la Villa y Corte de Madrid (1713–1775)." In *Devoción, paisanaje e identidad: Las cofradías y congregaciones de naturales en España y en América (siglos XVI–XIX)*, edited by Óscar Álvarez Gila, Alberto Angulo Morales, and Jon Ander Ramos Martínez, 199–226. Bilbao: UPV/EHU, 2014.

Angulo Morales, Alberto. "De la familia provincial a la atlántica: Hijos de las Provincias y Señorío: Reputación y éxito en la movilidad norteña (XVI–XIX)." In *Familias, trayectorias, desigualdades: Estudios de historia social en España y en Europa ss. XVI–XIX*, edited by Francisco García González, 179–200. Madrid: Sílex, 2021.

Angulo Morales, Alberto. "Embajadores, agentes, congregaciones y conferencias: la proyección exterior de las provincias vascas (siglos XV–XIX)." In *Delegaciones de Euskadi (1936–1975): Antecedentes históricos de los siglos XVI al XIX, origen y desarrollo*, 23–98. Vitoria-Gasteiz, Spain: Gobierno Vasco-Eusko Jaurlaritza, 2010.

Angulo Morales, Alberto. "Estanco y contrabando de tabaco en el País Vasco (1684–1876)." In *Tabaco y economía en el siglo XVIII*, edited by A. González Enciso and R. Torres Sánchez, 195–237. Pamplona, Spain: Eunsa, 1999.

Angulo Morales, Alberto. "Los frutos de la movilidad: La emigración norteña peninsular en Madrid y el Imperio (siglos XVII y XVIII)." *Obradoiro de Historia Moderna* 24 (2015): 113–39.

Angulo Morales, Alberto. "Las geografías epistolares de las élites vascongadas y la formación de comunidades ilustradas en el siglo

XVIII: La Real Congregación de San Ignacio y la Real Sociedad Bascongada de los Amigos del País." In *"Las cartas las inventó el afecto": Ensayos sobre epistolografía en el Siglo de las Luces*, edited by Rafael Padrón Fernández, 47–80. Santa Cruz de Tenerife, Spain: Ediciones Idea, 2013.

Angulo Morales, Alberto. "Los hidalgos norteños en el centro de un Imperio: Madrid (1638–1850). Negocios, política e identidad." In *Recuperando el Norte: Empresas, capitales y proyectos atlánticos en la economía imperial hispánica*, edited by Alberto Angulo Morales y Álvaro Aragón Ruano, 261–96. Bilbao: UPV/EHU, 2016.

Angulo Morales, Alberto. "Información, negociación y defensa: Las fronteras en las provincias exentas (XVI–XVII)." In *Dinámica de las fronteras en periodos de conflicto: El Imperio español (1640–1815)*, edited by Miguel Ángel Melón Jiménez, Miguel Rodríguez Cancho, and Isabel Testón Núñez, 154–67. Cáceres, Spain: Universidad de Extremadura, 2019.

Angulo Morales, Alberto. "El *institutional entangled global network* de navarros y vascongados en la defensa atlántica por la plata peruana del Seiscientos (Madrid, Potosí y Puno)." *Protohistoria* 35 (2021): 361–78.

Angulo Morales, Alberto. "Mercados y financieros vascos. El circuito de la plata y su control en el Seiscientos." In *Tesoreros, "arrendadores" y financieros en los reinos hispánicos: La Corona de Castilla y el Reino de Navarra (siglos XIV–XVII)*, edited by Ernesto García Fernández, 241–56. Madrid: Ministerio de Economía y Hacienda, Instituto de Estudios Fiscales, 2012.

Angulo Morales, Alberto. "Migration, Mobility and Voyages: A Case Study on the Use of Private Sources for the Understanding of Basque Migration in the Eighteenth Century." In *From the Records of my Deepest Memory. Personal Sources and the Study of European Migration, 18th–20th Centuries*, edited by Óscar Álvarez Gila y Alberto Angulo Morales, 13–40. Bilbao: UPV/EHU, 2016.

Angulo Morales, Alberto. "Otro 'imposible vencido': Hombres, provincias y reinos en la Corte en tiempos de Carlos II." In *Volver a la 'hora navarra': La contribución navarra a la construcción de la monarquía española en el siglo XVIII*, edited by Rafael Torres Sánchez, 33–72. Pamplona, Spain: Universidad de Navarra, 2010.

Angulo Morales, Alberto. *Las puertas de la vida y la muerte: La administración aduanera en las provincias vascas (1690–1780)*. Bilbao: UPV/EHU, 1994.

Angulo Morales, Alberto, and Álvaro Aragón Ruano. "No sólo pescado y harina a cambio de oro: Vascos en el comercio con los Estados Unidos durante el siglo XVIII." *Boletín americanista* 77 (2019): 147–66.

Angulo Morales, Alberto, and Álvaro Aragón Ruano. *Recuperando el Norte. Empresas, capitales y proyectos atlánticos en la economía imperial hispánica*. Bilbao: UPV/EHU, 2016.

Angulo Morales, Alberto, and Iker Echeberria Ayllón. "Furias de consumidores y voces femeninas: Las resistencias anti-fiscales en tierras de vasconia (1634–1804)." In *Resistencias campesinas en los espacios rurales de Europa y América durante la Edad Moderna*, edited by Rubén Castro Redondo and Pablo F. Luna, 341–74. La Plata, Argentina: Universidad Nacional de La Plata, Facultad de Humanidades y Ciencias de la Educación; Ensenada, Mexico: IdIHCS; Santander, Spain: Universidad de Cantabria, HisMundI 7, 2024.

Angulo Morales, Alberto, and Iker Echeberria Ayllón. "Herederas de la Ilustración vasca: El papel femenino en tiempos de revoluciones." In *Las mujeres en las revoluciones liberales atlánticas: Roles entre lealtades, independencias y patrias (1780–1873)*, edited by Alejandro Cardozo Uzcátegui, 195–227. Bogotá: Universidad Sergio Arboleda, 2023.

Angulo Morales, Alberto, and Iker Echeberria Ayllón. "Viviendo en la raya: Las mujeres y el mundo fronterizo en los Pirineos occidentales durante el Setecientos." *Príncipe de Viana* 272 (2018): 1179–94.

Anonymous [William Frankland]. *Una descripción de San Sebastián relativa a su gobierno, costumbres y comercio*. San Sebastián: Librería Internacional, 1985.

Aragón Ruano, Álvaro. "Euskal Herria 'itsastarra' lehen mundubiraren testuinguruan." In *Elkano eta lehen mundubira: 500 urte geroago*, 75–102. Getaria, Spain: Mundubira 500 Elkano Fundazioa, 2020.

Aragón Ruano, Álvaro. "Discrepancias en el seno de la burguesía guipuzcoana en torno a la libertad de comercio y el traslado de aduanas durante los siglos XVIII y XIX." *Hispania: Revista Española de Historia* 73, no. 245 (2013): 761–88.

Aragón Ruano, Álvaro. "Discursos de frontera en el Pirineo occidental durante la Edad Moderna." In *Una década prodigiosa. Beligerancia y negociación entre la Corona y las provincias vascas (1717–1728)*, edited by Álvaro Aragón Ruano and Alberto Angulo Morales, 155–74. Bilbao: UPV/EHU, 2019.

Aragón Ruano, Álvaro. "La evolución de la economía guipuzcoana en tiempos de Urdaneta: Un período de desarrollo y expansión entre supuestas crisis." In *Andrés de Urdaneta: Un hombre moderno*, edited by Susana Truchuelo García, 119–44. Ordizia, Spain: Ordiziako Udala, 2009.

Aragón Ruano, Álvaro. "'. . . Faltar y ausentarse con esto los naturales de esta provinçia y quedar despoblada y hierma, sin defensa alguna . . .': Discursos de frontera en Gipuzkoa durante la Edad Moderna." In *Naciones en el Estado-Nación: La formación cultural y política de naciones en la Europa contemporánea*, edited by Joseba Agirreazkuenaga Zigorraga and Eduardo J. Alonso Olea, 401–10. Barcelona: Editorial Base, 2014.

Aragón Ruano, Álvaro, and Alberto Angulo Morales. "Spanish Basque Country in Global Trade Networks in the Eighteenth Century." *International Journal of Maritime History* 25 (2013): 149–72.

Aramburu-Zudaire, José Miguel. "América y los vascos en la Edad Moderna: Una perspectiva historiográfica." *Vasconia* 34 (2005): 249–74.

Aranzadi, Juan. *Milenarismo vasco. Edad de Oro, etnia y nativismo*. Madrid: Taurus, 2000.

Arcos, Carol, and Alicia Salome. "Mujeres e Independencia en Chile: La cultura del trato y la escritura de cartas." *Teresa: Revista de Literatura Brasileira* 12–13 (2013): 205–21.

Arcos Herrera, Carol. "Sujetos de controversia: Aportes para una bibliografía sobre las mujeres en el siglo XVIII y la Ilustración." *Revista de Crítica Literaria Latinoamericana* 67 (2008): 111–22.

Areizaga, J. C., A. Iturbe, and I. Llano. "Los agavillados de 1607: Sobre los antecedentes urbanos de la Matxinada de la Sal." In *II Congreso de Historia de Euskal Herria*, 309–16. San Sebastián: Txertoa, 1988.

Arenas Frutos, Isabel. "Entre la mitra y la pluma: el sacerdote ilustrado Castorena y Ursúa (México, 1668–1733)." In *El Humanismo Español, su proyección en América y Canarias en la época del Humanismo*, edited by A. Martín Rodríguez and G. Santana Henríquez, 273–86. Las Palmas de Gran Canaria: Universidad de Las Palmas de Gran Canaria, 2006.

Arenas Frutos, Isabel. "La Ilustración y el nuevo universo cultural de México en la época del arzobispo Lorenzana." In *Humanismo y tradición clásica en España y América*, edited by J. M. Nieto Ibáñez, 463–90. León, Spain: Universidad de León, 2002.

Aresti Esteban, Nerea. "Género e identidad en la sociedad del siglo XVII." *Vasconia* 35 (2006): 49–62.

Arpal Poblador, Jesús. *La sociedad tradicional en el País Vasco: el estamento de los hidalgos en Guipúzcoa*. San Sebastián: Haranburu, 1979.

Arteche y Moro de Elexabeitia, José de. *La mujer en la Guerra de la Independencia*. Madrid: Hijos de J. A. García, 1903.

Astigarraga, Jesús. *Los ilustrados vascos: Ideas, instituciones y reformas económicas en España*. Barcelona: Crítica, 2003.

Ayerbe Iribar, María Rosa. "Manuel de Larramendi y la enseñanza femenina en el siglo XVIII: Constituciones del Seminario de niñas 'Nuestra Señora de la Soledad,' de Bergara (1741)." *Boletín de la Real Sociedad Bascongada de los Amigos del País* 64, no. 2 (2008): 795–815.

Azcona Pastor, José Manuel. *Identidad y estructura de la emigración vasca y navarra hacia Iberoamérica (siglos XVI–XXI)*. Madrid: Thomson Reuters-Aranzadi, 2015.

Azpiazu Elorza, José Antonio. "Los guipuzcoanos y Sevilla en la Alta Edad Moderna." *Itsas Memoria: Revista de Estudios Marítimos del País Vasco* 4 (2003): 207–13.

Azpiazu Elorza, José Antonio. *Mujeres vascas, sumisión y poder: La condición femenina en la Alta Edad Moderna*. San Sebastián: R&B, 1995.

Azpiazu Elorza, José Antonio. "Las mujeres vascas y el mar." *Itsas Memoria: Revista de Estudios Marítimos del País Vasco* 8 (2016): 811–29.

Bagües i Erriondo, Jon. "El conde de Peñaflorida, impulsor de la Ilustración musical en el País Vasco." *Musiker, Cuadernos de Música* 4 (1988): 106–48.

Balance y Perspectivas de los Estudios de las Mujeres y del Género. Madrid: Instituto de la Mujer, 2002.

Baldellou Monclús, Daniel, and José Antonio Salas Auséns. "Idiosincrasia del modelo de transmisión de la propiedad en el Antiguo Régimen:

el modelo de las familias del Pirineo." *Actas del I Congreso Internacional Jóvenes Investigadores Siglo de Oro*, (2012): 11–21.

Baldellou Monclús, Daniel, and José Antonio Salas Auséns. "Noviazgo y matrimonio en Aragón: Casarse en la Europa del Antiguo Régimen." *Revista de Historia Moderna: Anales de la Universidad de Alicante* 34 (2016): 79–105.

Baldellou Monclús, Daniel, and José Antonio Salas Auséns. "Transgresión y legalidad en el cortejo del siglo XVIII: El secuestro de mujeres en la diócesis de Zaragoza." *Studia histórica, Historia moderna* 38–1 (2016): 155–92.

Ballesteros Gaibrois, Manuel. "El vasco Diego de Gardoqui, primer embajador de España ante los Estados Unidos de América." In *Euskal Herria y el Nuevo Mundo: La contribución de los vascos a la formación de las Américas*, edited by Ronald Escobedo Mansilla, Ana de Zaballa Beascoechea, and Óscar Álvarez Gila, 305–18. Bilbao: UPV/EHU, 1996.

Barahona Arévalo, Renato. "A Seventeenth Century Vizcayan Sociopolitical Movement: The Salt-Tax Revolt." In *Euskal Herriaren historiari buruzko biltzarra*, 317–27. San Sebastián: Txertoa, Vol. 3, 1988.

Barbieri, Elena, and Rosa de Castro. "Ciudadanía y feminismo: Categorías a debatir." In *Actas de las XIII Jornadas Rosarinas de Antropología Socio-cultural*, 1–10. Rosario: Universidad de Rosario, 2016.

Baudot Monroy, María. "Asientos y política naval: El suministro de víveres a la Armada al inicio de la guerra contra Gran Bretaña, 1739–1741." *Estudia Histórica. Historia Moderna* 35 (2013): 127–58.

Becker, Anna. "Gender in the history of Early Modern Political thought." *Historical Journal* 60, no. 4 (2017): 843–63.

Bel Bravo, María Antonia. *Mujer y cambio social en la Edad Moderna*. Madrid: Encuentro, 2008.

Bernal Serna, Luis M. "Responsabilidades y conflictividad de las mujeres en las localidades portuarias (Vizcaya, 1550–1808)." *Itsas Memoria: Revista de Estudios Marítimos del País Vasco* 7 (2012): 197–210.

Birriel Salcedo, Margarita. "Sobrevivir al cónyuge: viudas y viudedad en la España Moderna." *Chronica Nova* 34 (2008): 7–12.

Bisha, Robin, Jehanne M. Gheith, Christine Holden, and William G. Wagner. *Russian Women: Experience & Expression: An Anthology of Sources*. Bloomington: Indiana University Press, 2002.

Bodelón, Encarna. "Feminismo y Derecho: Mujeres que van más allá de lo jurídico." In *Género y dominación: Críticas feministas del derecho y el poder*, edited by Gemma Nicolás and Encarna Bodelón, 95–116. Barcelona: Anthropos, 2009.

Bolufer Peruga, Mónica. "Afectos razonables: Equilibrios de la sensibilidad dieciochesca." In *La cultura de las emociones y las emociones en la cultura española contemporánea (siglos XVIII–XXI)*, edited by Luisa Elena Delgado, Pura Fernández, and Jo Labanyi, 35–56. Madrid: Cátedra, 2018.

Bolufer Peruga, Mónica. *Arte y artificio de la vida en común: Los modelos de comportamiento y sus tensiones en el siglo de las Luces*. Madrid: Marcial Pons, 2019.

Bolufer Peruga, Mónica. "En torno a la sensibilidad dieciochesca: Discursos, prácticas, paradojas." In *Las mujeres y las emociones en Europa y América: Siglos XVII–XIX*, edited by María Luisa Candau Chacón, 29–56. Santander, Spain: Universidad de Cantabria, 2016.

Bolufer Peruga, Mónica. "Josefa Amar e Inés Joyes: dos perspectivas femeninas sobre el matrimonio en el siglo XVIII." In *Historia de la mujer e historia del matrimonio*, edited by María Victoria López-Cordón and Montserrat Carbonell Esteller, 203–17. Murcia, Spain: Universidad de Murcia, 1997.

Bolufer Peruga, Mónica. "Modelar conductas y sensibilidades: Un campo abierto de indagación histórica." In *Educar los sentimientos y las costumbres: Una mirada desde la historia*, edited by Mónica Bolufer, Carolina Blutrach, and Juan Gomis, 7–17. Zaragoza, Spain: Institución Fernando el Católico, CSIC, 2014.

Bolufer Peruga, Mónica. "Sociabilidad mixta y civilización: Miradas desde España." In *Educar los sentimientos y las costumbres: Una mirada desde la historia*, edited by Mónica Bolufer, Carolina Blutrach, and Juan Gomis, 149–73. Zaragoza, Spain: Institución Fernando el Católico, CSIC, 2014.

Bolufer Peruga, Mónica, and Montserrat Cabré. "La Querella de las Mujeres: Nuevas perspectivas historiográficas." *Arenal* 20, no. 2 (2013): 235–341.

Bolufer Peruga, Mónica, and Isabel Morant Deusa. "Sobre la razón, la educación y el amor de las mujeres: Mujeres y hombres en la España y en la Francia de las Luces." *Studia Historica: Historia Moderna* 15 (1996): 179–208.

Bowles, Guillermo. *Introducción a la historia natural y a la geografía física de España*. Madrid: Imprenta de Francisco Manuel de Mena, 1775.

Brading, David A. *Mineros y comerciantes en el México borbónico (1763–1810)*. Mexico City: Fondo de Cultura Económica, 2015.

Brewster, Claire. "Women and the Spanish-American Wars of Independence: An overview." *Feminist Review* 79 (2005): 20–35.

Brown, Matthew. "Adventures, Foreign Women and Masculinity in the Colombian Wars of Independence." *Feminist Review* 79 (2005): 36–51.

Bruce, Beatrice, and Gabriela Gresores. "Cómo vivir en un mundo en llamas: Impacto de la Guerra de la Independencia en la cotidianeidad de las mujeres." *Cuadernos FHyCS-UNJu* 48 (2015): 13–27.

Bueno Carrera, José María. *La expedición española a Dinamarca, 1807–1808*. Madrid: Agualarga, 2000.

Caine, Barbara, and Glenda Sluga. *Género e Historia: Mujeres en el cambio sociocultural europeo, de 1780 a 1920*. Madrid: Narcea, 2000.

Candau Chacón, María Luisa. "Emociones diversas." In *Las mujeres y las emociones en Europa y América. Siglos XVII–XIX*, edited by María Luisa Candau Chacón, 11–26. Santander, Spain: Universidad de Cantabria, 2016.

Candau Chacón, María Luisa. "Literatura, género y moral en el Barroco hispano: Pedro de Jesús y sus consejos a 'señoras y demás mujeres.'" *Hispania Sacra* 127 (2011): 103–31.

Candau Chacón, María Luisa. "Las mujeres y las emociones en la Edad Moderna." In *El siglo XVIII en femenino: Las mujeres en el Siglo de las Luces*, edited by Manuel-Reyes García Hurtado, 113–50. Madrid: Síntesis, 2016.

Cantero Rosales, María Ángeles. "De 'perfecta casada' a 'ángel del hogar' o la construcción del arquetipo femenino en el XIX." *Revista Electrónica de Estudios Filológicos* 14 (2007).

Cantos Casenave, Marieta. "Entre la tertulia y la imprenta, la palabra encendida de una patriota andaluza, Frasquita Larrea (1775–1838)." In *Heroínas y patriotas: Mujeres de 1808*, edited by Irene Castells Oliván, Gloria Espigado Tocino, and María Cruz Romeo Mateo, 269–94. Madrid: Cátedra, 2009.

Cantos Casenave, Marieta. "La Literatura femenina en la Guerra de Independencia: A la ciudadanía por el patriotismo." *Revista HMiC* 8 (2010): 33–48.

Cantos Casenave, Marieta. "Mujeres en el Primer Liberalismo." In *La Constitución de 1812: Clave del liberalismo en Andalucía*, edited by Alberto Ramos Santana, 83–119. Seville, Spain: FPACEA, Junta de Andalucía, 2012.

Capel Martínez, Rosa María. "Mujer y educación en el Antiguo Régimen." *Historia de la Educación: Revista interuniversitaria* 26 (2007): 85–110.

Capel Martínez, Rosa María. "Preludio de una emancipación: la emergencia de la mujer ciudadana." *Cuadernos de Historia Moderna* 6 (2007): 155–79.

Capel Martínez, Rosa María, and Margarita Ortega. "La familia en la Edad Moderna." *Arenal: Revista de historia de las mujeres* 13, no. 1 (2006).

Cardozo Uzcátegui, Alejandro. "El lobby cisatlántico del cacao. La Real Compañía Guipuzcoana de Caracas y el poder vasco en la provincia de Venezuela." In *Recuperando el Norte: Empresas, capitales y proyectos atlánticos en la economía imperial hispánica*, edited by Alberto Angulo Morales y Álvaro Aragón Ruano, 195–216. Bilbao: UPV/EHU, 2016.

Castellanos, Gabriela. "Género, poder y postmodernidad: hacia un feminismo de la solidaridad." In *Desde las orillas de la política: Género y poder en América Latina*, edited by Lola G. Luna and Mercedes Vilanova, 21–48. Barcelona: Universidad de Barcelona, 1996.

Cava Mesa, Begoña. "Enlightenment figure, trader and diplomat: The historical contribution of Diego de Gardoqui to the Independence of the United States." In *Recovered Memories: Spain, New Orleans and the Support for the American Revolution*, edited by José Manuel Guerrero Acosta, 119–30. Madrid: Iberdrola, 2018.

Cava Mesa, María Jesús. *Un paseo por la historia de Bilbao*. Bilbao: Universidad de Deusto, 2008.

Cerdá Crespo, Jorge. *Conflictos coloniales: La Guerra de los Nueve Años 1739–1748*. Alicante, Spain: Universidad de Alicante, 2010.

Chambers, Sarah C. "¿Actoras políticas o ayudantes abnegadas? Repensando las actitudes hacia las mujeres durante las guerras de independencia hispanoamericana." In *L'Atlantíque Révolutionnaire*, edited by Clément Thibaud, Gabriel Entin, Alejandro Gómez, and Federica Morelli, 301–31. Bécherel: Les Perséides Editions, 2013.

Cherpak, Evelyn. "The Participation of Women in the Wars for Independence in Northern South America 1810–1824." *Minerva* 11, no. 3 (1993): 1–14.

Cid Carmona, Víctor J. "La Gaceta de México y la promoción de impresos españoles durante la primera mitad del siglo XVIII." *Titivillus* 1 (2015): 421–30.

Cierbide Martinena, Ricardo. "La Compañía Guipuzcoana de Caracas y los vascos en Venezuela durante el siglo XVIII." *Revista Internacional de Estudios Vascos* 42, no. 1 (1997): 63–75.

Ciriza Jofré, Alejandra. "Genealogías feministas: Sobre mujeres, revoluciones e Ilustración; Una mirada desde el Sur." *Estudios Feministas* 20, no. 3 (2012): 613–33.

Ciriza Jofré, Alejandra. "Pensar el bicentenario: Una lectura feminista sobre colonialidad, mujeres y emancipación." *Kairos: Revista de Temas sociales* 38 (2016): 118–25.

Clark, Katherine. "Visible Negotiations: Widowhood as a Category for Assessing Women's Lives and Work in Early Modern Europe." *Gender & History* 21, no. 1 (2009): 190–95.

Cogliano, Francis D., and Kirsten E. Phimister. *Revolutionary America, 1763–1815: A Source Book*. London: Taylor & Francis Group, 2010.

Corbalán De Celis y Durán, Juan. "Sobre la Expedición del marqués de la Romana y otros hechos de armas." (undated): 1–16.

Crawford, Katherine. "Revisiting Monarchy: Women and the Prospects for Power." *Journal of Women's History* 24, no. 1 (2012): 160–71.

Davies, Catherine, Claire Brewster, and Hilary Owen. *South American Independence: Gender, Politics, Text*. Liverpool, UK: Liverpool University Press, 2011.

Delgado, Luisa Elena, Pura Fernández, and Jo Labanyi. "Cartografía de las emociones en la cultura española contemporánea: teorías, prácticas y contextos culturales." In *La cultura de las emociones y las emociones en la cultura española contemporánea (siglos XVIII–XXI)*, edited by Luisa Elena Delgado, Pura Fernández, and Jo Labanyi, 9–33. Madrid: Cátedra, 2018.

Desplat, Christian. "Fiscalité et sédition à Bayonne et en Labourd." *Bulletin de la Société Sciences, Lettres et Arts de Bayonne* 132 (1976): 137–55.

Díaz de Durana, José Ramón. "La hidalguía universal en el País Vasco: Tópicos sobre sus orígenes y causas de su desigual generalización." *Cuadernos de Alzate* 31 (2004): 49–64.

Diccionario de Autoridades. Madrid: Real Academia Española, 1726–39.

Domínguez Martín, Rafael. *Cántabros en México: Historia de un éxito colectivo*. Santander, Spain: Gobierno de Cantabria, 2005.

Domínguez Nárez, Freddy. "Nación, pensamiento e intelligentsia en el movimiento de independencia de 1810 en México." *América: Cahiers du CRICCAL* 41 (2012): 43–50.

Dop, Pierre. "Une émeute de femmes à St-Jean-de-Luz en 1726." *Gure herria* 12 (1932): 267–73.

Duhet, Paule-Marie. *Las mujeres y la Revolución (1789–1794)*. Barcelona: Península, 1974.

Echeberria Ayllón, Iker. *Basque Women's Education in the 18th Century: An Atlantic Issue*. Reno: Center for Basque Studies, University of Nevada, 2023.

Echeberria Ayllón, Iker. *La plata embustera: Emociones y divorcio en la Guipúzcoa del siglo XVIII*. Bilbao: UPV/EHU, 2017.

Elliott, John H. *España, Europa y el mundo de ultramar (1500–1800)*. Madrid: Taurus, 2010.

Elliott, John H. *Imperios del mundo atlántico: España y Gran Bretaña en América, 1492–1830*. Madrid: Taurus, 2006.

Enciso Recio, Luis Miguel. *Las Sociedades Económicas en el Siglo de las Luces*. Madrid: Real Academia de la Historia, 2010.

Enríquez Fernández, José Carlos, and Javier Enríquez Fernández. "Comportamientos populares durante las machinadas vascas: Moral patibular y orden tradicional." In *II Congreso de Historia de Euskal Herria*, 341–48. San Sebastián: Txertoa, 1988.

Enríquez Fernández, José Carlos. "Cultura popular, Charivari y fiesta: Los procesos de regulación represiva de las tradiciones lúdicas de las clases plebeyas vizcaínas (siglos XVII–XIX)." *Zainak: Cuadernos de Antropología-Etnografía* 26 (2004): 525–45.

Erdozain Azpilikueta, Pilar, and Fernando Mikelarena Peña. "Algunas consideraciones en torno a la investigación del régimen de herencia troncal en la Euskal Herria tradicional." *Vasconia* 28 (1991): 71–91.

Espigado Tocino, Gloria. "Europeas y españolas contra Napoleón. Un estudio comparado." *Revista HMiC* 8 (2010): 49–63.

Espigado Tocino, Gloria. "Mujeres y ciudadanía: Del Antiguo Régimen a la Revolución Liberal." *Revista HMiC* 1 (2003): 171–193.

Espigado Tocino, Gloria. "Las mujeres y la política durante la Guerra de la Independencia." *Ayer* 86, no. 2 (2012): 67–88.

Espigado Tocino, Gloria. "Pasiones políticas: la representación de la mujer política en el siglo XIX." *Historia social* 81 (2015): 151–168.

Farge, Arlette. "La historia de las mujeres: Cultura y poder de las mujeres; Ensayo de historiografía." *Historia Social* 5 (1989): 79–101.

Fattaccia, Irene. "The Resilience and Boomerang Effect of Chocolate: A Product's Globalization and Commodification." In *Global Goods and the Spanish Empire, 1492–1824: Circulation, Resistance and Diversity*, edited by Bethany Aram and Bartolomé Yun-Casalilla, 255–73. London: Palgrave Macmillan, 2014.

Fernández Fonseca, María Jesús, and Ana Isabel Prado Antúnez. "Roles femeninos en la Bizkaia del siglo XIX: Aproximación a la situación de la mujer en el mundo laboral en ámbitos pesqueros urbanos." *Itsas Memoria* 3 (2000): 277–87.

Fernández García, Elena. "Transgresión total y transgresión parcial en las defensoras de la patria." *Mélanges de la Casa de Velázquez* 38 (2008): 135–54.

Fernández González, Fernando. "Castilla, Sevilla y el País Vasco en la segunda mitad del siglo XVIII." *Itsas Memoria. Revista de Estudios Marítimos del País Vasco* 4 (2003): 287–95.

Fernández González, Fernando. *Comerciantes vascos en Sevilla, 1650–1700*. Vitoria-Gasteiz, Spain: Diputación de Sevilla/Gobierno Vasco, 2000.

Franco Rubio, Gloria. "La contribución literaria de Moratín y otros hombres de letras al modelo de mujer doméstica." *Cuadernos de Historia Moderna* 6 (2007): 221–54.

Franco Rubio, Gloria. "El ejercicio del poder en la España del siglo XVIII." *Mélanges de la Casa de Velázquez* 35, no. 1 (2005): 1–20.

Fraser, Ronald. *La maldita guerra de España: Historia social de la Guerra de la Independencia, 1808–1814*. Barcelona: Crítica, 2006.

Frasquet, Ivana. "Actrices en la independencia de México: Buscando su lugar en la Historia." In *Jamás ha llovido reyes del cielo: De independencias, revoluciones y liberalismos en Iberoamérica*, edited by Ivana Frasquet, 209–22. Quito: Corporación Editorial Nacional, 2013.

Gálvez Ruiz, María Ángeles. "La construcción del nuevo Estado y la cuestión de las mujeres en México." *Chronica Nova* 38 (2012): 125–50.

Gárate Ojanguren, Montserrat. "Las cuentas de la Real Compañía Guipuzcoana de Caracas." *Moneda y Crédito* 153 (1980): 49–75.

Gárate Ojanguren, Montserrat. *La Real Compañía Guipuzcoana de Caracas*. San Sebastián: Sociedad Guipuzcoana de Ediciones y Publicaciones, 1990.

Gárate Ojanguren, Montserrat. "Remesas de capitales mexicanos a Europa en el siglo XIX: La participación vasca." In *Los vascos en las regiones de México: Siglos XVI–XX*, edited by Amaya Garritz, 281–94. México: UNAM, Tomo I, 1996.

García Fuentes, Lutgardo. "La crisis del siglo XVII y las remesas de caudales indianos desde Sevilla para el País Vasco." *Archivo hispalense: Revista histórica, literaria y artística* 84–255 (2001): 27–42.

García Fuentes, Lutgardo. *Los peruleros y el comercio de Sevilla con las Indias, 1580–1630*. Sevilla: Universidad de Sevilla, 1997.

García Fuentes, Lutgardo. "Los vascos en la Carrera de Indias en la Edad Moderna: una minoría dominante." *Temas Americanistas* 16 (2003): 29–49.

García Hurtado, M. "Mujeres y militares en el siglo XVIII: De discursos teóricos y realidad práctica." In *El siglo XVIII en femenino: Las mujeres en el Siglo de las Luces*, edited by M. García Hurtado, 327–436. Madrid: Síntesis, 2016.

García Jordán, Pilar, and Gabriela Dalla-Corte Caballero, "Mujeres y sociabilidad política en la construcción de los Estados nacionales." In *Historia de las mujeres en España y América Latina*, edited by Isabel Morant Deusa, 559–83. Madrid: Cátedra, Vol. 3, 2006.

García López, Ana Belén. "La participación de las mujeres en la independencia hispanoamericana a través de los medios de comunicación." *Historia y Comunicación Social* 16 (2011): 33–49.

García Rodríguez, María José. "La figura de la mujer en Lizardi: *Noches Tristes y Día Alegre y Don Catrín de la Fachenda*." *Cartaphilus: Revista de investigación y crítica estética* 13 (2014): 154–75.

García-Abásolo, Antonio. "Cofradías y hospitales de Filipinas (siglos XVI–XVIII)." In *Devoción, paisanaje e identidad: Las cofradías y congregaciones de naturales en España y en América (siglos XVI–XIX)*, edited by Óscar Álvarez Gila, Alberto Angulo Morales, and Jon Ander Ramos Martínez, 57–80. Bilbao: UPV/EHU, 2014.

García-Ayluardo, Clara. "El milagro de la Virgen: El desarrollo de los vascos como grupo de poder en la Nueva España." In *IV Seminario de Historia de la Real Sociedad Bascongada de los Amigos del País: "La RSBAP y Méjico,"* vol. 1, 439–57. Donostia–San Sebastián: RSBAP, 1993.

García-Prieto, Elisa. "La gestión femenina del patrimonio nobiliar: Doña Teresa de Saavedra y Zúñiga, condesa de Villalonso; Una aristócrata en los reinados de Felipe II y Felipe III." *Cuadernos de Historia Moderna* 41, no. 1 (2016): 109–28.

Gargallo, Francesca. "Las mujeres, sus ideas, sus escritos y sus actos en la Independencia nuestroamericana." In *Coloquio Políticas de la Alteridad*, 1–5. México: Universidad Autónoma de la Ciudad–Plantel del Valle de México, 2010.

Garmendia Arruebarrena, José. *Cádiz, los vascos y la carrera de Indias*. San Sebastián: Eusko Ikaskuntza, 1989.

Garmendia Arruebarrena, José. "La Real Compañía Guipuzcoana de Caracas y su contribución en Sevilla." *Cuadernos de Sección, Eusko Ikaskuntza, Sociedad de Estudios Vascos* 8 (1986): 48–58.

Garrido Asperó, María José. "Entre hombres te veas: Las mujeres de Pénjamo y la revolución de independencia." In *Disidencia y disidentes en la historia de México*, edited by Felipe Castro and Marcela Terrazas, 169–90. México: UNAM, 2003.

Girard, Philippe. "Rebels with a Cause: Women in the Haitian War of Independence, 1802–04." *Gender & History* 21, no. 1 (2009): 60–85.

Gomis Coloma, Juan. "Romances conyugales: Buenas y malas esposas en la literatura popular del siglo XVIII." *Tiempos Modernos* 18, no. 1 (2009): 1–26.

Gonzalbo Aizpuru, Pilar. "Por decisión o necesidad: La jefatura femenina en los hogares de México virreinal." *Revista de Historiografía* 26 (2017): 47–66.

Gonzalbo Aizpuru, Pilar. "La educación colonial: Una mirada reflexiva." *Revista Historia de la Educación Latinoamericana* 2 (2000): 180–88.

González Dios, Estíbaliz. "Gipuzkoa en la primera globalización (ss. XVI–XVIII)." In *Síntesis de la Historia de Gipuzkoa*, edited by Álvaro

Aragón Ruano and Iker Echeberria Ayllón, 269-362. Donostia: Diputación Foral de Gipuzkoa, 2017.

González, Maya. "La gabelle en Basse-Navarre: La saline d'Ugarre à l'époque de Louis XIV (1683-1692)." *Euskonews* 338 (2016).

Gorosabel, Pablo. *Noticias de las cosas memorables de Guipúzcoa.* Bilbao: La Gran Enciclopedia Vasca, 1972.

Gracia Rivas, Manuel. "En torno a la biografía de Blas de Lezo." *Itsas Memoria: Revista de Estudios Marítimos del País Vasco* 7 (2012): 487-522.

Guerrero Acosta, José Manuel. *Memorias de soldados españoles durante la Guerra de la Independencia (1806-1815).* Madrid: Ministerio de Defensa, Subdirección General de Documentación y Publicaciones, 2009.

Guzmán Pérez, Moisés. "Gertrudis Bocanegra y el Proceso de Construcción de la Heroína en México." In *Las mujeres en la Independencia de América Latina,* edited by Sara Beatriz Guardia, 59-73. Lima: CEMHAL, 2010.

Hernández Pérez, José Santos. "La manifestación de la Ilustración a través de los 'prospectos' de la prensa hispanoamericana." *El Argonauta español* 14 (2017).

Hernández Torres, Yelopattli. "Entre mesura y coquetería: Ilustración, prensa y maternidad en la Nueva España." *Forma: Revista d'estudis comparatius; Art, literatura, pensament* 12 (2015): 53-66.

Hernández Torres, Yelopattli. "Melindrosas, bárbaras y maternales: El oficio de las parteras en la discusión periodística de la 'Gaceta de México' y el 'Diario de México.'" *Letras Femeninas* 40, no. 2 (2014): 63-77.

Herzog, Tamar. "Private Organizations as Global Networks in Early Modern Spain and Spanish America." In *The Collective and the Public in Latin America: Cultural Identities and Political Order,* edited by Luis Roniger and Tamar Herzog, 117-33. Brighton, UK: Sussex Academic Press, 2000.

Hidle, Steve. "The Shaming of Margaret Knowley: Gossip, Gender and the Experience of Authority in Early Modern England." *Continuity and Change* 9, no. 3 (1994): 391-419.

Hilton Stow, Sylvia Lyn. "El conflicto anglo-español en Florida: Utopía y realismo en la política española, 1732-39." *Quinto centenario* 5 (1983): 97-130.

Hume, David. *Tratado de la naturaleza humana.* Madrid: Editorial Nacional, 1981.

Iglesias, Carmen. *Razón, sentimiento y utopía*. Barcelona: Galaxia Gutenberg, 2006.

Imízcoz Beunza, José María, ed. *Casa, familia y sociedad (País Vasco, España y América, siglos XV–XIX)*. Leioa, Spain: UPV/EHU, 2004.

Iñurrategui Rodríguez, José María. "Matxinada: El fuero y sus lecturas en la Guipúzcoa del Setecientos." In *El mundo hispánico en el Siglo de las Luces*, vol. 2, 805–16. Madrid: Universidad Complutense, 1996.

Jiménez Codinach, Guadalupe. "Algunos miembros de la Real Sociedad Bascongada y sus descendientes, amigos de la Independencia de la Nueva España." In *IV Seminario de Historia de la Real Sociedad Bascongada de los Amigos del País: "La RSBAP y Méjico,"* vol. 2, 841–69. Donostia–San Sebastián: RSBAP, 1993.

Johnson, Robert, and Maite Zubiaurre. *Antropología del pensamiento feminista español*. Madrid: Cátedra, 2012.

Jovellanos, Gaspar Melchor de. *Diarios*. Edited by Julio Somoza. Oviedo, Spain: Instituto de Estudios Asturianos, 1955.

Juliano, Dolores. *Excluidas y marginales*. Madrid: Cátedra, 2004.

La Real Sociedad Bascongada y América. Madrid: Fundación BBVA, 1992.

Ladd, Doris M. *La nobleza mexicana en la época de la independencia, 1780–1826*. Mexico City: Fondo de Cultura Económica, 1984.

Laffont, Jean-Luc. "Les femmes dans les revoltes populaires en France a l'époque moderne." *Memoires de l'Académie des sciences, inscriptions et belles lettres de Toulouse* 177 (2016): 163–82.

Lafon, Jean-Marc. "San Sebastián (1813): Bloqueos, sitios y destrucción." In *Los sitios en la Guerra de la Independencia: La lucha en las ciudades*, edited by Gonzalo Butrón Prida and Pedro Víctor Rújula López, 335–56. Madrid: Sílex, 2012.

Lafourcade, Maite. "L'autonomie administrative du Pays Basque de France sous l'Ancien Regime." *Boletín JADO* 19 (2010): 111–39.

Lamikiz, Xabier. "La matxinada de 1718 y su trasfondo socioeconómico." In *Una década prodigiosa: Beligerancia y negociación entre la Corona y las provincias vascas (1717–1728)*, edited by Álvaro Aragón Ruano and Alberto Angulo Morales, 95–123. Bilbao: UPV/EHU, 2019.

Landavazo, Marco Antonio. "La fidelidad al rey: Donativos y préstamos novohispanos para la guerra contra Napoleón." *HMex* 48, no. 3 (1999): 493–521.

Langue, Fréderique. *Los señores de Zacatecas: Una aristocracia minera del siglo XVIII novohispano.* Mexico City: Fondo de Cultura Económica, 1999.

Lara Ródenas, Manuel José de. "Un modelo ilustrado de educación para la mujer: José Isidoro Morales y la hija de José de Mazarredo." In *Las mujeres y el honor en la Europa Moderna,* edited by María Luisa Candau Chacón, 139–61. Huelva, Spain: Universidad de Huelva, 2014.

Larrañaga, Koldo. "Oihenart y el tema de los orígenes vascos." *Vasconia* 14 (1996): 115–43.

Larrinaga Rodríguez, Carlos. *San Sebastián, 1813: Historia y Memoria.* Donostia: Hiria Liburuak, 2013.

Lavrin, Asunción, ed. *Latin American Women: Historical Perspectives.* Westport, CT: Greenwood Press, 1978.

Lema Pueyo, José Ángel. "De 'Ipuzkoa' a la hermandad de villas de Gipuzkoa (ss. VI–VX)." In *Síntesis de la Historia de Gipuzkoa,* edited by Álvaro Aragón Ruano and Iker Echeberria Ayllón, 208–10. Donostia: Diputación Foral de Gipuzkoa, 2017.

León, Fray Luis de. *La Perfecta Casada.* Salamanca: Tomás de Alva librero, 1603.

López-Cordón, María Victoria. *Condición femenina y razón ilustrada: Josefa Amar y Borbón.* Zaragoza, Spain: Universidad de Zaragoza, 2006.

López-Cordón, María Victoria. "El espejo palatino o la malla de las damas: ¿Sociabilidad cortesana o cultura política?" In *El siglo XVIII en femenino: Las mujeres en el Siglo de las Luces,* edited by Manuel García Hurtado, 79–112. Madrid: Síntesis, 2016.

Lougee, Carolyn C. "'Its Frequent Visitor': Death at Boarding School in Early Modern Europe." In *Women's Education in Early Modern Europe: A History, 1500–1800,* edited by Barbara J. Whitehead. New York: Garland, 1999.

Ludlow Wiechers, Leonor. "Los vascos-mexicanos ante los gobiernos independientes: Relaciones financieras y políticas." In *IV Seminario de Historia de la Real Sociedad Bascongada de los Amigos del País: "La RSBAP y Méjico,"* vol. 1, 905–24. Donostia–San Sebastián: RSBAP, 1993.

Luque Alcaide, Elisa. "Asociacionismo vasco en la Nueva España: Modelo étnico-cultural." In *Los vascos en las regiones de México: Siglos XVI–XX*, edited by Amaya Garritz, vol. 2, 67–86. México: UNAM, 1996.

Luque Alcaide, Elisa. "La cofradía de Aránzazu de México (1681–1861): Continuidad de un proyecto." In *Devoción, paisanaje e identidad: Las cofradías y congregaciones de naturales en España y en América (siglos XVI–XIX)*, edited by Óscar Álvarez Gila, Alberto Angulo Morales, and Jon Ander Ramos Martínez, 227–46. Bilbao: UPV/EHU, 2014.

Luque Alcaide, Elisa. "Recursos de la Cofradía de Aránzazu de México ante la corona (1729–1763)." *Revista de Indias* 56, no. 206 (1996): 205–19.

Luque Alcaide, Elisa. "Relaciones intercontinentales de la Cofradía de Aránzazu de México." In *IV Seminario de Historia de la Real Sociedad Bascongada de los Amigos del País: "La RSBAP y Méjico,"* vol. 1, 459–81. Donostia–San Sebastián: RSBAP, 1993.

Madariaga Orbea, José. *Sociedad y Lengua Vasca en los siglos XVII y XVIII*. Bilbao: Euskailtzaindia, 2014.

Manrique, Cayetano, and Amalio Marichalar. *Historia de la legislación y recitaciones del Derecho Civil de España*. Vol. 8. Madrid: Imprenta Nacional, 1865.

Mantecón Movellán, Tomás Antonio. "El peso de la infrajudicialidad en el control del crimen durante la Edad Moderna." *Estudis. Revista de historia moderna* 28 (2002): 43–76.

Manzanos Arreal, Paloma, and Francisca Vives Casas. *La vida cotidiana de las mujeres en la Vitoria de los siglos XVIII y XIX*. Vitoria-Gasteiz, Spain: Ayuntamiento de Vitoria-Gasteiz, 2005.

Manzanos Arreal, Paloma, and Francisca Vives Casas. *Las mujeres en Vitoria-Gasteiz a lo largo de los siglos: Recorridos y biografías*. Vitoria-Gasteiz, Spain: Ayuntamiento de Vitoria-Gasteiz, 2001.

Martínez de Isasti, Lope. *Compendio historial de Guipúzcoa*. Bilbao: La Gran Enciclopedia Vasca, 1972.

Martínez I. Álvarez, Patrícia-Victòria. "Memoria feminista para pensar a Manuela Sáenz: Un recorrido por su política y sus territorios." *Debate Feminista* 65 (2023): 1–25.

Martínez Martínez, María del Carmen. "Cartas privadas de emigrantes en pleitos civiles." In *Cinco Siglos de Cartas: Historia y prácticas epistolares en las épocas moderna y contemporánea*, edited by Antonio Castillo Gómez and Verónica Sierra Blas, 187–202. Huelva, Spain: Universidad de Huelva, 2014.

Martín-Valdepeñas Yagüe, Elisa. "'Mis señoras traidoras': Las afrancesadas, una historia olvidada." *Revista HMiC* 8 (2010): 79–108.

Mata Montes de Oca, María Cristina. "Mujeres en el límite del periodo virreinal." In *Historia de las mujeres en México*, 47–67. Mexico City: Instituto Nacional de Estudios Históricos de las Revoluciones de México, 2015.

Mateos Varona, David. *Cartas desde Florida: Manuel Joaquín de Montiano, bilbaíno y gobernador de Florida (1739–1749) y de Panamá (1749–1759)*. Bilbao: Universidad de Deusto, Manuscript, 2009.

McCaa, Robert. "La viuda viva del México borbónico: sus voces, variedades y vejaciones." In *Familias novohispanas, siglos XVI al XIX*, edited by Pilar Gonzalbo Aizpuru, 299–324. Mexico City: Colegio de México, 1991.

McClelland, Averil E. *The Education of Women in the United States*. New York: Gerland, 1992.

Melón Jiménez, Miguel Ángel. *Los tentáculos de la Hidra: Contrabando y militarización del orden público en España (1784–1800)*. Madrid: Sílex, 2009.

Méndez Reyes, Salvador. "Los Fagoaga: magnates de las minas zacatecanas y la independencia." In *Los vascos en las regiones de México, siglos XVI–XX*, edited by Amaya Garritz, vol. 5, 297–308. Mexico City: UNAM, 1999.

Mendieta Garrrote, Eva. "Del silencio al alboroto: el control del lenguaje de la mujer en la Edad Moderna." *Memoria y Civilización* 18 (2015): 127–62.

Mendieta Garrrote, Eva. *In Search of Catalina de Erauso: The National and Sexual Identity of the Lieutenant Nun*. Reno: Center for Basque Studies, University of Nevada, 2019.

Mendieta Garrote, Eva, and Isabel Molina Martos. "Revuelta social en la Edad Moderna europea: Participación y discurso de las mujeres en la Matxinada de la sal de Bilbao (1631–1634)." *Vasconia* 42 (2018): 5–27.

Mojica, Sarah de. "La leyenda de Policarpa Salavarrieta." In *Entre el olvido y el recuerdo: iconos, lugares de memoria y cánones de la historia y la literatura en Colombia*, edited by Carlos Rincón, Sarah de Mojica, and Liliana Gómez, 139–78. Bogotá: Editorial Pontificia Universidad Javeriana, 2010.

Molina Petit, Cristina. *Dialéctica feminista de la Ilustración*. Barcelona: Anthropos, 1994.

Monreal Huegun, Beatriz. *Guipúzcoa en escritores y viajeros*. San Sebastián: Caja de Ahorros de Guipúzcoa, 1983.

Mora Valcárcel, Carmen de. "Una mujer de armas tomar: La coronela Juan de Azurduy." In *Milicia y sociedad ilustrada en España y América*, 501–8. Madrid: Deimos, 2003.

Morales, José Isidoro. *Comentarios de Don José Isidoro Morales al excelentísimo señor Don José de Mazarredo sobre la enseñanza de su hija*. Madrid: Imprenta de Don Gabriel de Sacha, 1796.

Morán, Daniel. "Las 'jacobinas de la revolución': Imágenes y representaciones de la mujer en la prensa de Buenos Aires (1810–1816)." *Tiempos Modernos* 37 (2018): 148–60.

Morán, Daniel, and Montserratt Rivera. "Libertadoras en tiempos de Revolución: La participación de las mujeres en la Independencia del Perú y América Latina." *Desde el Sur* 13, no. 1 (2021): 1–22.

Morant Deusa, Isabel. "El hombre y la mujer en el matrimonio: Moral y sentimientos familiares." In *Familia y organización social en Europa y América, siglos XV–XX*, edited by Francisco Chacón Jiménez, Juan Hernández Franco, and Francisco García González, 185–209. Murcia, Spain: Universidad de Murcia, 2007.

Morant Deusa, Isabel. "Mujeres ilustradas en el debate de la educación: Francia y España." *Cuadernos de Historia Moderna*, anejo 3 (2004): 59–84.

Morant Deusa, Isabel. "¿Qué es una mujer? O la condición sentimental de la mujer." In *Mujeres en la historia del pensamiento*, edited by Rosa María Rodríguez Magda, 147–52. Barcelona: Anthropos, 1997.

Moreno Almárcegui, José Antonio, and Ana Zabalza Seguín. *El origen histórico de un sistema de heredero único: El prepirineo navarro, 1540–1739*. Pamplona, Spain: Rialp, 1999.

Moring, Beatrice, and Richard Wall. *Widows in European Economy and Society, 1600–1920*. Woodbridge, UK: Boydell Press, 2017.

Munibe, Xabier María de. "Historia de la Real Sociedad Bascongada." *Revista Internacional de Estudios Vascos* 22 (1931): 443–82.

Muriel, Josefina. "Los arzobispos vascos y sus obras dedicadas a las mujeres novohispanas." In *Los vascos en las regiones de México: Siglos XVI–XX*, edited by Amaya Garritz, vol. 4, 55–72. Mexico City: UNAM, 1999.

Muriel, Josefina. "Las instituciones educativas de los vascos para mujeres de México: Época Colonial." In *IV Seminario de Historia de la Real Sociedad Bascongada de los Amigos del País: "La RSBAP y Méjico,"* vol. 1, 316–423. Donostia–San Sebastián: RSBAP, 1993.

Muriel, Josefina. "La música en las instituciones femeninas existente en el Archivo Histórico del Colegio de San Ignacio de Loyola, Vizcaínas." In *Una Mujer, Un Legado, Una Historia: Homenaje a Josefina Muriel*, 221–26. Mexico City: Universidad Autónoma de México, 2000.

Muriel, Josefina. *La sociedad novohispana y sus colegios de niñas*. Tomo 2, *Fundaciones del siglo XVII y XVIII*. Mexico City: UNAM, 2004.

Muriel, Josefina. "La transmisión cultural en la familia criolla novohispana." In *Familias novohispanas, siglos XVI al XIX*, edited by Pilar Gonzalbo Aizpuru, 109–22. Mexico City: Colegio de México, 1991.

Murugarrren Zamora, Luis. *1813, San Sebastián incendiada: Británicos y portugueses*. San Sebastián: Sociedad Guipuzcoana de Ediciones y Publicaciones, 1993.

Nash, Margaret A. *Women's Education in the United States, 1780–1840*. New York: Palgrave Macmillan, 2005.

Nash, Margaret A. "Young Ladies' Academy of Philadelphia." In *Historical Dictionary of Women's Education in the United States*, ed. Linda Eisenmann, 498–99. Westport, CT: Greenwood Press, 1998.

Nausia Primoulier, Amaia. "Las viudas y las segundas nupcias en la Europa moderna: Últimas aportaciones." *Memoria y Civilización* 9 (2006): 233–60.

Nicolas, Jean. *La rébellion française: Mouvements populaires et conscience sociale*. Paris: Gallimard, 2008.

Notitia Vasconiae: Historiadores, juristas y pensadores políticos de Vasconia; Antigüedad, Edad Media y Moderna. Madrid: Fundación Iura Vasconiae, Marcial Pons, 2019.

Oliván Santaliestra, Laura. "Gobierno, género y legitimidad en las regencias de Isabel de Borbón y Mariana de Austria." *Historia y política* 31 (2014): 21–48.

Oliván Santaliestra, Laura. "Por una historia diplomática de las mujeres en la Edad Moderna." In *Autoridad, poder e influencia. Mujeres que hacen historia*, edited by H. Gallego Franco and M. C. García Herrero, 61–77. Baracelona: Icaria, 2017.

Oliveri Korta, Oihane. "El gran gobierno de la dicha señora. Economía doméstica y mujer en el estamento hidalgo guipuzcoano." In *Economía doméstica y redes sociales en el Antiguo Régimen*, edited by José María Imízcoz Beunza and Oihane Oliveri Korta, 89–118. Madrid: Sílex, 2010.

Oliveri Korta, Oihane. "Mujer, casa y familia en el estamento hidalgo guipuzcoano del siglo XVI." *Arenal* 13, no. 1 (2006): 39–59.

O'Phelan Godoy, Scarlett. "Las viudas de empresarios mineros en el Perú borbónico." *Histórica* 27, no. 2 (2003): 357–81.

Ortega del Cerro, Pablo. "Forging Social Links through the Navy: Elite Family Connections across the Spanish Atlantic, 1750–1810." *Atlantic Studies* 17, no. 2 (2020): 206–226.

Ortega López, Margarita. "Estrategias de defensa de las mujeres de la sociedad popular española del siglo XVIII." *Arenal* 5, no. 2 (1998): 277–305.

Otazu, Alfonso de, and José Ramón Díaz de Durana. *El espíritu emprendedor de los vascos*. Madrid: Sílex, 2008.

Palacio Montiel, Celia del. "La participación femenina en la Independencia de México." In *Historia de las mujeres en México*, 69–92. Mexico City: Instituto Nacional de Estudios Históricos de las Revoluciones de México, 2015.

Palacios Fernández, Emilio. *La mujer y las letras en la España del siglo XVIII*. Madrid: Laberinto, 2002.

Palacios Fernández, Emilio. "Proyección de la ilustración vasca en América." *Revista Internacional de Estudios Vascos* 43 (1998): 33–60.

Panera Rico, Carmen María. "La edad de la Ilustración en España. Lazos de fortuna, devoción y saber entre el País Vasco y América." *Itsas Memoria: Revista de Estudios Marítimos del País Vasco* 3 (2000): 711–27.

Pani, Erika. "'Ciudadana y muy ciudadana'? Women and the State in Independent Mexico, 1810–30," *Gender and History* 18-1 (2006): 5-19.

Pascua Sánchez, María José de la. "Una aproximación a la Historia de la familia como espacio de afectos y desafectos: El mundo hispánico del Setecientos." *Chronica Nova* 27 (2000): 131–66.

Pascua Sánchez, María José de la. "La escritura privada y la representación de las emociones." In *Educar los sentimientos y las costumbres: Una mirada desde la historia*, edited by Mónica Bolufer, Carolina Blutrach, and Juan Gomis, 81–107. Zaragoza, Spain: Institución Fernando el Católico, CSIC, 2014.

Pascua Sánchez, María José de la. "Vivir en soledad, vivir en compañía: Las mujeres y el mundo familiar en el siglo XVIII hispánico." In *El siglo XVIII en femenino: Las mujeres en el Siglo de las Luces*, edited by Manuel-Reyes García Hurtado, 151–90. Madrid: Síntesis, 2016.

Pateman, Carole. "Críticas feministas a la dicotomía público/privado." In *Perspectivas feministas en teoría política*, edited by Carme Castells, 31–52. Barcelona: Paidós, 1996.

Pearce, Adrian J. *El comercio británico con Hispanoamérica*. Mexico City: Colegio de México, 2017.

Pélaquier, Élie. "Les mouvements anti-fiscaux en Languedoc d'après les archives de la Cour des Comptes, Aides et Finances de Montpellier (1660–1789)." *Annales du Midi* 111, no. 125 (1999): 5–29.

Peralta Ruiz, Víctor. *Patrones clientes y amigos: El poder burocrático indiano en la España del siglo XVIII*. Madrid: CSIC, 2006.

Perdices de Blas, Luis. "Mujer, educación y mercado de trabajo en el proyecto reformista de Pablo de Olavide." *ICE: Revista de Economía* 852 (2010): 99–111.

Perdices de Blas, Luis. *Pablo de Olavide (1725–1803), el ilustrado*. Madrid: Universidad Complutense, 1993.

Pérez Herrero, Pedro. "Los beneficiarios del reformismo borbónico: Metrópoli versus élites novohispanas." *Historia Mexicana* 41, no. 2 (1991): 207–64.

Pérez Samper, María de los Ángeles. "Espacios y prácticas de sociabilidad en el siglo XVIII: Tertulias, refrescos y cafés de Barcelona." *Cuadernos de Historia Moderna* 26 (2001): 11–55.

Pérez San Vicente, Guadalupe. *Análisis Paleográfico sobre el Acta de Independencia*. Mexico City: UNAM, 1961.

Pérez Vejo, Tomás. "El retrato como arma de poder: La representación de vizcaínos y montañeses en la Nueva España del siglo XVIII." In *Devoción, paisanaje e identidad. Las cofradías y congregaciones de naturales en España y en América (siglos XVI–XIX)*, edited by Óscar

Álvarez Gila, Alberto Angulo Morales, and Jon Ander Ramos Martínez, 289–316. Bilbao: UPV/EHU, 2014.

Pérez-Fuentes Hernández, Pilar. *"Ganadores de pan" y "amas de casa": Otra mirada sobre la industrialización vasca.* Bilbao: UPV/EHU, 2004.

Pescador, Juan Javier. "La familia Fagoaga y los matrimonios en la Ciudad de México en el siglo XVIII." In *Familias novohispanas, siglos XVI a XIX*, edited by Pilar Gonzalbo Aizpuru, 203–26. Mexico City: Colegio de México, 1991.

Pía Taracena, María. "La migración dorada: una familia vizcaína encuentra fama y fortuna en la ciudad de México a finales del siglo XVIII y siglo XIX. El caso de los Bassoco." In *Los vascos en las regiones de México: Siglos XVI–XX*, vol. 4, edited by Amaya Garritz, 217–29. México: UNAM, 1999.

Piquero Zarauz, Santiago. "El siglo XVI, época dorada de los movimientos migratorios guipuzcoanos de media y larga distancia durante la Edad Moderna,". In *La lucha de bandos en el País Vasco, de los Parientes Mayores a la Hidalguía Universal*, edited by José Ramón Díaz de Durana Ortiz de Urbina, 399-423. Bilbao: UPV/EHU, 1998.

Pita Pico, Roger. "Resistencia y reivindicaciones de las mujeres en las guerras de independencia de Colombia: una aproximación a través de sus cartas y reclamaciones." *Arenal* 26, no. 2 (2019): 609–30.

Polo Sánchez, Julio Juan. "Vascos y montañeses. Arte, poder e identidades nacionales en el virreinato de Nueva España." *Acta Artis. Estudis d'Art Modern* 3 (2015): 63–73.

Polónia, Amélia. "El rostro oculto de la aventura de Magalhaes/Elcano: El protagonismo femenino en sociedades marítimas portuguesas en el siglo XVI." In *Más allá del mito y la epopeya: El País Vasco y la expedición Magallanes-Elcano en el contexto de la primera globalización*, edited by A. Angulo, Ó. Álvarez, Á. Aragón, and A. Zaballa, 99–127. Madrid: Dykinson, 2022.

Porres Marijuán, Charo. "Elites, poder provincial y reformismo borbónico en el País Vasco del siglo XVIII." In *Élites y poder en las monarquías ibéricas: Del siglo XVIII al primer liberalismo*, edited by María López Díaz, 129–54. Madrid: Biblioteca Nueva, 2013.

Porres Marijuán, Charo. "El poder y los conflictos sociales." In *Historia del País Vasco. Edad Moderna (siglos XVI–XVIII)*, edited by A. Angulo

Morales, C. Porres Marijuán, and I. Reguera, 237–89. Donostia: Hiria, 2004.

Poska, Allyson M. "The Case for Agentic Gender Norms for Women in Early Modern Europe." *Gender and History* 30, no. 2 (2018): 354–65.

Poska, Allyson M. *Women and Authority in Early Modern Spain: The Peasants of Galicia*. Oxford: Oxford University Press, 2005.

Puleo, Alicia H. *La Ilustración olvidada: La polémica de los sexos en el siglo XVIII*. Barcelona: Anthropos, 1993.

Ramírez Maya, Carmina. "En el prisma de la Independencia: Los vascos en México." In *Los vascos en las Independencias Americanas*, edited by Óscar Álvarez Gila, 217–46. Bogotá: Fundación Centro Vasco Euskal Etxea, 2010.

Ramos y Ramos, Pedro, and Magdalena Rius de la Pola. "Tres momentos en la vida del Colegio de las Vizcaínas." In *Los vascos en las regiones de México: Siglos XVI–XX*, vol. 4, edited by Amaya Garritz, 103–16. Mexico City: UNAM, 1999.

Recarte Barriola, Maite. *Ilustración vasca y renovación educativa: La Real Sociedad Bascongada de los Amigos del País*. Salamanca: Universidad Pontificia de Salamanca, RSBAP, 1990.

Recarte Barriola, Maite. "Ideario pedagógico de la Real Sociedad Bascongada de los Amigos del País, según los discursos de sus Juntas Generales." In *I Seminario de historia de la Real Sociedad Bascongada de los Amigos del País*, 311–22. San Sebastián: RSBAP, 1986.

Rey Castelao, Ofelia. "Las viudas de Galicia a finales del Antiguo Régimen." *Chronica Nova* 34 (2008): 91–122.

Rilova Jericó, Carlos. "Vida de un general de las Guerras Napoleónicas, Gabriel de Mendizábal e Iraeta (1764–1838)." *Boletín de Estudios Históricos de San Sebastián* 45 (2012): 199–248.

Rivera de Jesús, N. "La participación de las mujeres en la Guerra de Independencia de las Trece Colonias." In *X Congreso Virtual sobre Historia de las Mujeres*, 741–57. Jaén, Spain: Archivo Histórico Diocesano de Jaén, 2018.

Robinson, Barry Matthew. "La reclusión de mujeres rebeldes: El recogimiento en la guerra de independencia mexicana, 1810–1819." *Fronteras de la Historia* 15, no. 2 (2010): 225–44.

Robles Do Campo, C. "Los infantes de España bajo la Ley Sálica." *Anales de la Real Academia Matritense de Heráldica y Genealogía* 10 (2007): 305–56.

Rodríguez Mirabal, Adelina. "La España reformista de comienzos del siglo XVIII y la nueva orientación del comercio ultramarino (El caso de la Compañía Guipuzcoana de Caracas)." *Ensayos Históricos: Anuario del Instituto de Estudios Hispánicos* 13 (2001): 39–54.

Rodríguez, Jaime E. "La Revolución Francesa y la Independencia de México." In *La Revolución Francesa en México*, edited by Solange Alberro, Alicia Hernández Chávez, and Elías Trabulse, 137–53. Mexico City: Colegio de México, 1993.

Romeo Mateo, María Cruz. "Españolas en la guerra de 1808: Heroínas recordadas." In *Heterodoxas, guerrilleras y ciudadanas: Resistencias femeninas en la España moderna y contemporánea*, edited by Mercedes Yusta e Ignacio Peiró, 63–83. Zaragoza, Spain: Institución Fernando el Católico, CSIC, 2015.

Romero Peña, Aleix. "Mariano Luis de Urquijo, testigo y protagonista involuntario del motín de la Zamacolada (1804)." *Brocar* 33 (2009): 115–47.

Roquero Ussía, María Rosario. "El convento y la política matrimonial de la burguesía donostiarra." *Boletín de Estudios Históricos de San Sebastián* 47 (2014): 119–45.

Roquero Ussía, María Rosario. "La Real Compañía Guipuzcoana de Caracas: La mujer donostiarra y la emigración a Ultramar (siglo XVIII)." *Boletín de Estudios Históricos de San Sebastián* 48 (2015): 109–82.

Rousseau, Jean-Jacques. *Emilio o de la educación*. Barcelona: Fontanella, 1973.

Ruiz Astiz, Javier. "Cencerradas y matracas en Navarra durante el Antiguo Régimen: funciones y objetivos." *Hispania* 73-245 (2013): 733-60.

Ruiz Astiz, Javier. "Herramientas de transmisión comunitaria: Libelos y pasquines en la Navarra moderna." *Historia y Comunicación Social* 14 (2009): 87–110.

Ruiz Astiz, Javier. "La participación de las mujeres en los desórdenes públicos: Análisis de su presencia en la Navarra moderna." *Sancho el Sabio* 33 (2010): 11–34.

Ruiz de Gordejuela Urquijo, Jesús. "Los vascos y navarros en México en el tránsito de colonia a nación." In *Del espacio cantábrico al mundo americano: Perspectivas sobre migración, etnicidad y retorno*, edited by Óscar Álvarez Gila and Juan Bosco Amores Carredano, 249–63. Bilbao: UPV/EHU, 2015.

Ruiz de Gordejuela Urquijo, Jesús. "Los Voluntarios de Fernando VII de Ciudad de México: ¿Baluarte de la capital y confianza del reino?" *Revista de Indias* 262 (2014): 751–82.

Rustighi, Lorenzo. "The Good Prince or the Good Mother: Reassessing the Question of Gender in Rousseau's Political Theory." *Gender and History* 30, no. 1 (2018): 30–51.

Saladino García, Alberto. "La Real Sociedad Bascongada de los Amigos del País y las publicaciones periódicas del siglo XVIII en Nueva España." In *IV Seminario de Historia de la Real Sociedad Bascongada de los Amigos del País: "La RSBAP y Méjico,"* vol. 2, 729–36. Donostia–San Sebastián: RSBAP, 1993.

Sales Gelabert, Tomeu. "Crítica y teoría feminista: Por una nueva agenda feminista." *Astrolabio: Revista Internacional de Filosofía* 20 (2017): 179–91.

Sánchez Arreseigor, Juan José. *Vascos contra Napoleón*. Madrid: Editorial Actas, 2010.

Sánchez de Madariaga, Elena. "Caridad, devoción e identidad de origen: Las cofradías de naturales y nacionales en el Madrid de la Edad Moderna." In *Devoción, paisanaje e identidad: Las cofradías y congregaciones de naturales en España y en América (Siglos XVI–XIX)*, edited by Óscar Álvarez Gila, Alberto Angulo Morales, and Jon Ander Ramos Martínez, 17–32. Bilbao: UPV/EHU, 2014.

Sánchez Erauskin, Miren. "Plan y ordenanzas de un seminario o casa de educación de señoritas: El proyecto de la Real Sociedad Bascongada de los Amigos del País." In *I Seminario de historia de la Real Sociedad Bascongada de los Amigos del País*, 323–48. San Sebastián: RSBAP, 1986.

Sánchez González, Dolores del Mar. "El virrey Miguel José de Azanza y la conspiración de los machetes ¿Primer intento de independencia mexicana?" In *Una crisis atlántica: España, América y los acontecimientos de 1808*, edited by Concepción Navarro Azcue, Arrigo Amadori, and Miguel Luque Talaván, 29–38. Madrid: Universidad Complutense, 2010.

Sanchís Vidal, Amelia, and María José Ramos Rovi. "Afrancesadas y majas: Presentes en la guerra e invisibles en las Cortes. Análisis feminista." *Raudem: Revista de Estudios de las Mujeres* 2 (2014): 172–89.

Sarabia Viejo, María Justina. "Humanismo y Ciencia: José Antonio de Alzate y las 'Gacetas de Literatura de México' (1788–1795)." In *El Humanismo Español, su proyección en América y Canarias en la época del Humanismo*, edited by A. Martín Rodríguez and G. Santana Henríquez, 287–300. Las Palmas de Gran Canaria, Spain: Universidad de Las Palmas de Gran Canaria, 2006.

Sarrailh, Jean. *La España ilustrada de la segunda mitad del siglo XVIII*. Mexico City: Fondo de Cultura Económica, 1957.

Saura Sánchez, Alfonso. "Acercamiento literario y biográfico a Pedro Ángel de Gorostiza y Cepeda: documentos y pistas sueltas." *Literatura Mexicana* 18, no. 2 (2007): 97–120.

Sazatornil Ruiz, Luis, ed. *Arte y mecenazgo indiano: Del Cantábrico al Caribe*. Gijón, Spain: Ediciones Trea, 2007.

Serra Sánchez, Clara. "El feminismo a principios del siglo XXI: Sobre hechos y derechos en clave ilustrada." In *XLVII Congreso de Filosofía Joven*, 1–10. Murcia, Spain: Universidad de Murcia, 2010.

Sierra, María. "Entre emociones y política: la historia cruzada de la virilidad romántica." *Rúbrica Contemporánea* 4, no. 7 (2015): 11–25.

Sullivan, Constance A. "Las escritoras del siglo XVIII." In *Breve historia feminista de la literatura española (en lengua castellana)*, vol. 4, edited by Iris M. Zavala, 305–30. Barcelona: Anthropos, 1997.

Sullivan, Constance A. "Gender, Text, and Cross-Dressing: The Case of 'Beatriz Cienfuegos' and La Pensadora Gaditana." *Dieciocho* 18, no. 1 (1995): 27–47.

Taxin, Amy. "La participación de la mujer en la Independencia: El caso de Manuela Sáenz." *Procesos: Revista Ecuatoriana de Historia* 14 (1999): 85–113.

Tellechea Idígoras, José Ignacio. "La Cofradía de Nuestra Señora de Aránzazu en la ciudad de México (1681–1794)." In *Las huellas de Aránzazu en América*, edited by Óscar Álvarez Gila and Idoia Arrieta Elizalde, 43–54. Donostia: Lankidetzan, 2004.

Tellechea Idígoras, José Ignacio. *El Colegio de las Vizcaínas de México y el Real Seminario de Vergara*. Vitoria-Gasteiz., Spain: Eusko Jaurlaritza-Gobierno Vasco, 1992.

Tellechea Idígoras, José Ignacio. "El padre Larramendi, S. J., confesor de Mariana de Neoburgo." *Hispania* 28 (1969): 627–70.

Terán Elizondo, María Isabel, and Sonia Ibarra Valdez. "Crítica y ¿defensa? de las mujeres en un 'sermón' satírico novohispano prohibido por la Inquisición (1795)." *Edad de Oro* 38 (2019): 293–314.

Thompson, Edward P. *Tradición, revuelta y conciencia de clase: Estudios sobre la crisis de la sociedad preindustrial*. Barcelona, Crítica, 1984.

Torales Pacheco, María Cristina. *La Compañía de Comercio de Francisco Ignacio de Yraeta (1767–1797)*. Mexico City: IMCE, 1985.

Torales Pacheco, María Cristina. "La familia Yraeta, Yturbe e Ycaza." In *Familias novohispanas, siglos XVI al XIX*, edited by Pilar Gonzalbo Aizpuru, 181–202. Mexico City: Colegio de México, 1991.

Torales Pacheco, María Cristina. *Ilustrados en la Nueva España: Los socios de la Real Sociedad Bascongada de los Amigos del País*. Mexico City: Universidad Iberoamericana, 2001.

Torales Pacheco, María Cristina. "Presencia en México de los socios europeos de la RSBAP." In *La Bascongada y Europa: Actas del V Seminario de Historia de la Real Sociedad Bascongada de los Amigos del País*, edited by Guadalupe Rubio de Urquía and María Montserrat Gárate Ojanguren, 441–62. Donostia–San Sebastián: RSBAP, 1999.

Torales Pacheco, María Cristina. "Los socios de la Real Sociedad Bascongada de los Amigos del País en México." In *IV Seminario de Historia de la Real Sociedad Bascongada de los Amigos del País. "La RSBAP y Méjico,"* vol. 1, 81–116. Donostia–San Sebastián: RSBAP, 1993.

Torales Pacheco, María Cristina. "Tres viudas de la elite novohispana en el siglo XVIII." In *Viudas en la Historia*, 205–27. Mexico, City: CONDUMEX, 2002.

Truchuelo García, Susana. "Fronteras marítimas en la Monarquía de los Habsburgo. El control de la costa cantábrica." *Manuscrits. Revista d'història moderna* 32 (2014): 33–60.

Truchuelo García, Susana. "'Junta de la frontera y junta de la tierra': Una propuesta reformista de Guipúzcoa ante las dificultades del último cuarto del siglo XVI." *Obradoiro de Historia Moderna* 16 (2007): 161–85.

Turiso Sebastián, Jesús. "Emigración, comerciantes y comercio en la región de Veracruz entre 1778–1822." *Naveg@mérica* 22 (2019): 1–25.

Tutino, John. "Breaking New Spain, 1808–1821: Remaking Power, Production and Patriarchy before Iguala." *Mexican Studies* 37, no. 3 (2021): 367–93.

Txueka Isasti, Fernando. "El Colegio de Pilotos Vizcaínos de Cádiz: La otra historia marítima de los vascos; Del Mare Nostrum al Pacífico." *Itsas Memoria: Revista de Estudios Marítimos del País Vasco* 8 (2016): 591–645.

Tyrrell, Ian. "Reflections on the Transnational Turn in United States History: Theory and Practice." *Journal of Global History* 4, no. 3 (2009): 453–74.

Ucelay Da Cal, Enric. "Agustina, la dama del cañón: El topos de la heroína fálica y el invento del patriotismo." In *Heroínas y patriotas: Mujeres de 1808*, edited by Irene Castells Oliván, Gloria Espigado Tocino, and María Cruz Romeo Mateo, 193–268. Madrid: Cátedra, 2009.

Ugalde, Ana Isabel, Pilar Aristizabal, Pablo Lekue, and María Teresa Vizcarra. "Mujeres vascas improvisadoras: Las *bertsolaris* del mundo tradicional (siglos XV–XIX)." *Arenal* 27, no. 1 (2020): 141–72.

Urra Olazabal, Manuela. *La Compañía de María en Bergara: Dos siglos de Historia*. Vitoria-Gasteiz, Spain: Gobierno Vasco, 1999.

Urra Olazabal, Manuela. *La educación de la mujer y la Compañía de María en el País Vasco: Siglos XVIII y XIX*. Orden de la Compañía de María Nuestra Señora: Ediciones Lestonnac, 2016.

Usunáriz Garayoa, Jesús María. "Cartas de amor y cartas de emigrantes como prueba judicial en España (siglos XVI–XVIII)." *Hispanic Research Journal: Iberian and Latin American Studies* 16, no. 14 (2015): 296–310.

Usunáriz Garayoa, Jesús María. "'Nere Andrea, beti memorien daukedana': Amores y desamores de ultramar en el siglo XVIII." In *Navarra y el nuevo mundo*, edited by María del Mar Larraza Micheltorena, 77–96. Pamplona, Spain: Mintzoa, 2016.

Usunáriz Garayoa, Jesús María. "Un aspecto de la emigración navarra al Nuevo Mundo durante el siglo XVIII: las remesas indianas." *Príncipe de Viana* 13 (1991): 383–92.

Valcárcel, Amelia. "Moralización de la política." *Revista del Centro de Estudios Constitucionales* 8 (1991): 147–65.

Valverde Lamsfús, Lola. *Entre el deshonor y la miseria: Infancia abandonada en Guipúzcoa y Navarra; Siglos XVIII y XIX*. Bilbao: Universidad del País Vasco, 1994.

Los vascos y América: Actas de las Jornadas sobre el comercio vasco con América en el siglo XVIII y la Real Compañía Guipuzcoana de Caracas en el II centenario de Carlos II. Bilbao: Fundación Banco de Vizcaya, 1980.

Vega Toscano, Ana. "La música en el espacio femenino del siglo XVIII español." In *El siglo XVIII en femenino: Las mujeres en el Siglo de las Luces*, edited by Manuel-Reyes García Hurtado, 293–304. Madrid: Síntesis, 2016.

Verju, Anne, and Catherine Dhaussy. "De l'action féminine en période de révolte(s) etrévolution(s), 1770–1802." In *Révoltes et révolutions en Europe (Russie incluse) et aux Amériques de 1773 à 1802 en dissertations corrigées*, edited by A. Jollet, 56–71. Paris: Ellipses, 2005.

Veyrin, Philippe. *Les Basques: De Labourd, de Soule et de la Basse Navarre, leur histoire et leurs traditions*. Grenoble, France: Arthaud, 1947.

Vidal-Abarca López, Juan. "Linajes alaveses: Los Aguirre: Marqueses de Montehermoso." *Boletín de la Institución Sancho el Sabio* XIX (1975): 181–244.

Vilalta, María José. "Historia de las mujeres y memoria histórica: Manuela Sáenz interpela a Simón Bolívar (1822–1830)." *European Review of Latin American and Caribbean Studies* 93 (2012): 61–78.

Viñao Frago, Antonio. "La influencia de Campomanes, Olavide y Cabarrús en la educación." In *Historia de la educación en España y América*, edited by B. Delgado Criado, 657–68. Madrid: Morata, 1993.

Vivas Pineda, Gerardo. *La aventura naval de la Compañía Guipuzcoana de Caracas*. Caracas: Fundación Polar, 1998.

Vivas Pineda, Gerardo. "La Compañía Guipuzcoana de Caracas: Los buques y sus hombres." In *Los vascos y América: Actas de las Jornadas sobre el comercio vasco con América en el siglo XVIII y la Real Compañía Guipuzcoana de Caracas en el II centenario de Carlos II*, 307–58. Bilbao: Fundación Banco de Vizcaya, 1980.

Von Wobeser, Gisela. "La Consolidación de Vales Reales como factor determinante de la lucha de Independencia en México, 1804–1808." *HMex* 61, no. 2 (2006): 373–425.

Wiesner-Hanks, Merry E. "Crossing Borders in Transnational Gender History." *Journal of Global History* 6 (2011): 357–79.

Wollstonecraft, Mary. *Vindicación de los derechos de la mujer.* Madrid: Istmo, 2005.

Young, Iris Marion. "Vida política y diferencia de grupo: Una crítica del ideal de ciudadanía universal." In *Perspectivas feministas en teoría política,* edited by Carme Castells, 99–126. Barcelona: Paidós, 1996.

Yturbide, Pierre. "Una émeute des femmes d'Hasparren en 1784." *Revista Internacional de Estudios Vascos* 1 (1908): 195–202.

Zabala Montoya, Mikel. "La rebelión del Estanco de la Sal (Bizkaia, 1631/34): Una revisión." *Boletín de la Real Academia de la Historia* 204, no. 1 (2007): 45–128.

Zabalza Seguín, Ana. "El heredero ideal: Prácticas sucesorias en la Navarra pirenaica durante la Edad Moderna (1550–1725)." In *Actas del Congreso Internacional de la Población: V Congreso de la ADEH,* edited by David Sven Reher Sullivan, 239–50. Logroño, Spain: 1999.

Zárate Toscano, Verónica. "Estrategias familiares de los nobles de origen vasco en la Nueva España." In *Los vascos en las regiones de México. Siglos XVI–XX,* vol. 2, edited by Amaya Garritz, 223–37. México: UNAM, 1999.

Zirón Pérez, Antonio. "Antropología filosófica y afectividad." In *Cultura y afectividad. Aproximaciones antropológicas y filosóficas al estudio de las emociones,* edited by Edith Calderón Rivera and Antonio Zirón Pérez, 11–19. Mexico City: Universidad Autónoma Metropolitana, 2018.

INDEX

Acedo y Sarria, María Pilar, Marquise of Montehermoso, 81
afrancesadas, 82
Aguirre, Ortuño de, Marquis of Montehermoso, 81
Aguirre Ortés de Velasco, José María, 52
Alamán, Lucas, 67, 111
Aldama, Juan, 66
Alegía, María Josefa, 83
Allende, Ignacio, 66
Alocución a las matronas del Socorro (Bolívar), 119–20
Álvarez, Casta, 93
Álvarez, María Tomasa, 88
Álvarez, Martínez I., 142, 148
Alzate, José Antonio de, 68
Alzate y Ramírez, José Antonio de, 50
Amezola, Margarita Zúñiga de, 76
Amorós, Celia, 133
Ángeles Zandaeta, María de los, 129
Aragón, Agustina de, 93
Arana, Enrique de, 8
Aránzazu Brotherhood, 66
Aristiguieta, Josefa, 35
Aroca, Joaquina, 89
Arrazola, Eugenia, 87
Arteche y Moro de Elexabeita, José Gómez, 106
Astiz, Javier Ruiz, 2
Azanza, Miguel José de, 82, 83
Azlor y Echeverz, Ignacia de, 84
Azlor y Villavicencio, Josefa de, Marquise of Ayerbe, 84
Azurduy, Juana de, 89, 91, 127

Baroness of Beniparell, 86
Barre, Poullain de la, 133
Basque country: agriculture, 4; Atlantic-centric economy, 5; female preeminence, 23–28
Basque network in America, 5
Basque women: armed combat, 90–96; in Atlantic Revolutions, 73–96; citizenship exclusion, 131–38; emotions, 27–28; female canons, 47–52; heroines, 103–12; in military, 33–35; Olazabal y Veroiz, María Teresa de, 35–42; punishment suffered by, 126–29; riots, 7–9; sailing, 26–27; silence of, 6; smuggling, 23–24; speech, 9–10; subsistence riots, 1–2; "support" for the crown, 65–69; virile attributes of, 25–27, 117–24

Basques in Mexico, 59–61
Bassoco, Antonio, 76, 77
Bastidas, Micaela, 11
bateleras, 24
Bates, Mrs., 24
Belén school, 67
Belgrano, Manuel, 110, 127
Bentham, Jeremy, 132
Berneo riot, 7–8
Berrio y Zaldívar, Miguel de, 74
bertso, 9–10
Bocanegra, Gertrudis, 91, 145
Bolívar, Simón, 95, 105, 111, 118–20, 122, 127
Bonaparte, José, 42
Bonaparte, Joseph, 81, 82
Bonaparte, Napoleon. See Napoleon Bonaparte
Boussingault, Jean-Baptiste, 91, 118
Bowles, Guillermo, 26
Bravo, Nicolás, 91
Brewster, Claire, 147
Brotherhood of Aránzazu, 68–69
Brotherhood of San Ignacio of Madrid, 61
Brown, Matthew, 39
Bruce, Beatrice, 108, 149

Cabañas, Juan Ruiz de, 68
Cabarrús, Francisco, 82
Calleja, Félix, 127
Calvo, Teresa, 85
Camacho, Carmen, 88
Camejo, Josefa, 91–92
Cañizares, Manuela, 89
Carlos IV, 38

Carmen Silva, María del, 84
Carmen Uriarte, María del, 84
Cartesianism, 132–33
Castelli, Juan José, 89
Castilla, Count Ruiz de, 92
Castorena Ursúa y Goyeneche, Juan Ignacio María de, 50, 68
Catherine the Great, 49
Cepeda, Rosario, 83
Charron, Claude, 8
Cienfuegos, Beatriz, 51, 84
Claessens, Magdalena de, 24
Clavijo y Fajardo, José, 51
Colegio de las Vizcaínas, 60–61
Córdoba y Moncada, Don José Joaquin Fernández de, 74
Countess of San Mateo de Valparaíso, 74
Crawford, Katherine, 87
Creole origin, 107–8

Descartes, René, 104, 132
domesticated feminity, 49
Domínguez, Miguel, 76
Doumonstier, General, 92
Duke of Wellington, 93

Echegaray y Garibay, Francisca Xaviera de, 78
Elcano, Juan Sebastián, 3
Elias, Norbert, 132
Empecinado, Don Juan Martín El, 86
English, Mary, 35
Erauso, Catalina de, 94
Espalza, Bárbara, 128
Espigado, Gloria, 103–4

Espigado, Tocino, 110
Esteban, Francisca, 85
Euskal Herria, 23–24

Fagoaga, Manuela de, 74
Fandiño, Juan León de, 33
Farge, Arlette, 122–23
femininity: Hispanic, 110; national feeling and identity, 104–5
feminist memory, 142
Ferdinand VII, King of Spain, 79, 80, 84
Fernández de Lizardi, José Joaquín, 136
Flores y Aramburu, Juan José, 126
Foucault, Michel, 132
Francis Xavier, Saint, 60
Frankland, William, 25

Gaceta de Buenos Aires, 105
Gaceta de Caracas, 109
Gaceta de Lima, 108–9
Gamarra, Agustín de, 119
Gamarra, Francisco, 127
Gorostiza, Pedro Miguel de, 83
Gouges, Olympe, 132
Goyeneche, José Manuel, 91
Gresores, Gabriela, 108, 149

Haramboure, Abbot, 9
Hasparren riot, 9
heroines, 103–12
Hidalgo, Miguel, 11, 65
Hidle, Steve, 7
Hispanic feminism, 110
Huarte, Ana, 79

Hugo, Abel, 81
Hugo, Victor, 26–27, 81
Humboldt, Alexander von, 26
Hume, David, 104

Ibaibarriaga, Martina de, 92–93
Ignatius of Loyola, Saint, 60
Iraeta, Ana Maria, 79, 148
Isabella of Bourbon, 117
Iturbide, Agustin de, 79, 127
Iturbide, José Joaquín, 68
Iturriaga, Manuel, 66
Iturriza, Juan Ramón de, 26
Izazaga, José María, 66

Jenkins, Robert, 33
Jofré, Ciriza, 108, 135
Josefa, Doña, 75
Joseph I, 80
Juntas Generales de Guipúzcoa, 23

Kant, Immanuel, 132

L.M.P., 84
La musjuer en la Guerra de la Independencia (Arteche y Moro de Elexabeita), 106
La Pola, Policarpa, 146
Labourd, 10
Lagarde, Commissioner, 128
Larraín, María de, 92
Larramendi, Manuel de, 27–28, 51, 122
Larrea, Frasquita, 83
Lavrin, Asunción, 111
Lazcano, María Josefa, 75

León, Fray Luis de, 6, 47
Lizardi, José Joaquín Fernández de, 109–10, 120, 138
Lizarralde, María Josefa, 128
Loaiza, Mercedes, 87
Longa y Anchía, Francisco de, 93
López, García, 111
Louis II, 38

Manifesto de Cartagena (Bolívar), 105
Maria Luisa, Queen Regent, 38
Mariana, Queen of Neuburg, 27
Marmolejo de Aldama, María Josefa, 127
Marquis of Jaral de Berrio, 74
Marquis of Montehermoso, 48, 51–52
Marquis of San Miguel de Aguayo, 68
Marquise of Apartado, 74
Marquise of Castañiza, 74
Marquise of Legarda, 82
Marquise of San Miguel de Aguayo, 40
Martínez, Capel, 134
Martínez, Manuel, 82
Martínez, María Josefa, 91
Matxinada of 1718, 8
Maya, Ramírez, 66
Mazarredo, José de, 81, 82
McGregor, Gregor, 35
Medina, Manuela, 91
Mendionde riot, 10
Mendizábal e Iraeta, Gabriel de, 73–74, 78
Mexico, Basques in, 59–61

Michelena, Francisca, 128
Michelena, José Mariano, 66
Mier, Ana María Iraeta de, 76
Mina, Xavier, 145
Mojica, Sarah de, 146
Monteagudo, Matías, 89
Montiano, Manuel Joaquín de, 32, 33, 52, 110
Montiano, Teresa de, 52
Morelos, José María, 67
Moreno, Mariano, 89
Morillo, Pablo, 35
motherhood, 124
Moyúa, María Antonia de, 81, 83
Muriel, Josefina, 66

Nabio, Angela, 86
Napoleon Bonaparte, 34, 39, 41, 105, 106, 128
Nava, Antonia, 91

Ochoa, Antonia de, 128
Olano, Carmen, 128
Olavide, Pablo de, 48–49, 105, 109, 135–36, 149
Olazabal y Veroiz, María Teresa de, 35–42, 47, 50–51, 81
Orendáin, Dolores, 109
Ortiz, Josefa, 66, 87, 145

Palacios, Josefa, 89
Palma, Ricardo, 118
Panes, Ana Josefa Zabaleta de, 78
Pani, Erika, 135, 137
Pasajes bateleras, 24
Pateman dilemma, 134
Philip IV, 117

Ramírez, Juana, 89, 91
RCGC, 23, 24
Riofrío, María Josefa, 128
Rivera, María Fermina, 91
Rocafuerte, Vicente, 126
Roche, Domínguez, 111, 119, 146
Rodriguez, Güera, 145
Roo, Andrés Quintana, 111
Rousseau, Jean-Jacques, 7, 49, 104
RSBAP, 48, 49, 50, 52, 61, 68
Ruiz, Juana, 92

Sáenz, Manuela, 91, 111, 118–19, 145
Saint Jean de Luz riot, 8–9
Salavarrieta, Policarpa, 87, 111–12, 119, 126
Salazar, Manuela de, Marquise of La Alameda, 81
salon culture, 88
Salt Rebellion of Biscay, 7
San Sebastián, 24–25
Sánchez de Thompson, Mariquita, 89
Sancho, Manuela, 93
Santa Anna, Antonio López, 69
Santamaría, Manuela Sanz de, 89
Santander, Francisco, 35
Sara riot, 9
seductress, 87–88
Sermón, 117–18
sexuality, 147
smuggling, 23–24
social motherhood, 49, 86–87
Socorro, New Granada, revolt, 11
Spanish War of Independence, 41–42, 73

spying, 87–88
Sucre, Antonio José, 91, 127

Tellería, María Ángela, 93
thalassocracy, 3
Thompson, E. P., 2
Tocino, Espigado, 83, 143
Toro de Lazarín, Mariana de, 89
Treaty of Aranjuez, 34
Túpac Amaru II, 11, 89
Tyrell, Ian, 143

Ugarre riot, 8
Ulloa, Manuel López de, 84
universal nobility, 4
Urdaneta, Andrès de, 3
Ureta, Carmen, 87
Uriondo, Manuel Pérez, 127
Urquijo, Mariano Luis de, 82
Urrea, Margarita de, 35

Valdelomar, Abraham, 119
Valencegui, María Agueda de, 81–82, 127
Veeduría del Contrabando, 7
Venegas, Francisco Xavier, 89
Vera, Joaquín José de Vera, 34, 36–37, 38, 40
Vergara, María Josefa, 75–76
Vergara y Aizpuru, Manuela Sáenz de, 87, 126
Vicario, Leona, 111, 128, 145
Vicario, María Leona, 67
Vicuña y Echave, Josefa Luisa de, 84
Virgin of Aránzazu, 60
Virgin of Guadalupe, 67
Vives, Juan Luis, 6

Vizarrón y Eguiarreta, Juan Antonio de, 67
Vizcaínas school, 66
Vizcaya Salt Rebellion, 5–6

Wiesner-Hanks, Merry E., 23, 113
Wollstonecraft, Mary, 132, 133
Wollstonecraft dilemma, 134
women's throne, 7

Yermo, María Josefa Yermo de, 76

Zabala, Dolores, 128
Zabaleta, María Soledad Esain de, 78
Zambrano, Manuel, 128
Zárate, Rosa, 128
Zubiaga, Francisca de, 119, 127

www.ingramcontent.com/pod-product-compliance
Lightning Source LLC
Chambersburg PA
CBHW020737230426
43665CB00009B/472